GEORGE ELIOT

Collected Poems

GEORGE ELIOT

Collected Poems

Edited with an introduction
by Lucien Jenkins

SKOOB BOOKS PUBLISHING
LONDON

Introduction: © Lucien Jenkins
Cover painting: © Mick Finch

Published by
SKOOB BOOKS PUBLISHING LTD
11a-15 Sicilian Avenue
off Southampton Row
Holborn
London WC1 2QH

ISBN 1 871438 35 7 Cloth
ISBN 1 871438 40 3 Paper

Typeset by Moss Database in ITC Garamond
Printed in Singapore

CONTENTS

INTRODUCTION

(i)

Mary Ann Evans was born at South Farm on the estate of Arbury Hall in Warwickshire, where her father was a farm manager, on 2 November 1819. She was the youngest surviving child of Robert Evans and grew up particularly close to her brother Isaac. While at school she came under the evangelical influence of the principal teacher, Maria Lewis. After moving to a school in Coventry, run by the Baptist Miss Franklins, Mary Ann Evans, who often styled herself 'Marian', underwent a conversion experience, that is, a realisation of personal sinfulness and yet of personal salvation through the redemptive achievement of Christ's sacrifice at Calvary. Events witnessed by the young Marian Evans while living at Nuneaton and Coventry formed the basis of her first published work of fiction. The three tales in *Scenes of Clerical Life* were apparently so undisguisedly based upon actual happenings and individuals that many saw through the fiction and recognised the historical sources: the novelist's biographer G. S. Haight tells how a priest, reading the story of Amos Barton in *Blackwood's Magazine*, found himself so clearly portrayed that he suspected his daughter of having written the account !

Following this evangelical Christian experience, the period of the novelist's twenties included the friendship of the free-thinker Charles Bray which contributed powerfully to the process by which she became the humanist she later was. Her first published works were articles in *The Westminster Review* and translations from German philosophy: Strauss's *Life of Jesus (Das Leben Jesu)* in 1846 and Feuerbach's *Essence of Christianity (Das Wesen des Christentums)* in 1854. At the house of the publisher John Chapman, where she lodged, she met the man with whom

1

she was to live as wife, although unmarried, until his death: George Henry Lewes. He was already married and thus not free to wed, but it was a devoted relationship from 1853 onwards. It was he who encouraged her to write fiction and he who sent her 'The Sad Fortunes of the Revd Amos Barton' to his own publisher, John Blackwood, who accepted it and published it in *Blackwood's Magazine*. When he asked for the author's name, he was told it was by 'George Eliot'. 'George' was of course Lewes's name. 'Eliot' was apparently chosen as being easy to pronounce and remember. Her fiction of the 1850's was closely based on her own experiences and those events she had witnessed. Her middle period, from which her poems largely come, is generally characterised as a period of uncertainty and casting around. This is the period of the 'historical novel' *Romola* and the 'political novel' *Felix Holt*. Dividing a writer's life into periods in this way, though useful, should only be done with the greatest hesitation. But it does seem to be the case that the period of the 1860's was a difficult time, a time of search. The work from this period, *Romola*, *Felix Holt* and *The Spanish Gypsy*, all had a disappointing reception compared with the immense success of George Eliot's first three works of fiction, *Scenes of Clerical Life*, *Adam Bede* and *Mill on the Floss*. In 1869 she began writing *Middlemarch*, but this was soon overshadowed by the illness and then death of Lewes's son Thornton. Work on the novel came to a halt. It was at this time that George Eliot wrote the 'Brother and Sister' sonnets and the narrative poem 'The Legend of Jubal', which were published in 1874 by Blackwood. After completing *Middlemarch* and *Daniel Deronda* in the 1870's, a new catastrophe struck with the death in November 1878 of George Henry Lewes. Her loyal publisher coaxed her to continue working and she corrected the proofs of the volume of pseudonymous essays, *Impressions of Theophrastus Such*, but Blackwood himself died in 1879. That same year the novelist married a man more than twenty years younger than herself, John Walker Cross. It was the occasion of a letter of congratulation from her brother Isaac, to whom as a girl she had been so devoted but from whom she had been for so many years estranged. (The 'Brother and Sister' poems and the novel *Mill on the Floss* both deal with this relationship with her brother.) She herself died in 1880, after only seven months of legitimate marriage.

(ii)

George Eliot published two volumes of poetry, *The Spanish Gypsy* and *The Legend of Jubal and Other Poems*. Of the four long poems in the *Jubal* collection of 1874, it was the dramatic poem 'Armgart' that Henry James considered the best. It concerns itself with a much-praised prima donna who in the midst of her success first receives and refuses a proposal of marriage from Graf Dornberg and then falls victim to an illness which deprives her of the singing voice which had been the foundation of her independence. The argument of the Graf in putting to her his proposal is that more than in ambition,

> A woman's rank
> Lies in the fulness of her womanhood:
> Therein alone she is royal.

Armgart replies coolly:

> Woman, thy desire
> Shall be that all superlatives on Earth
> Belong to men, save the one highest kind –
> To be a mother.

The Graf seeks to domesticate Armgart's talent, but she refuses this. He seeks to prove her gifts to be in conflict with her sex, that being an artist makes her less a woman.

3

This she rejects:

> I am an artist by my birth −
> By the same warrant that I am a woman.

Nature, which the Graf would recruit to his side, is ranged by Armgart on hers, declaring that her gifts as well as her gender come from that source:

> O blessed Nature !
> Let her be arbitress; she gave me voice
> Such as she only gives a woman child,
> Best of its kind, gave me ambition too . . .

Yet George Eliot cannot be said to be siding with Armgart, even though she makes her well able to refute the Graf's arguments. Nor is she offering us Armgart as the voice of a new womanhood. A second voice speaks up as Armgart is distressed by the consequences of her illness. Walpurga, her attendant and cousin, tells her that talent and success had taken her away from her fellow women and the ordinary 'thwarted life' and accuses her of egotism. Armgart takes a step away from the self-absorption of ambition and self-pity alike, but not into marriage. Like Deronda she takes up a duty to others: she will teach music. The choice of the town in which she will work is also important: it is the one that Walpurga had left to serve her. In the decision to serve others, Armgart has learnt a new possibility of independence without egotism.

'Armgart' can usefully be considered George Eliot's reply to Byron. Lord Byron's poetry and its heroes were the object of her consistent dislike:

> Byron and his poetry have become more and more repugnant
> to me of late years (I read a good deal of him a little while ago,
> in order to form a fresh judgement).

(Letters V 54)

In her novel *Felix Holt*, written a few years before 'Armgart', Mr Lyons is entertaining the young radical to tea when Felix spots a volume of Byron's poems. Esther admitting to a 'great admiration for Byron', Felix Holt, in a judgement surely reflecting George Eliot's own, declares him to be 'A misanthropic debauchee . . . whose notion of a hero was that he should disorder his stomach and despise mankind'. Armgart is a Byronic figure in her adoption of a posture of permanent rebellion and her refusal to accept an authority outside of her own will:

> An inborn passion gives a rebel's right:
> I would rebel and die in twenty worlds
> Sooner than bear the yoke of thwarted life . . . .

She insists that her involvement in art is not out of service to music but simply out of the desire for self-expression. The Graf declares that:

> She bears
> Caesar's ambition in her delicate breast,
> And nought to still it with but quivering song !

Walpurga replies though:

> She often wonders what her life had been
> Without that voice for channel to her soul.
> She says, it must have leapt through all her limbs –
> Made her a Maenad – made her snatch a brand
> And fire some forest, that her rage might mount
> In crashing roaring flames through half a land,
> Leaving her still and patient for a while.

George Eliot does not have a heroine like Elizabeth Barrett Browning's Aurora Leigh: no woman in her fiction is a writer. Armgart the opera singer is her portrait of a creative woman possessed of exceptional gifts. Ellen Moers has remarked that: 'the miracle of operatic performance served as could no other to show off a woman's genius.' (*Literary Women*)

(iii)

The novel most centred around the theme of singing is of course *Daniel Deronda*. When Gwendolen Harleth is considering a career to make herself independent it is as a singer that she sees herself. Klesmer offsets her dilettante, essentially amateurish attitude with advice about hard work and self-sacrifice of an artistic career. Meanwhile both Daniel's mother and his bride Mirah turn out to be Jewish singers. Klesmer is the great apologist for the concept of art not as egotistical self-glorification and a vehicle for personal ambition but as an ideal unselfishly to be served. K. M. Newton has argued that Klesmer's concept of art and Mordecai's vision of the organic nation (he is a committed Jewish nationalist) are similar in offering the ego 'a means of definition in devoting itself to the service of a higher ideal'. Deronda finds his own identity in his discovery of his own Jewishness, which leads him to marry not Gwendolen but Mirah and to further the Zionist cause of founding a Jewish national homeland.

The discovery by Deronda that he is a Jew is closely prefigured by the story of Fedalma in *The Spanish Gypsy*, which came out six years before *Daniel Deronda* began appearing. Fedalma is brought up among the Spanish nobility and then on the eve of her marriage is reclaimed by her Gypsy father who is engaged in open conflict with the society in which his daughter has been brought up. The fairy tale element of the child brought up in ignorance of its own parentage is a very basic and frequently recurring theme in George Eliot's work. In addition to Deronda and Fedalma, there is Eppie in *Silas Marner*, who is the child of a secret marriage, and who is found and brought up by Silas. In *Felix Holt*, Rufus Lyon brings up the orphaned Esther as his daughter, while Harold Transome discovers he is not the son of his mother's husband but of the despised lawyer Jermyn with whom, many years before, she had an affair. The question of parentage, the theme of genetic parents and foster parents, of mysterious origins, reflects a concern with identity and purpose. Now this is by no means an uncommon literary conceit. In nineteenth-century fiction heroines and heroes frequently discover themselves to be the children of aristocrats and accordingly come into their inheritance as a reward for vicissitudes previously met. Heroines and heroes that prove their worth had long been rewarded by promotion, as in the case of Richardson's *Pamela*, or restoration, as in the case of Maria Edgeworth's *Patronage* and of course Goldsmith's *The Vicar of Wakefield*. But Esther does not accept the reward offered in *Felix Holt*: she renounces her inheritance and rejects the self-intested courtship of Harold Transome. Moreover the inheritance discovered by Fedalma and Deronda is not a reward, it is not a restoration. *Pamela* and *Patronage* end with stability at last achieved. *Daniel Deronda* and *The Spanish Gypsy* both end with the rejection of worldly reward and satisfaction. Fedalma has declared tellingly:

> I will not take a heaven
> Haunted by shrieks of far-off misery.

(iv)

The tone of George Eliot's poem is one of resolution not of triumph. The discovery of identity in this case is not the achievement of peace. On the contrary, it is the beginning of duty. Deronda and Fedalma both choose a life of service to their oppressed nations, the Jews and the Gypsies. The recollections of F. W. H. Myers of a conversation with George Eliot show the significance that duty had for her:

> I remember how, at Cambridge, I walked with her once in the Fellows' Garden of Trinity, on an evening of rainy May; and she . . . taking as her text the three words . . . *God*, *Immortality*, *Duty*, – pronounced, with terrible earnestness how inconceivable was the *first*, how unbelievable the *second*, and yet how peremptory and absolute the *third* . . . I listened, and night fell; her grave majestic countenance turned towards me like a sibyl's in the gloom . . .

7

It is in her 'O May I Join the Choir Invisible' that George Eliot comes closest to writing an openly religious poem, dealing directly with her own faith, one in which she attempts to meet head on the question of that immortality she considered so 'unbelievable'. The poem, in which the theme of music and song again plays an important role, was actually set by more than half a dozen composers and adapted as a Positivist hymn. (Although Martha S. Vogeler considers it 'was in fact probably not much sung by Comtist congregations'.)

The poem asserts the continuing life of 'the immortal dead', not in the form of a Christian afterlife of individual existence but in the relationship of the dead with the lives of men and women whom they affect and whom, by their example, they encourage away from narrow egocentricity to 'generosity', 'deeds of daring rectitude', 'thoughts sublime' and 'vaster issues'. This philosophy is close to the motivation of Zarca, the Gypsy leader in *The Spanish Gypsy* who declares:

> The Zíncali have no god
> Who speaks to them and calls them his, unless
> I, Zarca, carry living in my frame
> The power divine that chooses them and saves.

This duty, to which Fedalma is called, the duty of constructing for ourselves and our descendants the necessary tradition which a bankrupt Christianity has left us without, is in 'the choir invisible' seen as a wider human need, not limited to the Zíncali.

The poem is one example of the nineteenth-century attempt to winnow Christianity, to discover that 'Essence of Christianity' which was the title and subject of George Eliot's translation of Feuerbach. George Eliot here seeks to discover something divine and to that end apotheosises, declares Martha Vogeler, 'not man but only his best qualities — which for Feuerbach constituted the essence of

8

Christianity'. It is an essentially optimistic, organic poem, one which is attempting to show, as Wordsworth had attempted, that human life formed a part of an integrated, patterned universe. The image of this integration and pattern is of course music. Where in life 'our rarer, better, truer self' had 'sobbed religiously in yearning song', now, the individual soul takes up its place in the choir invisible:

> So to live is heaven:
> To make undying music in the world,
> Breathing as beauteous order that controls
> With growing sway the growing life of man.

The opening half lines of the second and third strophes declare a certainty in this immortality: 'So to live is heaven', 'This is the life to come'.

'O May I Join the Choir Invisible' is not the only poem in the collection *The Legend of Jubal and Other Poems* that deals with religious faith, death and music. In the title poem we are shown the mythical story, taken from Genesis, of the invention by Jubal of the lyre and hence of song. After his years-long wanderings he returns home to find his name worshipped as the divine inventor of music, but for his attempts to draw attention to himself and claim the credit that is his due, he is attacked by the crowd of worshippers for blasphemy. Only in dying does he leave behind the egotistical desire for recognition and become the god that the crowd had worshipped.

The poem 'Stradivarius' deals with the same issue but from a different angle. Whereas the egotistical and lazy artist Naldo acts the wastrel, the self-effacing violin maker perfects his craft. The gratitude of violin players for his life and work is his immortality and his religious faith is expressed in his dedication to perfection in his craft. He sees himself in this work as God's hands:

9

> . . . heresy or not, if my hand slacked
> I should rob God − since He is fullest good −
> Leaving a blank instead of violins.
> I say, not God Himself can make man's best
> Without best men to help him.

(v)

The sonnet sequence 'Brother and Sister' is an autobiographical account of the author's childhood and her recollection of that intimate relationship she had once had with her brother Isaac. (In this it is closely bound up with the novel *Mill on the Floss* written ten years before and uses some similar material.) The poems recollect a time of wild flowers and intimacy with the natural world: It is a Wordsworthian poem, and as with Wordsworth the poetry of recollection is not simply nostalgic and its purpose is not merely to recall. 'Memory', as K. M. Newton reminds us, 'is (an) essential aspect of George Eliot's organicism'. The recollection of things past is part of the process of organic continuity within the individual life, the continuity between a formative past and a present identity. The separation from his past suffered by Silas in *Silas Marner*, the ignorance of their origins of Daniel Deronda, Fedalma, Eppie, Harold Transome and Esther Lyons poses a challenge to those individuals. Even when he has found a place in society through the redemptive work of the child Eppie, who reminds him of his little sister for whom he had cared 'when he was a small boy without shoes and stockings', even after the tale has unfolded Silas still feels the need to go back to the pace of his origins, back to Lantern Yard from which, like Adam from Eden, he was harshly cast out.

Wordsworthian in philosophy, 'Brother and Sister' is Wordsworthian in tone also. It emphasises the slowness of childhood days in the country. Sonnet 6, with the little

10

sister sitting by the canal, contains the quiet, slow fifth line in which the long, open vowels create in sound the scene: 'Slowly the barges floated into view'. 'The Legend of Jubal', which concerns itself with the childhood of the human race, declares:

> Man's life was spacious in the early world:
> It paused, like some slow ship with sail unfurled
> Waiting on seas by scarce a wavelet curled . . .

This is a world of amplitude of time and space, a generous world not threatened by urban bustle. The idyll in 'Jubal' is first hurt by the accidental killing by Lamech of his own son, through which the children of Cain first learn about death. At the end, Jubal finds 'dread Change' has altered the home he left. The homestead has become a town:

> His memory saw a small foot-trodden way,
> His eyes a broad far-stretching paven road
> Bordered with many a tomb and fair abode;
> The little city that once nestled low
> As buzzing groups about some central glow,
> Spread like a murmuring crowd o'er plain and steep,
> Or monster huge in heavy-breathing sleep.

The end of the sequence 'Brother and Sister' declares that 'School parted us'. The final sonnet, like 'Jubal', speaks of change as a grim force:

> . . . the dire years whose awful name is Change
> Had grasped our souls still yearning in divorce,
> And pitiless shaped them in two forms that range
> Two elements which sever their life's course.

Time and change threaten identity but memory maintains the integrity of the individual. The sixth sonnet, listing details of the landscape, asserts their significance to the author:

> The wide-arched bridge, scented elder flowers,
> The wondrous watery rings that died too soon,
> The echoes of the quarry, the still hours
> With white robe sweeping-on the shadeless noon,
> > Were but my growing self, are part of me,
> > My present Past, my root of piety.

This word 'piety' is one of great Wordsworthian significance, particularly in such a context. In his poem about his own reactions to seeing a rainbow, Wordsworth declares the reaction to be one of the constant factors in his life and then tells us:

> The child is father of the man
> And I could wish my days to be
> Bound each to each by natural piety.

There in a nutshell are the two themes: of natural piety and of the days being bound together. 'Brother and Sister' is a celebration not only of childhood but of life. The nineteenth century was of course an age of scientific discovery and speculation, when geologists and naturalists were preparing the greatest shock to the orthodox interpretation of Genesis since Galileo. George Eliot was familiar with the debate over the nature of the universe and the scientific assertion that it was not created and stable but dynamic and developing. But although, reading Darwin's *Origin of Species* in December 1859, she acknowledged its achievement and importance, she felt its limitations:

> . . . to me the Development theory and all other explanations of processes by which things come to be, produce a feeble impression compared with the mystery that lies under the processes.

> (*Letters* III 127).

This sense of the mystery, of the numinous, is central to George Eliot's work. The third sonnet shows the two children walking away from their mother into the trees, where:

> . . . over all the dark rooks cawing flew,
> And made a happy strange solemnity,
> A deep-toned chant from life unknown to me.

Childhood has in these sonnets and elsewhere a further spiritual significance worth considering. Wordsworth had written of God as being not only the father to whom we go in death but as the home from which we come by being born:

> Our birth is but a sleep and a forgetting:
> The Soul that rises with us, our life's Star,
> > Hath had elsewhere its setting,
> > > And cometh from afar:
> > Not in entire forgetfulness,
> > And not in utter nakedness,
> But trailing clouds of glory do we come
> > From God, who is our home:
> Heaven lies about us in our infancy!
> Shades of the prison house begin to close
> > Upon the growing boy
> But He beholds the light, and whence it flows,
> > He sees it in his joy;
> The Youth, who daily farther from the east
> > Must travel, still is Nature's Priest,
> > > And by the vision splendid
> > > Is on his way attended;
> At length the Man perceives it die away,
> And fade into the light of common day.

The poem from which this is taken, the Ode 'Intimations of Immortality from Recollections of Early Childhood', takes as its epigraph Wordsworth's own three lines on 'natural piety' quoted above and makes explicit a mythology which lies behind the George Eliot sonnets without ever being explained. For the childhood days of the sequence are not being recalled because of their having been pleasant, but because they were in some sense sacred, the sacredness of childhood deriving from childhood's closer proximity to God. Thus the force of 'Change' or 'School' is part of the

13

process that causes our forgetting. Childhood is further seen as the period of creation both of the core of identity and of language.

> Thus rambling we were schooled in deepest lore,
> And learned the meanings that give words a soul,
> The fear, the love, the primal passionate store,
> Whose shaping impulses make manhood whole.

George Eliot's declaration 'These hours were seed to all my after good' recalls Wordsworth's:

> Fair seedtime had my soul and I grew up
> Foster'd alike by beauty and by fear;

> *(The Prelude* 1 305-6/301-2)

The biggest difference though between the Wordsworth poems and those of George Eliot is the almost unshadowed quality of the later author's work. She may in her phrase 'the fear, the love' imitate Wordsworth's 'by beauty and by fear', but the only frightening event of the sequence is being startled one time by a Gypsy's 'dark smile'. Wonderful though these sonnets are, the absence of any shade to cast them into relief leaves them finally without the authority of Wordsworth's autobiographical writing, where nature is a parent capable not only of benign approval but also of threat. George Eliot's nature is a force exclusively maternal and embracing.

In 'Brother and Sister' the parent that is seen is the mother who watches her departing children with 'the benediction of her gaze' in the third sonnet. The process by which the child draws on nature is described in the fifth sonnet, where 'infant gladness':

> Took easily as warmth a various food
> To nourish the sweet skill of loving much.

The image is that of the child being nursed. In *The Spanish Gypsy*, where the only parent is the father, the absent mother is supplied by the landscape, 'Broad-breasted Spain'. In the poem 'Agatha' the image is even more openly used:

> Come with me to the mountains, not where rocks
> Soar harsh above the troops of hurrying pines,
> But where the earth spreads soft and rounded breasts
> To feed her children; where the generous hills
> Lift a green isle betwixt the sky and plain
> To keep some Old World things aloof from change.

Here, as in 'Brother and Sister', the safety of the relationship of the child with the protective mother is threatened by 'change'. Perhaps one should remember that the background to the writing of the sonnets is the death of Lewes's son Thornie and thus understand the determination George Eliot shows to keep her eye fixed on the light and avoid the shadow. Death, naturally for one with no faith in a Christian afterlife, posed a great question to George Eliot. It was a question to which she struggled to provide answers. One answer lay in her poem 'The Choir Invisible'. Following the death of her partner Lewes she established the George Henry Lewes Studentship in Physiology in Cambridge: it was a form of immortality, another way of answering the question.

(vi)

In stark contrast to this fully lit world of the sonnets is the poem 'In a London drawingroom'. With its urban setting, its atmosphere is unrelieved cloud and shadow and the poem is dominated by the vocabulary of darkness and gloom. For Bernard Paris, the poem is one of George Eliot's best and he has speculated that it is the poem's very bleakness that caused her not to publish it. The world evoked is one of isolation, it is the world of T. S. Eliot's 'The Waste Land', a London in which crowds hurry by and no human contact is possible:

> All hurry on and look upon the ground,
> Or glance unmarking at the passers by
> The wheels are hurrying too, cabs, carriages
> All closed, in multiplied identity.

Compare that to T. S. Eliot's lines:

> Under the brown fog of a winter's dawn,
> A crowd flowed over London Bridge, so many,
> I had not thought death had undone so many.
> Sighs short and infrequent were exhaled,
> And each man kept his eyes before his feet.

If the poem looks forward to 'The Waste Land', it also looks back to Wordsworth and once again it is the Ode 'Intimations of Immortality' that is alluded to. For when George Eliot writes:

> The world seems one huge prison-house and court
> Where men are punished at the slightest cost,
> With lowest rate of colour, warmth and joy

it is impossible not to recall Wordsworth's:

> Shades of the prison-house begin to close
> Upon the growing boy.

The urban gloom of 'In a London drawingroom' confirms the Wordsworthian view of the idyllic sonnets, that the organic, integrated life of the child in the country reveals all that is missing from the hollow, alienated and dulled adult life in the city.

(vii)

George Eliot's poems are sketches (only in *The Spanish Gypsy* does she attempt in verse a work on the scale of her novels) and reading them is often like looking through a painter's sketchbook. Sentimentality is the greatest threat to George Eliot's work as a poet. A slightly sweetened sadness is dangerously close to flavouring some of her work and perhaps 'How Lisa Loved the King' does not escape the saccharine.

On the question of the sadness that permeates these poems – and it might be said to be most felt where it is most excluded – one would do well to recall a sentence from *Romola*:

> The pressing problem for Romola just then was . . . to keep alive that flame of unselfish emotion by which a life of sadness might still be a life of active love.

In a sense we are returned to the memoir of F. W. H. Myers, that while God and Immortality were inconceivable and unbelievable, Duty alone was peremptory and absolute. It is this that is the subject to which George Eliot returns over and over in her poems: how to live a life of active love despite the absence of God and immortality.

NOTE ON THE TEXT

The purpose of this edition is to provide an accurate and readable text of all those poems by George Eliot which have survived. The shorter poems, whether published in her lifetime or not, are collected in Part One and placed, as far as possible, in chronological order. Where dates are available they have been given after each poem; conjectural dates have been placed in parentheses.

The Spanish Gypsy, composed and revised over too long a period easily to fit into this chronology, is in Part Two, and the brief preface and the notes that follow the poem are the author's own. The largely undatable epigraphs to the novels are in Part Three. An Appendix gives the order of the poems as they appeared in the 1874 and 1878 editions of *The Legend of Jubal*.

Yale University Library's collection of George Eliot manuscript material in the Beinecke Rare Book and Manuscript Library includes letters and an autograph manuscript notebook, in which a number of unpublished or uncollected poems are to be found. The notebook, catalogues MS Vault, Eliot 7, contains, in addition to prose writings, 'In a London Drawingroom', 'Ex Oriente Lux', 'Arms ! To Arms !' (a translation from a Spanish poem), 'In the South', five fragments, 'I grant you ample leave', 'Erinna', 'The Death of Moses', 'Master in loving' (here printed as one of the fragments), ''Mid my gold-brown curls', and 'Sweet Evenings Come and Go, Love'. One of the five fragments is the epigraph to Chapter 57 of *Daniel Deronda* and therefore does not appear in Part One with the other four. 'The Death of Moses' and 'Sweet Evenings Come and Go, Love' were both published in the 1878 edition of *The Legend of Jubal*, the former in a heavily revised version. Lines 5-12 of 'Erinna' were used by George Eliot as the epigraph to Chapter 51 of *Daniel Deronda*:

appearing in Part One in the context of the poem, they have not been repeated in Part Three of this edition.

'Farewell' appears in a letter to Maria Lewis dated 17 July 1839. It was then printed in the *Christian Observer* in January 1840. 'Sonnet' appears in a letter to Maria Lewis dated 4 September 1839. 'Question and Answer' (a translation of a German poem) appears in a letter to Maria Lewis dated 1 October 1840 and was printed in Cross's *Life*, 1885. 'Mid the rich store of nature's gifts to man' also appears in a letter to Maria Lewis, dated 19 February 1842, and in Cross's *Life*. 'As tu vu la lune' appears in a letter to Mr and Mrs Charles Bray and Sara Sophia Hennel dated 20 August 1849.

Some of the poems of George Eliot are impossible to date with any certainty. To regard 'Sweet Evenings Come and Go, Love' as belonging to the Spanish group of 1866-67, as Creel does, would be to beg the question of why it was omitted from *The Spanish Gypsy* for which, Creel suggests, it was written. Moreover, if 'Sweet Evenings Come and Go, Love', one of the four poems added to the 1878 edition of *The Legend of Jubal and Other Poems*, dates from the 1860's and could thus have been included in the original 1874 edition, one is left with the unanswered question of why, excluded from the earlier edition, it was included in the later. A better, more Ockhamist, conclusion is that the poem dates from between 1874 and 1878. 'Self and Life' has been linked by Creel to the time of George Eliot's 'marriage' to Lewes and by Secor to the dying of Thornie. The later date is again to be preferred because an earlier dating would, as with 'Sweet Evenings Come and Go, Love', leave open the question of why the author would exclude the poem in 1874 only to include it in 1878.

'The Death of Moses', ''Mid my gold-brown curls' (based on a Hebrew poem by Jehuda Ha-Levi) and Mordecai's Hebrew Verses (influenced by Jehuda Ha-Levi) form a

Hebrew group dating from the months leading up to December 1875, when Book Five of *Daniel Deronda* was being finished.

A second poem included in Part One which is taken from one of George Eliot's novels is 'Will Ladislaw's Song'. This is from *Middlemarch*, chapter 47. George Creel suggests it may be a fragment of a song written for *The Spanish Gypsy*. This poem is, despite doubts, put with the 'Spanish' poems, as belonging to the period of George Eliot's visit to Spain in 1867 and the resumption of work on the dramatic poem.

Questions of dating are usefully discussed by George W. Creel, Bernard J. Paris and Cynthia Ann Secor and by Gordon S. Haight in his biography of George Eliot. To these studies, and to the others listed in *Further Reading*, this edition is indebted.

Nothing has been included from George Eliot's school notebook, which was discovered in a Wiltshire bookshop in 1943. Although there are a number of unattributed poems there, these turn out to be by poets admired by the young Mary Ann Evans. The unattributed poem 'On Being Called a Saint' is considered by Gordon S. Haight as being 'probably written by Mary Ann herself' and its being left incomplete does go some way to suggest this. Haight describes and discusses the notebook in the first chapter of his biography.

The text of published work follows that of the Cabinet Edition, the production of which George Eliot herself supervised. The poems from the letters and the notebook appear here by kind permission of the Beinecke Rare Book and Manuscript Library, for whose help and co-operation I am very grateful.

FURTHER READING

Eliot, George: *The Spanish Gypsy*, Edinburgh and London, 1868.

Eliot, George: *The Legend of Jubal and Other Poems*, Edinburgh and London, 1874.

The Works of George Eliot, Cabinet Edition, 24 vols, Edinburgh and London, 1878-85.

The George Eliot Letters, ed. Gordon S. Haight, 7 vols, New Haven, 1954-55 and 1979.

Blake, Kathleeen: 'Armgart – George Eliot on the Woman Artist', *Victorian Poetry* 18 (1980), 75-80.

Creel, George W.: *The Poetry of George Eliot*, unpublished dissertation, University of California, Berkeley, 1948.

Cross, John W.: *George Eliot's Life as Related in Her Letters and Journals*, 3 vols, Edinburgh and London, 1885.

Haight, Gordon S.: *George Eliot, A Biography*, Oxford, 1968.

Moers, Ellen: *Literary Women*, 2nd edn. London, 1978.

Newton, K. M.: *George Eliot: Romantic Humanist*, London, 1981.

Paris, Bernard J.: 'George Eliot's Unpublished Poetry', *Studies in Philology*, 56 (1959), 539-58.

Secor, Cynthia Ann: *The Poems of George Eliot*, unpublished dissertation, Cornell University, 1969.

Siff, David H.: *The Choir Invisible: the Relation of George Eliot's Poetry and Fiction*, unpublished dissertation, New York University, 1968.

Vogeler, Martha S.: 'The Choir Invisible: the Poetics of Humanistic Poets' in *George Eliot, A Centenary Tribute*, ed. Gordon S. Haight and Rosemary T. VanArsdel, London 1982.

THE SHORTER POEMS

(FAREWELL)

"Knowing that shortly I must put off this tabernacle"

(2 Peter i. 14)

As o'er the fields by evening's light I stray,
I hear a still, small whisper – "Come away" !
Thou must to this bright, lovely world soon say
         Farewell !

The mandate I'd obey, my lamp prepare,
Gird up my garments, give my soul to pray'r,
And say to earth and all that breathe earth's air
         Farewell !

Thou sun, to whose parental beam I owe
All that has gladden'd me while here below, –
Moon, stars, and covenant confirming bow,
         Farewell !

Ye verdant meads, fair blossoms, stately trees,
Sweet song of birds, and soothing hum of bees, –
Refreshing odours, wafted on the breeze,
         Farewell !

Ye patient servants of creation's lord
Whose mighty strength is govern'd by his word,
Who raiment, food and help in toil afford,
         Farewell !

Ye feebler, freer tribes, that people air,
Fairy like insects, making buds your lair,
Ye that in water shine, and frolic there,
         Farewell !

25

Books that have been to me as chest of gold,
Which, miser like, I secretly have told,
And for them love, health, friendship, peace have sold,
                                        Farewell !

Blest volume ! whose clear truth-writ page, once known,
Fades not before heaven's sunshine or hell's moan,
To thee I say not, of earth's gifts alone,
                                        Farewell !

Dear kindred, whom the lord to me has given,
Must the dear tie that binds us, now be riven?
No ! say I *only* till we meet in heaven,
                                        Farewell !

There shall my newborn senses find new joy,
New sounds, new sights my eyes and ears employ,
Nor fear that word that here brings sad alloy,
                                        Farewell !

(July) 1839

SONNET

Oft, when a child, while wand'ring far alone,
That none might rouse me from my waking dream,
And visions with which fancy still would teem
Scare by a disenchanting earthly tone;
If, haply, conscious of the present scene,
I've marked before me some untraversed spot
The setting sunbeams had forsaken not,
Whose turf appeared more velvet-like and green
Than that I walked and fitter for repose:
But ever, at the wished-for place arrived,
I've found it of those seeming charms deprived
Which from the mellowing power of distance rose:
To my poor thought, an apt though simple trope
Of life's dull path and earth's deceitful hope.

(*September*) *1839*

"Where blooms, O my Father, a thornless rose ?"
    "That can I not tell thee, my child;
Not one on the bosom of earth e'er grows,
    But wounds whom its charms have beguiled."

"Would I'd a rose on my bosom to lie !
    But I shrink from the piercing thorn;
I long, but dare not its point defy,
    I long, and I gaze forlorn."

"Not so, O my child, round the stem again
    Thy resolute fingers entwine –
Forego not the joy for its sister pain,
    Let the rose, the sweet rose, be thine !"

(September) 1840

"Mid the rich store of nature's gifts to man
Each has his loves, close wedded to his soul
By fine associations' golden links.
As the Great Spirit bids creation teem
With conscious being and intelligence,
So man His miniature resemblance gives
To matter's every form a speaking soul,
An emanation from his spirit's fount,
The impress true of its peculiar seal.
Here finds he thy best image, sympathy !"

(February) *1842*

As tu vu la lune se lever
Dans un ciel d'azur sans voile ?
Mille gouttes de rosée réflechissent
Sa lumière, comme autant d'étoiles.

Un violet du printemps cueilles
Et le caches bien dans ton sein,
De la delicieuse odeur
Tu et tes vêtements seront pleins.

Ainsi lorsqu'une belle âme se montre
Elle revêtit tant de ses charmes: –
Ainsi son souvenir gardons
Quoique, hélas ! il tire nos larmes.

20 August 1849

A MINOR PROPHET

I have a friend, a vegetarian seer,
By name Elias Baptist Butterworth,
A harmless, bland, disinterested man,
Whose ancestors in Cromwell's day believed
The Second Advent certain in five years,
But when King Charles the Second came instead,
Revised their date and sought another world:
I mean – not heaven but – America.
A fervid stock, whose generous hope embraced
The fortunes of mankind, not stopping short
At rise of leather, or the fall of gold,
Nor listening to the voices of the time
As housewives listen to a cackling hen,
With wonder whether she has laid her egg
On their own nest-egg. Still they did insist
Somewhat too wearisomely on the joys
Of their Millennium, when coats and hats
Would all be of one pattern, books and songs
All fit for Sundays, and the casual talk
As good as sermons preached extempore.

And in Elias the ancestral zeal
Breathes strong as ever, only modified
By Transatlantic air and modern thought.
You could not pass him in the street and fail
To note his shoulders' long declivity,
Beard to the waist, swan-neck, and large pale eyes;
Or, when he lifts his hat, to mark his hair
Brushed back to show his great capacity –
A full grain's length at the angle of the brow
Proving him witty, while the shallower men
Only seem witty in their repartees.

Not that he's vain, but that his doctrine needs
The testimony of his frontal lobe.
On all points he adopts the latest views;
Takes for the key of universal Mind
The "levitation" of stout gentlemen;
Believes the Rappings are not spirits' work,
But the Thought-atmosphere's, a steam of brains
In correlated force of raps, as proved
By motion, heat, and science generally;
The spectrum, for example, which has shown
The self-same metals in the sun as here;
So the Thought-atmosphere is everywhere:
High truths that glimmered under other names
To ancient sages, whence good scholarship
Applied to Eleusinian mysteries –
The Vedas – Tripitaka – Vendidad –
Might furnish weaker proof for weaker minds
That Thought was rapping in the hoary past,
And might have edified the Greeks by raps
At the greater Dionysia, if their ears
Had not been filled with Sophoclean verse.
And when all Earth is vegetarian –
When, lacking butchers, quadrupeds die out,
And less Thought-atmosphere is reabsorbed
By nerves of insects parasitical,
Those higher truths, seized now by higher minds
But not expressed (the insects hindering)
Will either flash out into eloquence,
Or better still, be comprehensible
By rappings simply, without need of roots.

'Tis on this theme – the vegetarian world –
That good Elias willingly expands:
He loves to tell in mildly nasal tones
And vowels stretched to suit the widest views,

The future fortunes of our infant Earth –
When it will be too full of human kind
To have the room for wilder animals.
Saith he, Sahara will be populous
With families of gentlemen retired
From commerce in more Central Africa,
Who order coolness as we order coal,
And have a lobe anterior strong enough
To think away the sand-storms. Science thus
Will leave no spot on this terraqueous globe
Unfit to be inhabited by man,
The chief of animals: all meaner brutes
Will have been smoked and elbowed out of life.
No lions then shall lap Caffrarian pools,
Or shake the Atlas with their midnight roar:
Even the slow, slime-loving crocodile,
The last of animals to take a hint,
Will then retire for ever from a scene
Where public feeling strongly sets against him.
Fishes may lead carnivorous lives obscure,
But must not dream of culinary rank
Or being dished in good society.
Imagination in that distant age,
Aiming at fiction called historical,
Will vainly try to reconstruct the times
When it was men's preposterous delight
To sit astride live horses, which consumed
Materials for incalculable cakes;
When there were milkmaids who drew milk from cows
With udders kept abnormal for that end
Since the rude mythopoeic period
Of Aryan dairymen, who did not blush
To call their milkmaid and their daughter one –
Helplessly gazing at the Milky Way,
Nor dreaming of the astral cocoa-nuts

Quite at the service of posterity.
'Tis to be feared, though, that the duller boys,
Much given to anachronisms and nuts,
(Elias has confessed boys will be boys)
May write a jockey for a centaur, think
Europa's suitor was an Irish bull,
Æsop a journalist who wrote up Fox,
And Bruin a chief swindler upon 'Change.
Boys will be boys, but dogs will all be moral,
With longer alimentary canals
Suited to diet vegetarian.
The uglier breeds will fade from memory,
Or, being palaeontological,
Live but as portraits in large learned books,
Distasteful to the feelings of an age
Nourished on purest beauty. Earth will hold
No stupid brutes, no cheerful queernesses,
No naïve cunning, grave absurdity.
Wart-pigs with tender and parental grunts,
Wombats much flattened as to their contour,
Perhaps from too much crushing in the ark,
But taking meekly that fatality;
The serious cranes, unstung by ridicule;
Long-headed, short-legged, solemn-looking curs,
(Wise, silent critics of a flippant age);
The silly straddling foals, the weak-brained geese
Hissing fallaciously at sound of wheels –
All these rude products will have disappeared
Along with every faulty human type.
By dint of diet vegetarian
All will be harmony of hue and line,
Bodies and minds all perfect, limbs well-turned,
And talk quite free from aught erroneous.

Thus far Elias in his seer's mantle:
But at this climax in his prophecy
My sinking spirits, fearing to be swamped,
Urge me to speak. "High prospects these, my friend,
Setting the weak carnivorous brain astretch;
We will resume the thread another day."
"To-morrow," cries Elias, "at this hour ? "
"No, not to-morrow – I shall have a cold –
At least I feel some soreness – this endemic –
Good-bye."
        No tears are sadder than the smile
With which I quit Elias. Bitterly
I feel that every change upon this earth
Is bought with sacrifice. My yearnings fail
To reach that high apocalyptic mount
Which shows in bird's-eye view a perfect world,
Or enter warmly into other joys
Than those of faulty, struggling human kind.
That strain upon my soul's too feeble wing
Ends in ignoble floundering: I fall
Into short-sighted pity for the men
Who living in those perfect future times
Will not know half the dear imperfect things
That move my smiles and tears – will never know
The fine old incongruities that raise
My friendly laugh; the innocent conceits
That like a needless eyeglass or black patch
Give those who wear them harmless happiness;
The twists and cracks in our poor earthenware,
That touch me to more conscious fellowship
(I am not myself the finest Parian)
With my coevals. So poor Colin Clout,
To whom raw onion gives prospective zest,
Consoling hours of dampest wintry work,
Could hardly fancy any regal joys

Quite unimpregnate with the onion's scent:
Perhaps his highest hopes are not all clear
Of waftings from that energetic bulb:
'Tis well that onion is not heresy.
Speaking in parable, I am Colin Clout.
A clinging flavour penetrates my life –
My onion is imperfectness: I cleave
To nature's blunders, evanescent types
Which sages banish from Utopia.
"Not worship beauty ?" say you. Patience, friend !
I worship in the temple with the rest;
But by my hearth I keep a sacred nook
For gnomes and dwarfs, duck-footed waddling elves
Who stitched and hammered for the weary man
In days of old. And in that piety
I clothe ungainly forms inherited
From toiling generations, daily bent
At desk, or plough, or loom, or in the mine,
In pioneering labours for the world.
Nay, I am apt when floundering confused
From too rash flight, to grasp at paradox,
And pity future men who will not know
A keen experience with pity blent,
The pathos exquisite of lovely minds
Hid in harsh forms – not penetrating them
Like fire divine within a common bush
Which glows transfigured by the heavenly guest,
So that men put their shoes off; but encaged
Like a sweet child within some thick-walled cell,
Who leaps and fails to hold the window-bars,
But having shown a little dimpled hand
Is visited thenceforth by tender hearts
Whose eyes keep watch about the prison walls.
A foolish, nay, a wicked paradox !
For purest pity is the eye of love

Melting at sight of sorrow; and to grieve
Because it sees no sorrow, shows a love
Warped from its truer nature, turned to love
Of merest habit, like the miser's greed.
But I am Colin still: my prejudice
Is for the flavour of my daily food.
Not that I doubt the world is growing still
As once it grew from Chaos and from Night;
Or have a soul too shrunken for the hope
Which dawned in human breasts, a double morn,
With earliest watchings of the rising light
Chasing the darkness; and through many an age
Has raised the vision of a future time
That stands an Angel with a face all mild
Spearing the demon. I too rest in faith
That man's perfection is the crowning flower,
Toward which the urgent sap in life's great tree
Is pressing, – seen in puny blossoms now,
But in the world's great morrows to expand
With broadest petal and with deepest glow.

Yet, see the patched and plodding citizen
Waiting upon the pavement with the throng
While some victorious world-hero makes
Triumphal entry, and the peal of shouts
And flash of faces 'neath uplifted hats
Run like a storm of joy along the streets !
He says, "God bless him !" almost with a sob,
As the great hero passes; he is glad
The world holds mighty men and mighty deeds;
The music stirs his pulses like strong wine,
The moving splendour touches him with awe –
'Tis glory shed around the common weal,
And he will pay his tribute willingly,
Though with the pennies earned by sordid toil.

Perhaps the hero's deeds have helped to bring
A time when every honest citizen
Shall wear a coat unpatched. And yet he feels
More easy fellowship with neighbours there
Who look on too; and he will soon relapse
From noticing the banners and the steeds
To think with pleasure there is just one bun
Left in his pocket, that may serve to tempt
The wide-eyed lad, whose weight is all too much
For that young mother's arms: and then he falls
To dreamy picturing of sunny days
When he himself was a small big-cheeked lad
In some far village where no heroes came,
And stood a listener 'twixt his father's legs
In the warm fire-light, while the old folk talked
And shook their heads and looked upon the floor;
And he was puzzled, thinking life was fine –
The bread and cheese so nice all through the year
And Christmas sure to come. Oh that good time !
He, could he choose, would have those days again
And see the dear old-fashioned things once more.
But soon the wheels and drums have all passed by
And tramping feet are heard like sudden rain:
The quiet startles our good citizen;
He feels the child upon his arms, and knows
He is with the people making holiday
Because of hopes for better days to come.
But Hope to him was like the brilliant west
Telling of sunrise in a world unknown,
And from that dazzling curtain of bright hues
He turned to the familiar face of fields
Lying all clear in the calm morning land.
Maybe 'tis wiser not to fix a lens
Too scrutinising on the glorious times
When Barbarossa shall arise and shake

His mountain, good King Arthur come again,
And all the heroes of such giant soul
That, living once to cheer mankind with hope,
They had to sleep until the time was ripe
For greater deeds to match their greater thought.
Yet no ! the earth yields nothing more Divine
Than high prophetic vision — than the Seer
Who fasting from man's meaner joy beholds
The paths of beauteous order, and constructs
A fairer type, to shame our low content.
But prophecy is like potential sound
Which turned to music seems a voice sublime
From out the soul of light; but turns to noise
In scrannel pipes, and makes all ears averse.

The faith that life on earth is being shaped
To glorious ends, that order, justice, love
Mean man's completeness, mean effect as sure
As roundness in the dew-drop — that great faith
Is but the rushing and expanding stream
Of thought, of feeling, fed by all the past.
Our finest hope is finest memory,
As they who love in age think youth is blest
Because it has a life to fill with love.
Full souls are double mirrors, making still
An endless vista of fair things before
Repeating things behind: so faith is strong
Only when we are strong, shrinks when we shrink.
It comes when music stirs us, and the chords
Moving on some grand climax shake our souls
With influx new that makes new energies.
It comes in swellings of the heart and tears
That rise at noble and at gentle deeds —
At labours of the master-artist's hand
Which, trembling, touches to a finer end,

Trembling before an image seen within.
It comes in moments of heroic love,
Unjealous joy in joy not made for us –
In conscious triumph of the good within
Making us worship goodness that rebukes.
Even our failures are a prophecy,
Even our yearnings and our bitter tears
After that fair and true we cannot grasp;
As patriots who seem to die in vain
Make liberty more sacred by their pangs.

Presentiment of better things on earth
Sweeps in with every force that stirs our souls
To admiration, self-renouncing love,
Or thoughts, like light, that bind the world in one:
Sweeps like the sense of vastness, when at night
We hear the roll and dash of waves that break
Nearer and nearer with the rushing tide,
Which rises to the level of the cliff
Because the wide Atlantic rolls behind
Throbbing respondent to the far-off orbs.

2-27 January 1865

IN A LONDON DRAWINGROOM

The sky is cloudy, yellowed by the smoke.
For view there are the houses opposite
Cutting the sky with one long line of wall
Like solid fog: far as the eye can stretch
Monotony of surface and of form
Without a break to hang a guess upon.
No bird can make a shadow as it flies,
For all is shadow, as in ways o'erhung
By thickest canvass, where the golden rays
Are clothed in hemp. No figure lingering
Pauses to feed the hunger of the eye
Or rest a little on the lap of life.
All hurry on and look upon the ground,
Or glance unmarking at the passers by
The wheels are hurrying too, cabs, carriages
All closed, in multiplied identity.
The world seems one huge prison-house and court
Where men are punished at the slightest cost,
With lowest rate of colour, warmth and joy.

(*December 1865*)

TWO LOVERS

Two lovers by a moss-grown spring:
    They leaned soft cheeks together there,
    Mingled the dark and sunny hair,
And heard the wooing thrushes sing.
                O budding time !
                O love's blest prime !

Two wedded from the portal stept:
    The bells made happy carollings,
    The air was soft as fanning wings,
White petals on the pathway slept.
                O pure-eyed bride !
                O tender pride !

Two faces o'er a cradle bent:
    Two hands above the head were locked;
    These pressed each other while they rocked,
Those watched a life that love had sent.
                O solemn hour !
                O hidden power !

Two parents by the evening fire:
    The red light fell about their knees
    On heads that rose by slow degrees
Like buds upon the lily spire.
                O patient life !
                O tender strife !

The two still sat together there,
  The red light shone about their knees;
  But all the heads by slow degrees
Had gone and left that lonely pair.
                    O voyage fast !
                    O vanished past !

The red light shone upon the floor
  And made the space between them wide;
  They drew their chairs up side by side,
Their pale cheeks joined, and said, "Once more!"
                    O memories !
                    O past that is !

September 1866

When first the earth broke from her parent ring
Trembling an instant ere her separate life
Had found the unfailing pulse of night and day,
Her inner half that met the effusive Sun
Had earlier largesse of his rays and thrilled
To the celestial music of the dawn
While yet the western half was cold and sad,
Shivering beneath the whisper of the stars.
So Asia was the earliest home of light:
The little seeds first germinated there,
Birds first made bridals, and the year first knew
Autumnal ripeness. Ever wandering sound
That dumbly throbbed within the homeless vast
Took sweet imprisonment in song and speech –
Like light more beauteous for shattering,
Parted melodious in the trembling throat
Of the first matin bird; made utterance
From the full-rounded lips of that young race
Who moved by the omnipresent Energy
Dividing towards sublimer union,
Clove sense and image subtilly in twain,
Then wedded them, till heavenly Thought was born.

1866

ARMS ! TO ARMS !

(From Depping's Spanish Ballads)

With two thousand Moorish horsemen
  Reduan lays waste the plain,
Seizes all the herds and pushes
  Past the frontier of Jasa;
Spies the turrets of the city −
  Arrow-swift he leaves them far,
Scours the fruitful lands dividing
  All the towered holds of war.
    And Baeza's bells high swinging
    Arms ! to Arms ! in haste are ringing.

On he marches in such silence,
  Seems as it had been agreed
'Twixt the mutely hanging trumpet
  And the hushed, unneighing steed.
But at last the watchman posted
  Darkly like the stars at noon
Send their threatening signals onward:
  Torch to torch is answering soon
    And Baeza's bells high swinging
    Arms ! to Arms ! in haste are ringing.

Night is in their van to shroud them
    With her banners floating black,
But behind them are the bonfires
    They have left upon their track:
Flames that wave instead of harvests,
    Coiling round the cottage wall,
Fiery serpents that illumine
    Ruin's wicked festival.
        And Baeza's bells high swinging
        Arms ! to Arms ! in haste are ringing.

Towards the front of sudden danger
    All the brave prepare to go:
Cavaliers take polished lances,
    Men afoot the trusty bow,
Proud Jaen sends forth her nobles,
    Hurrying townsmen spread alarm,
Humming, swarming, sharp'ning weapons,
    Angry wasps at threat of harm.
        And Baeza's bells high swinging
        Arms ! to Arms ! in haste are ringing.

Now the gates of morn are open
    And the Christians ope their gates;
Meet the Moor at half a league thence,
    Clashing weapons, clashing hates.
With the din the air is maddened,
    Echoes hurry in dismay,
Fifes are shrieking, drums are roaring
    Men are shouting, horses neigh.
        And Baeza's bells high swinging
        Arms ! to Arms ! in haste are ringing.

1866

IN THE SOUTH

O gentle brightness of late autumn morns !
The dear Earth like a patient matron left
By all she loved and reared, still smiles and loves.
The fields low-shorn gleam with a paler gold,
The olives stretch their shadows; on the vines
Forgotten bunches breathe out mellowness,
And little apples poised upon their stems
Laugh sparkling high above the mounting sun.
Each delicate blade and bossy arching leaf
Is silvered with the dew; the plough o'erturns
The redolent earth, and with slow-broadening belt
Of furrowed brownness, makes mute prophecy.
The far off rocks take breathing colours, bathed
In the aërial ocean of clear blue;
The palm soars in the silence, and the towers
And scattered villages seem still to sleep
In happy morning dreams.

1867

(WILL LADISLAW'S SONG)

O me, O me, what frugal cheer
  My love doth feed upon !
A touch, a ray, that is not here,
  A shadow that is gone:

A dream of breath that might be near,
  An inly-echoed tone,
The thought that one may think me dear,
  The place where one was known,

The tremor of a banished fear,
  An ill that was not done –
O me, O me, what frugal cheer
  My love doth feed upon !

From Middlemarch, *Book V, Chapter 47.*

'O MAY I JOIN THE CHOIR INVISIBLE'

Longum illud tempus, quum non ero, magis me movet,
quam hoc exiguum. – CICERO, ad Att., xii. 18.

O may I join the choir invisible
Of those immortal dead who live again
In minds made better by their presence: live
In pulses stirred to generosity,
In deeds of daring rectitude, in scorn
For miserable aims that end with self,
In thoughts sublime that pierce the night like stars,
And with their mild persistence urge man's search
To vaster issues.
        So to live is heaven:
To make undying music in the world,
Breathing as beauteous order that controls
With growing sway the growing life of man.
So we inherit that sweet purity
For which we struggled, failed, and agonised
With widening retrospect that bred despair.
Rebellious flesh that would not be subdued,
A vicious parent shaming still its child
Poor anxious penitence, is quick dissolved;
Its discords, quenched by meeting harmonies,
Die in the large and charitable air.
And all our rarer, better, truer self,
That sobbed religiously in yearning song,
That watched to ease the burthen of the world,
Laboriously tracing what must be,
And what may yet be better – saw within
A worthier image for the sanctuary,
And shaped it forth before the multitude
Divinely human, raising worship so

To higher reverence more mixed with love –
That better self shall live till human Time
Shall fold its eyelids, and the human sky
Be gathered like a scroll within the tomb
Unread for ever.

              This is life to come,
Which martyred men have made more glorious
For us who strive to follow. May I reach
That purest heaven, be to other souls
The cup of strength in some great agony,
Enkindle generous ardour, feed pure love,
Beget the smiles that have no cruelty –
Be the sweet presence of a good diffused,
And in diffusion ever more intense.
So shall I join the choir invisible
Whose music is the gladness of the world.

August 1867

Come with me to the mountain, not where rocks
Soar harsh above the troops of hurrying pines,
But where the earth spreads soft and rounded breasts
To feed her children; where the generous hills
Lift a green isle betwixt the sky and plain
To keep some Old World things aloof from change.
Here too 'tis hill and hollow: new-born streams
With sweet enforcement, joyously compelled
Like laughing children, hurry down the steeps,
And make a dimpled chase athwart the stones;
Pine woods are black upon the heights, the slopes
Are green with pasture, and the bearded corn
Fringes the blue above the sudden ridge:
A little world whose round horizon cuts
This isle of hills with heaven for a sea,
Save in clear moments when southwestward gleams
France by the Rhine, melting anon to haze.
The monks of old chose here their still retreat,
And called it by the Blessed Virgin's name,
Sancta Maria, which the peasant's tongue,
Speaking from out the parent's heart that turns
All loved things into little things, has made
Sanct Märgen, – Holy little Mary, dear
As all the sweet home things she smiles upon,
The children and the cows, the apple-trees,
The cart, the plough, all named with that caress
Which feigns them little, easy to be held,
Familiar to the eyes and hand and heart.
What though a Queen ? She puts her crown away
And with her little Boy wears common clothes,
Caring for common wants, remembering
That day when good Saint Joseph left his work

To marry her with humble trust sublime.
The monks are gone, their shadows fall no more
Tall-frocked and cowled athwart the evening fields
At milking-time; their silent corridors
Are turned to homes of bare-armed, aproned men,
Who toil for wife and children. But the bells,
Pealing on high from two quaint convent towers,
Still ring the Catholic signals, summoning
To grave remembrance of the larger life
That bears our own, like perishable fruit
Upon its heaven-wide branches. At their sound
The shepherd boy far off upon the hill,
The workers with the saw and at the forge,
The triple generation round the hearth, –
Grandames and mothers and the flute-voiced girls, –
Fall on their knees and send forth prayerful cries
To the kind Mother with the little Boy,
Who pleads for helpless men against the storm,
Lightning and plagues and all terrific shapes
Of power supreme.
Within the prettiest hollow of these hills,
Just as you enter it, upon the slope
Stands a low cottage neighboured cheerily
By running water, which, at farthest end
Of the same hollow, turns a heavy mill,
And feeds the pasture for the miller's cows,
Blanchi and Nägeli, Veilchen and the rest,
Matrons with faces as Griselda mild,
Coming at call. And on the farthest height
A little tower looks out above the pines
Where mounting you will find a sanctuary
Open and still; without, the silent crowd
Of heaven-planted, incense-mingling flowers;
Within, the altar where the Mother sits
'Mid votive tablets hung from far-off years

By peasants succoured in the peril of fire,
Fever, or flood, who thought that Mary's love,
Willing but not omnipotent, had stood
Between their lives and that dread power which slew
Their neighbour at their side. The chapel bell
Will melt to gentlest music ere it reach
That cottage on the slope, whose garden gate
Has caught the rose-tree boughs and stands ajar;
So does the door, to let the sunbeams in;
For in the slanting sunbeams angels come
And visit Agatha who dwells within, –
Old Agatha, whose cousins Kate and Nell
Are housed by her in Love and Duty's name,
They being feeble, with small withered wits,
And she believing that the higher gift
Was given to be shared. So Agatha
Shares her one room, all neat on afternoons,
As if some memory were sacred there
And everything within the four low walls
An honoured relic.
                        One long summer's day
An angel entered at the rose-hung gate,
With skirts pale blue, a brow to quench the pearl,
Hair soft and blonde as infants', plenteous
As hers who made the wavy lengths once speak
The grateful worship of a rescued soul.
The angel paused before the open door
To give good day. "Come in," said Agatha.
I followed close, and watched and listened there.
The angel was a lady, noble, young,
Taught in all seemliness that fits a court,
All lore that shapes the mind to delicate use,
Yet quiet, lowly, as a meek white dove
That with its presence teaches gentleness.
Men called her Countess Linda; little girls

In Freiburg town, orphans whom she caressed,
Said Mamma Linda: yet her years were few,
Her outward beauties all in budding time,
Her virtues the aroma of the plant
That dwells in all its being, root, stem, leaf,
And waits not ripeness.

                          "Sit," said Agatha.
Her cousins were at work in neighbouring homes
But yet she was not lonely; all things round
Seemed filled with noiseless yet responsive life,
As of a child at breast that gently clings:
Not sunlight only or the breathing flowers
Or the swift shadows of the birds and bees,
But all the household goods, which, polished fair
By hands that cherished them for service done,
Shone as with glad content. The wooden beams
Dark and yet friendly, easy to be reached,
Bore three white crosses for a speaking sign;
The walls had little pictures hung a-row,
Telling the stories of Saint Ursula,
And Saint Elizabeth, the lowly queen;
And on the bench that served for table too,
Skirting the wall to save the narrow space,
There lay the Catholic books, inherited
From those old times when printing still was young
With stout-limbed promise, like a sturdy boy.
And in the farthest corner stood the bed
Where o'er the pillow hung two pictures wreathed
With fresh-plucked ivy: one the Virgin's death,
And one her flowering tomb, while high above
She smiling bends and lets her girdle down
For ladder to the soul that cannot trust
In life which outlasts burial. Agatha
Sat at her knitting, aged, upright, slim,
And spoke her welcome with mild dignity.

She kept the company of kings and queens
And mitred saints who sat below the feet
Of Francis with the ragged frock and wounds;
And Rank for her meant Duty, various,
Yet equal in its worth, done worthily.
Command was service; humblest service done
By willing and discerning souls was glory.
　　Fair Countess Linda sat upon the bench,
Close fronting the old knitter, and they talked
With sweet antiphony of young and old.

AGATHA. You like our valley, lady? I am glad
　　You thought it well to come again. But rest –
　　The walk is long from Master Michael's inn.

COUNTESS LINDA. Yes, but no walk is prettier.

AGATHA.　　　　　　　　　　　　　It is true:
　　There lacks no blessing here, the waters all
　　Have virtues like the garments of the Lord,
　　And heal much sickness; then, the crops and cows
　　Flourish past speaking, and the garden flowers,
　　Pink, blue, and purple, 'tis a joy to see
　　How they yield honey for the singing bees.
　　I would the whole world were as good a home.

COUNTESS LINDA.
　　And you are well off, Agatha ? – your friends
　　Left you a certain bread: is it not so?

AGATHA. Not so at all, dear lady. I had nought,
　　Was a poor orphan; but I came to tend
　　Here in this house, an old afflicted pair,
　　Who wore out slowly; and the last who died,
　　Full thirty years ago, left me this roof

And all the household stuff. It was great wealth;
And so I had a home for Kate and Nell.

COUNTESS LINDA.
But how, then, have you earned your daily bread
These thirty years ?

AGATHA.   O, that is easy earning.
We help the neighbours, and our bit and sup
Is never failing: they have work for us
In house and field, all sorts of odds and ends,
Patching and mending, turning o'er the hay,
Holding sick children, – there is always work;
And they are very good, – the neighbours are:
Weigh not our bits of work with weight and scale,
But glad themselves with giving us good shares
Of meat and drink; and in the big farm-house
When cloth comes home from weaving, the good wife
Cuts me a piece, – this very gown, – and says:
"Here, Agatha, you old maid, you have time
To pray for Hans who is gone soldiering:
The saints might help him, and they have much to do,
'Twere well they were besought to think of him."
She spoke half jesting, but I pray, I pray
For poor young Hans. I take it much to heart
That other people are worse off than I, –
I ease my soul with praying for them all.

COUNTESS LINDA. That is your way of singing, Agatha;
Just as the nightingales pour forth sad songs,
And when they reach men's ears they make men's hearts
Feel the more kindly.

AGATHA.   Nay, I cannot sing:
My voice is hoarse, and oft I think my prayers

Are foolish, feeble things; for Christ is good
Whether I pray or not, – the Virgin's heart
Is kinder far than mine; and then I stop
And feel I can do nought towards helping men,
Till out it comes, like tears that will not hold,
And I must pray again for all the world.
'Tis good to me, – I mean the neighbours are:
To Kate and Nell too. I have money saved
To go on pilgrimage the second time.

COUNTESS LINDA. And do you mean to go on pilgrimage
    With all your years to carry, Agatha ?

AGATHA. The years are light, dear lady: 'tis my sins
    Are heavier than I would. And I shall go
    All the way to Einsiedeln with that load:
    I need to work it off:

COUNTESS LINDA.   What sort of sins,
    Dear Agatha ? I think they must be small.

AGATHA. Nay, but they may be greater than I know;
    'Tis but dim light I see by. So I try
    All ways I know of to be cleansed and pure.
    I would not sink where evil spirits are.
    There's perfect goodness somewhere: so I strive.

COUNTESS LINDA. You were the better for that pilgrimage
    You made before ? The shrine is beautiful;
    And then you saw fresh country all the way.

AGATHA. Yes, that is true. And ever since that time
    The world seems greater, and the Holy Church
    More wonderful. The blessed pictures all,
    The heavenly images with books and wings,

Are company to me through the day and night.
The time ! the time ! It never seemed far back,
Only to father's father and his kin
That lived before him. But the time stretched out
After that pilgrimage: I seemed to see
Far back, and yet I knew time lay behind,
As there are countries lying still behind
The highest mountains, there in Switzerland.
O, it is great to go on pilgrimage !

COUNTESS LINDA.

Perhaps some neighbours will be pilgrims too,
And you can start together in a band.

AGATHA. Not from these hills: people are busy here,
The beasts want tendance. One who is not missed
Can go and pray for others who must work.
I owe it to all neighbours, young and old;
For they are good past thinking, – lads and girls
Given to mischief, merry naughtiness,
Quiet it, as the hedgehogs smooth their spines,
For fear of hurting poor old Agatha.
'Tis pretty: why, the cherubs in the sky
Look young and merry, and the angels play
On citherns, lutes, and all sweet instruments.
I would have young things merry. See the Lord !
A little baby playing with the birds;
And how the Blessed Mother smiles at him.

COUNTESS LINDA. I think you are too happy, Agatha,
To care for heaven. Earth contents you well.

AGATHA. Nay, nay, I shall be called, and I shall go
Right willingly. I shall get helpless, blind,
Be like an old stalk to be plucked away:

The garden must be cleared for young spring plants.
'Tis home beyond the grave, the most are there,
All those we pray to, all the Church's lights, –
And poor old souls are welcome in their rags:
One sees it by the pictures. Good Saint Ann,
The Virgin's mother, she is very old,
And had her troubles with her husband too.
Poor Kate and Nell are younger far than I,
But they will have this roof to cover them.
I shall go willingly; and willingness
Makes the yoke easy and the burden light.

COUNTESS LINDA.
When you go southward in your pilgrimage,
Come to see me in Freiburg, Agatha.
Where you have friends you should not go to inns.

AGATHA. Yes, I will gladly come to see you, lady.
And you will give me sweet hay for a bed,
And in the morning I shall wake betimes
And start when all the birds begin to sing.

COUNTESS LINDA.
You wear your smart clothes on the pilgrimage,
Such pretty clothes as all the women here
Keep by them for their best: a velvet cap
And collar golden-broidered ? They look well
On old and young alike.

AGATHA.   Nay, I have none, –
Never had better clothes than these you see.
Good clothes are pretty, but one sees them best
When others wear them, and I somehow thought
'Twas not worth while. I had so many things
More than some neighbours, I was partly shy

Of wearing better clothes than they, and now
I am so old and custom is so strong
'Twould hurt me sore to put on finery.

Countess Linda. Your grey hair is a crown, dear Agatha.
Shake hands; good-bye. The sun is going down,
And I must see the glory from the hill.

I stayed among those hills; and oft heard more
Of Agatha. I liked to hear her name,
As that of one half grandame and half saint,
Uttered with reverent playfulness. The lads
And younger men all called her mother, aunt,
Or granny, with their pet diminutives,
And bade their lasses and their brides behave
Right well to one who surely made a link
'Twixt faulty folk and God by loving both:
Not one but counted service done by her,
Asking no pay save just her daily bread.
At feasts and weddings, when they passed in groups
Along the vale, and the good country wine,
Being vocal in them, made them quire along
In quaintly mingled mirth and piety,
They fain must jest and play some friendly trick
On three old maids; but when the moment came
Always they bated breath and made their sport
Gentle as feather-stroke, that Agatha
Might like the waking for the love it showed.
Their song made happy music 'mid the hills,
For nature tuned their race to harmony,
And poet Hans, the tailor, wrote them songs
That grew from out their life, as crocuses
From out the meadow's moistness. 'Twas his song
They oft sang, wending homeward from a feast, –

The song I give you. It brings in, you see,
Their gentle jesting with the three old maids.

Midnight by the chapel bell !
Homeward, homeward all, farewell !
I with you, and you with me,
Miles are short with company.
Heart of Mary, bless the way,
Keep us all by night and day !

Moon and stars at feast with night
Now have drunk their fill of light.
Home they hurry, making time
Trot apace, like merry rhyme.
Heart of Mary, mystic rose,
Send us all a sweet repose !

Swiftly through the wood down hill,
Run till you can hear the mill.
Toni's ghost is wandering now,
Shaped just like a snow-white cow.
Heart of Mary, morning star,
Ward off danger, near or far !

Toni's waggon with its load
Fell and crushed him in the road
'Twixt these pine-trees. Never fear !
Give a neighbour's ghost good cheer.
Holy Babe, our God and Brother,
Bind us fast to one another !

Hark ! the mill is at its work,
Now we pass beyond the murk
To the hollow, where the moon
Makes her silvery afternoon.
> *Good Saint Joseph, faithful spouse,*
> *Help us all to keep our vows !*

Here the three old maidens dwell,
Agatha and Kate and Nell;
See, the moon shines on the thatch,
We will go and shake the latch.
> *Heart of Mary, cup of joy,*
> *Give us mirth without alloy !*

Hush, 'tis here, no noise, sing low,
Rap with gentle knuckles − so !
Like the little tapping birds,
On the door; then sing good words.
> *Meek Saint Anna, old and fair,*
> *Hallow all the snow-white hair !*

Little maidens old, sweet dreams !
Sleep one sleep till morning beams.
Mothers ye, who help us all,
Quick at hand, if ill befall.
> *Holy Gabriel, lily-laden,*
> *Bless the aged mother-maiden !*

Forward, mount the broad hillside
Swift as soldiers when they ride.
See the two towers how they peep,
Round-capped giants, o'er the steep.
> *Heart of Mary, by thy sorrow,*
> *Keep us upright through the morrow !*

Now they rise quite suddenly
Like a man from bended knee,
Now Saint Märgen is in sight,
Here the roads branch off – good night !
Heart of Mary, by thy grace,
Give us with the saints a place !

December 1868 – January 1869

HOW LISA LOVED THE KING

Six hundred years ago, in Dante's time,
Before his cheek was furrowed by deep rhyme –
When Europe, fed afresh from Eastern story,
Was like a garden tangled with the glory
Of flowers hand-planted and of flowers air-sown,
Climbing and trailing, budding and full-blown,
Where purple bells are tossed amid pink stars,
And springing blades, green troops in innocent wars,
Crowd every shady spot of teeming earth,
Making invisible motion visible birth –
Six hundred years ago, Palermo town
Kept holiday. A deed of great renown,
A high revenge, had freed it from the yoke
Of hated Frenchmen, and from Calpe's rock
To where the Bosporus caught the earlier sun,
'Twas told that Pedro, King of Aragon,
Was welcomed master of all Sicily,
A royal knight, supreme as kings should be
In strength and gentleness that make high chivalry.

Spain was the favourite home of knightly grace,
Where generous men rode steeds of generous race;
Both Spanish, yet half Arab, both inspired
By mutual spirit, that each motion fired
With beauteous response, like minstrelsy
Afresh fulfilling fresh expectancy.
So when Palermo made high festival,
The joy of matrons and of maidens all
Was the mock terror of the tournament,
Where safety with the glimpse of danger blent,
Took exaltation as from epic song,
Which greatly tells the pains that to great life belong.

And in all eyes King Pedro was the king
Of cavaliers: as in a full-gemmed ring
The largest ruby, or as that bright star
Whose shining shows us where the Hyads are.
His the best jennet, and he sat it best;
His weapon, whether tilting or in rest,
Was worthiest watching, and his face once seen
Gave to the promise of his royal mien
Such rich fulfilment as the opened eyes
Of a loved sleeper, or the long-watched rise
Of vernal day, whose joy o'er stream and meadow flies.

But of the maiden forms that thick enwreathed
The broad piazza and sweet witchery breathed,
With innocent faces budding all arow
From balconies and windows high and low,
Who was it felt the deep mysterious glow,
The impregnation with supernal fire
Of young ideal love – transformed desire,
Whose passion is but worship of that Best
Taught by the many-mingled creed of each young breast?
'Twas gentle Lisa, of no noble line,
Child of Bernardo, a rich Florentine,
Who from his merchant-city hither came
To trade in drugs; yet kept an honest fame,
And had the virtue not to try and sell
Drugs that had none. He loved his riches well,
But loved them chiefly for his Lisa's sake,
Whom with a father's care he sought to make
The bride of some true honourable man: –
Of Perdicone (so the rumour ran),
Whose birth was higher than his fortunes were;
For still your trader likes a mixture fair
Of blood that hurries to some higher strain
Than reckoning money's loss and money's gain.

And of such mixture good may surely come:
Lords' scions so may learn to cast a sum,
A trader's grandson bear a well-set head,
And have less conscious manners, better bred;
Nor, when he tries to be polite, be rude instead.

'Twas Perdicone's friends made overtures
To good Bernardo: so one dame assures
Her neighbour dame who notices the youth
Fixing his eyes on Lisa; and in truth
Eyes that could see her on this summer day
Might find it hard to turn another way.
She had a pensive beauty, yet not sad;
Rather, like minor cadences that glad
The hearts of little birds amid spring boughs;
And oft the trumpet or the joust would rouse
Pulses that gave her cheek a finer glow,
Parting her lips that seemed a mimic bow
By chiselling Love for play in coral wrought,
Then quickened by him with the passionate
  thought,
The soul that trembled in the lustrous night
Of slow long eyes. Her body was so slight,
It seemed she could have floated in the sky,
And with the angelic choir made symphony;
But in her cheek's rich tinge, and in the dark
Of darkest hair and eyes, she bore a mark
Of kinship to her generous mother earth,
The fervid land that gives the plumy palm-trees birth.

She saw not Perdicone; her young mind
Dreamed not that any man had ever pined
For such a little simple maid as she:
She had but dreamed how heavenly it would be
To love some hero noble, beauteous, great,

Who would live stories worthy to narrate,
Like Roland, or the warriors of Troy,
The Cid, or Amadis, or that fair boy
Who conquered everything beneath the sun,
And somehow, some time, died at Babylon
Fighting the Moors. For heroes all were good
And fair as that archangel who withstood
The Evil One, the author of all wrong –
That Evil One who made the French so strong;
And now the flower of heroes must be he
Who drove those tyrants from dear Sicily,
So that her maids might walk to vespers tranquilly.

Young Lisa saw this hero in the king,
And as wood-lilies that sweet odours bring
Might dream the light that opes their modest eyne
Was lily-odoured, – and as rites divine,
Round turf-laid altars, or 'neath roofs of stone,
Draw sanctity from out the heart alone
That loves and worships, so the miniature
Perplexed of her soul's world, all virgin pure,
Filled with heroic virtues that bright form,
Raona's royalty, the finished norm
Of horsemanship – the half of chivalry:
For how could generous men avengers be,
Save as God's messengers on coursers fleet ? –
These, scouring earth, made Spain with Syria meet
In one self world where the same right had sway,
And good must grow as grew the blessed day.
No more; great Love his essence had endued
With Pedro's form, and entering subdued
The soul of Lisa, fervid and intense,
Proud in its choice of proud obedience
To hardship glorified by perfect reverence.

Sweet Lisa homeward carried that dire guest,
And in her chamber through the hours of rest
The darkness was alight for her with sheen
Of arms, and plumèd helm, and bright between
Their commoner gloss, like the pure living spring
'Twixt porphyry lips, or living bird's bright wing
'Twixt golden wires, the glances of the king
Flashed on her soul, and waked vibrations there
Of known delights love-mixed to new and rare:
The impalpable dream was turned to breathing flesh,
Chill thought of summer to the warm close mesh
Of sunbeams held between the citron-leaves,
Clothing her life of life. Oh, she believes
That she could be content if he but knew
(Her poor small self could claim no other due)
How Lisa's lowly love had highest reach
Of wingèd passion, whereto wingèd speech
Would be scorched remnants left by mounting flame.
Though, had she such lame message, were it blame
To tell what greatness dwelt in her, what rank
She held in loving ? Modest maidens shrank
From telling love that fed on selfish hope;
But love, as hopeless as the shattering song
Wailed for loved beings who have joined the throng
Of mighty dead ones. . . . Nay, but she was weak –
Knew only prayers and ballads – could not speak
With eloquence save what dumb creatures have,
That with small cries and touches small boons crave.

She watched all day that she might see him pass
With knights and ladies; but she said, "Alas !
Though he should see me, it were all as one
He saw a pigeon sitting on the stone
Of wall or balcony: some coloured spot
His eye just sees, his mind regardeth not.

I have no music-touch that could bring nigh
My love to his soul's hearing. I shall die,
And he will never know who Lisa was −
The trader's child, whose soaring spirit rose
As hedge-born aloe-flowers that rarest years disclose.

"For were I now a fair deep-breasted queen
A-horseback, with blonde hair, and tunic green
Gold-bordered, like Costanza, I should need
No change within to make me queenly there;
For they the royal-hearted women are
Who nobly love the noblest, yet have grace
For needy suffering lives in lowliest place,
Carrying a choicer sunlight in their smile,
The heavenliest ray that pitieth the vile.
My love is such, it cannot choose but soar
Up to the highest; yet for evermore,
Though I were happy, throned beside the king,
I should be tender to each little thing
With hurt warm breast, that had no speech to tell
Its inward pang, and I would soothe it well
With tender touch and with a low soft moan
For company: my dumb love-pang is lone,
Prisoned as topaz-beam within a rough-garbed stone."

So, inward-wailing, Lisa passed her days.
Each night the August moon with changing phase
Looked broader, harder on her unchanged pain;
Each noon the heat lay heavier again
On her despair; until her body frail
Shrank like the snow that watchers in the vale
See narrowed on the height each summer morn;
While her dark glance burnt larger, more forlorn,
As if the soul within her all on fire
Made of her being one swift funeral pyre.

Father and mother saw with sad dismay
The meaning of their riches melt away:
For without Lisa what would sequins buy ?
What wish were left if Lisa were to die ?
Through her they cared for summers still to come,
Else they would be as ghosts without a home
In any flesh that could feel glad desire.
They pay the best physicians, never tire
Of seeking what will soothe her, promising
That aught she longed for, though it were a thing
Hard to be come at as the Indian snow,
Or roses that on alpine summits blow –
It should be hers. She answers with low voice,
She longs for death alone – death is her choice;
Death is the King who never did think scorn,
But rescues every meanest soul to sorrow born.

Yet one day, as they bent above her bed
And watched her in brief sleep, her drooping head
Turned gently, as the thirsty flowers that feel
Some moist revival through their petals steal,
And little flutterings of her lids and lips
Told of such dreamy joy as sometimes dips
A skyey shadow in the mind's poor pool.
She oped her eyes, and turned their dark gems full
Upon her father, as in utterance dumb
Of some new prayer that in her sleep had come.
"What is it, Lisa ?" "Father, I would see
Minuccio, the great singer; bring him me."
For always, night and day, her unstilled thought
Wandering all o'er its little world, had sought
How she could reach, by some soft pleading touch,
King Pedro's soul, that she who loved so much
Dying, might have a place within his mind –
A litle grave which he would sometimes find

And plant some flower on it − some thought, some
   memory kind.
Till in her dream she saw Minuccio
Touching his viola, and chanting low
A strain that, falling on her brokenly,
Seemed blossoms lightly blown from off a tree,
Each burthened with a word that was a scent −
Raona, Lisa, love, death, tournament;
Then in her dream she said, "He sings of me −
Might be my messenger; ah, now I see
The king is listening −" Then she awoke,
And, missing her dear dream, that new-born longing
   spoke.

She longed for music: that was natural;
Physicians said it was medicinal;
The humours might be schooled by true consent
Of a fine tenor and fine instrument;
In brief, good music, mixed with doctor's stuff,
Apollo with Asklepios − enough !
Minuccio, entreated, gladly came.
(He was a singer of most gentle fame −
A noble, kindly spirit, not elate
That he was famous, but that song was great −
Would sing as finely to this suffering child
As at the court where princes on him smiled.)
Gently he entered and sat down by her,
Asking what sort of strain she would prefer −
The voice alone, or voice with viol wed;
Then, when she chose the last, he preluded
With magic hand, that summoned from the strings
Aerial spirits, rare yet vibrant wings
That fanned the pulses of his listener,
And waked each sleeping sense with blissful stir.
Her cheek already showed a slow faint blush,

But soon the voice, in pure full liquid rush,
Made all the passion, that till now she felt,
Seem but cool waters that in warmer melt.
Finished the song, she prayed to be alone
With kind Minuccio; for her faith had grown
To trust him as if missioned like a priest
With some high grace, that when his singing ceased
Still made him wiser, more magnanimous
Than common men who had no genius.

So laying her small hand within his palm,
She told him how that secret glorious harm
Of loftiest loving had befallen her;
That death, her only hope, most bitter were,
If when she died her love must perish too
As songs unsung and thoughts unspoken do,
Which else might live within another breast.
She said, "Minuccio, the grave were rest,
If I were sure, that lying cold and lone,
My love, my best of life, had safely flown
And nestled in the bosom of the king;
See, 'tis a small weak bird, with unfledged wing.
But you will carry it for me secretly,
And bear it to the king, then come to me
And tell me it is safe, and I shall go
Content, knowing that he I love my love doth know."

Then she wept silently, but each large tear
Made pleading music to the inward ear
Of good Minuccio. "Lisa, trust in me,"
He said, and kissed her fingers loyally;
"It is sweet law to me to do your will,
And ere the sun his round shall thrice fulfil,
I hope to bring you news of such rare skill
As amulets have, that aches in trusting bosoms still."

He needed not to pause and first devise
How he should tell the king; for in nowise
Were such love-message worthily bested
Save in fine verse by music renderèd.
He sought a poet-friend, a Siennese,
And "Mico, mine," he said, "full oft to please
Thy whim of sadness I have sung thee strains
To make thee weep in verse: now pay my pains,
And write me a canzòn divinely sad,
Sinlessly passionate and meekly mad
With young despair, speaking a maiden's heart
Of fifteen summers, who would fain depart
From ripening life's new-urgent mystery –
Love-choice of one too high her love to be –
But cannot yield her breath till she has poured
Her strength away in this hot-bleeding word
Telling the secret of her soul to her soul's lord."

Said Mico, "Nay, that thought is poesy,
I need but listen as it sings to me.
Come thou again to-morrow." The third day
When linkèd notes had perfected the lay,
Minuccio had his summons to the court
To make, as he was wont, the moments short
Of ceremonious dinner to the king.
This was the time when he had meant to bring
Melodious message of young Lisa's love:
He waited till the air had ceased to move
To ringing silver, till Falernian wine
Made quickened sense with quietude combine,
And then with passionate descant made each ear incline.

Love, thou didst see me, light as morning's breath,
Roaming a garden in a joyous error,
Laughing at chases vain, a happy child,
Till of thy countenance the alluring terror
In majesty from out the blossoms smiled,
From out their life seeming a beauteous Death.

O Love, who so didst choose me for thine own,
Taking this little isle to thy great sway,
See now, it is the honour of thy throne
That what thou gavest perish not away,
Nor leave some sweet remembrance to atone
By life that will be for the brief life gone:
Hear, ere the shroud o'er these frail limbs be thrown –
Since every king is vassal unto thee,
My heart's lord needs must listen loyally –
O tell him I am waiting for my Death !

Tell him, for that he hath such royal power
'Twere hard for him to think how small a thing,
How slight a sign, would make a wealthy dower
For one like me, the bride of that pale king
Whose bed is mine at some swift-nearing hour.
Go to my lord, and to his memory bring
That happy birthday of my sorrowing
When his large glance made meaner gazers glad,
Entering the bannered lists: 'twas then I had
The wound that laid me in the arms of Death.

Tell him, O Love, I am a lowly maid,
No more than any little knot of thyme
That he with careless foot may often tread;
Yet lowest fragrance oft will mount sublime
And cleave to things most high and hallowèd,
As doth the fragrance of my life's springtime,

My lowly love, that soaring seeks to climb
Within his thought, and make a gentle bliss,
More blissful than if mine, in being his:
So shall I live in him and rest in Death.

The strain was new. It seemed a pleading cry,
And yet a rounded perfect melody,
Making grief beauteous as the tear-filled eyes
Of little child at little miseries.
Trembling at first, then swelling as it rose,
Like rising light that broad and broader grows,
It filled the hall, and so possessed the air
That not one breathing soul was present there,
Though dullest, slowest but was quivering
In music's grasp, and forced to hear her sing.
But most such sweet compulsion took the mood
Of Pedro (tired of doing what he would).
Whether the words which that strange meaning bore
Were but the poet's feigning or aught more,
Was bounden question, since their aim must be
At some imagined or true royalty.
He called Minuccio and bade him tell
What poet of the day had writ so well;
For though they came behind all former rhymes,
The verses were not bad for these poor times.
"Monsignor, they are only three days old,"
Minuccio said; "but it must not be told
How this song grew, save to your royal ear."
Eager, the king withdrew where none was near,
And gave close audience to Minuccio,
Who meetly told that love-tale meet to know.
The king had features pliant to confess
The presence of a manly tenderness −
Son, father, brother, lover, blent in one,
In fine harmonic exaltation −

The spirit of religious chivalry.
He listened, and Minuccio could see
The tender, generous admiration spread
O'er all his face, and glorify his head
With royalty that would have kept its rank
Though his brocaded robes to tatters shrank.
He answered without pause, "So sweet a maid,
In nature's own insignia arrayed,
Though she were come of unmixed trading blood
That sold and bartered ever since the Flood,
Would have the self-contained and single worth
Of radiant jewels born in darksome earth.
Raona were a shame to Sicily,
Letting such love and tears unhonoured be:
Hasten, Minuccio, tell her that the king
To-day will surely visit her when vespers ring."

Joyful, Minuccio bore the joyous word,
And told at full, while none but Lisa heard,
How each thing had befallen, sang the song,
And like a patient nurse who would prolong
All means of soothing, dwelt upon each tone,
Each look, with which the mighty Aragon
Marked the high worth his royal heart assigned
To that dear place he held in Lisa's mind.
She listened till the draughts of pure content
Through all her limbs like some new being went –
Life, not recovered, but untried before,
From out the growing world's unmeasured store
Of fuller, better, more divinely mixed.
'Twas glad reverse: she had so firmly fixed
To die, already seemed to fall a veil
Shrouding the inner glow from light of senses pale.

Her parents wondering see her half arise –
Wondering, rejoicing, see her long dark eyes
Brimful with clearness, not of 'scaping tears,
But of some light ethereal that enspheres
Their orbs with calm, some vision newly learnt
Where strangest fires erewhile had blindly burnt.
She asked to have her soft white robe and band
And coral ornaments, and with her hand
She gave her locks' dark length a backward fall,
Then looked intently in a mirror small,
And feared her face might perhaps displease the king;
"In truth," she said, "I am a tiny thing;
I was too bold to tell what could such visit bring."
Meanwhile the king, revolving in his thought
That virgin passion, was more deeply wrought
To chivalrous pity; and at vesper bell,
With careless mien which hid his purpose well,
Went forth on horseback, and as if by chance
Passing Bernardo's house, he paused to glance
At the fine garden of this wealthy man,
This Tuscan trader turned Palermitan:
But, presently dismounting, chose to walk
Amid the trellises, in gracious talk
With this same trader, deigning even to ask
If he had yet fulfilled the father's task
Of marrying that daughter whose young charms
Himself, betwixt the passages of arms,
Noted admiringly. "Monsignor, no,
She is not married; that were little woe,
Since she has counted barely fifteen years;
But all such hopes of late have turned to fears;
She droops and fades; though for a space quite brief –
Scarce three hours past – she finds some strange relief."
The king avised: " 'Twere dole to all of us,
The world should lose a maid so beauteous;

Let me now see her; since I am her liege lord,
Her spirits must wage war with death at my strong
   word."
In such half-serious playfulness, he wends,
With Lisa's father and two chosen friends,
Up to the chamber where she pillowed sits
Watching the open door, that now admits
A presence as much better than her dreams,
As happiness than any longing seems.
The king advanced, and, with a reverent kiss
Upon her hand, said, "Lady, what is this ?
You, whose sweet youth should others' solace be,
Pierce all our hearts, languishing piteously.
We pray you, for the love of us, be cheered,
Nor be too reckless of that life, endeared
To us who know your passing worthiness,
And count your blooming life as part of our life's bliss."
Those words, that touch upon her hand from him
Whom her soul worshipped, as far seraphim
Worship the distant glory, brought some shame
Quivering upon her cheek, yet thrilled her frame
With such deep joy she seemed in paradise,
In wondering gladness, and in dumb surprise
That bliss could be so blissful: then she spoke –
"Signor, I was too weak to bear the yoke,
The golden yoke of thoughts too great for me;
That was the ground of my infirmity.
But now, I pray your grace to have belief
That I shall soon be well, nor any more cause grief."

The king alone perceived the covert sense
Of all her words, which made one evidence
With her pure voice and candid loveliness,
That he had lost much honour, honouring less
That message of her passionate distress.

He stayed beside her for a little while
With gentle looks and speech, until a smile
As placid as a ray of early morn
On opening flower-cups o'er her lips was borne.
When he had left her, and the tidings spread
Through all the town how he had visited
The Tuscan trader's daughter, who was sick,
Men said, it was a royal deed and catholic.

And Lisa ? she no longer wished for death;
But as a poet, who sweet verses saith
Within his soul, and joys in music there,
Nor seeks another heaven, nor can bear
Disturbing pleasures, so was she content,
Breathing the life of grateful sentiment.
She thought no maid betrothed could be more blest;
For treasure must be valued by the test
Of highest excellence and rarity,
And her dear joy was best as best could be;
There seemed no other crown to her delight
Now the high loved one saw her love aright.
Thus her soul thriving on that exquisite mood,
Spread like the May-time all its beauteous good
O'er the soft bloom of neck, and arms, and cheek,
And strengthened the sweet body, once so weak,
Until she rose and walked, and, like a bird
With sweetly rippling throat, she made her spring joys
    heard.
The king, when he the happy change had seen,
Trusted the ear of Constance, his fair queen,
With Lisa's innocent secret, and conferred
How they should jointly, by their deed and word.
Honour this maiden's love, which, like the prayer
Of loyal hermits, never thought to share
In what it gave. The queen had that chief grace

Of womanhood, a heart that can embrace
All goodness in another woman's form;
And that same day, ere the sun lay too warm
On southern terraces, a messenger
Informed Bernardo that the royal pair
Would straightway visit him and celebrate
Their gladness at his daughter's happier state,
Which they were fain to see. Soon came the king,
On horseback, with his barons, heralding
The advent of the queen in courtly state;
And all, descending at the garden gate,
Streamed with their feathers, velvet, and brocade,
Through the pleached alleys, till they, pausing, made
A lake of splendour 'mid the aloes grey –
When, meekly facing all their proud array,
The white-robed Lisa with her parents stood,
As some white dove before the gorgeous brood
Of dapple-breasted birds born by the Colchian flood.

The king and queen, by gracious looks and speech,
Encourage her, and thus their courtiers teach
How this fair morning they may courtliest be
By making Lisa pass it happily.
And soon the ladies and the barons all
Draw her by turns, as at a festival
Made for her sake, to easy, gay discourse,
And compliment with looks and smiles enforce;
A joyous hum is heard the gardens round;
Soon there is Spanish dancing and the sound
Of minstrel's song, and autumn fruits are pluckt;
Till mindfully the king and queen conduct
Lisa apart to where a trellised shade
Made pleasant resting. Then King Pedro said –
"Excellent maiden, that rich gift of love
Your heart hath made us, hath a worth above

All royal treasures, nor is fitly met
Save when the grateful memory of deep debt
Lies still behind the outward honours done:
And as a sign that no oblivion
Shall overflood that faithful memory,
We while we live your cavalier will be,
Nor will we ever arm ourselves for fight,
Whether for struggle dire or brief delight
Of warlike feigning, but we first will take
The colours you ordain, and for your sake
Charge the more bravely where your emblem is;
Nor will we ever claim an added bliss
To our sweet thoughts of you save one sole kiss.
But there still rests the outward honour meet
To mark your worthiness, and we entreat
That you will turn your ear to proffered vows
Of one who loves you, and would be your spouse.
We must not wrong yourself and Sicily
By letting all your blooming years pass by
Unmated: you will give the world its due
From beauteous maiden and become a matron true.''

Then Lisa, wrapt in virgin wonderment
At her ambitious love's complete content,
Which left no further good for her to seek
Than love's obedience, said with accent meek –
"Monsignor, I know well that were it known
To all the world how high my love had flown,
There would be few who would not deem me mad,
Or say my mind the falsest image had
Of my condition and your lofty place.
But heaven has seen that for no moment's space
Have I forgotten you to be the king,
Or me myself to be a lowly thing –
A little lark, enamoured of the sky,

That soared to sing, to break its breast, and die.
But, as you better know than I, the heart
In choosing chooseth not its own desert,
But that great merit which attracteth it;
'Tis law, I struggled, but I must submit,
And having seen a worth all worth above,
I loved you, love you, and shall always love.
But that doth mean, my will is ever yours,
Not only when your will my good insures,
But if it wrought me what the world calls harm –
Fire, wounds, would wear from your dear will a charm.
That you will be my knight is full content,
And for that kiss – I pray, first for the queen's consent.''

Her answer, given with such firm gentleness,
Pleased the queen well, and made her hold no less
Of Lisa's merit than the king had held.
And so, all cloudy threats of grief dispelled,
There was betrothal made that very morn
'Twixt Perdicone, youthful, brave, well-born,
And Lisa, whom he loved; she loving well
The lot that from obedience befell.
The queen a rare betrothal ring on each
Bestowed, and other gems, with gracious speech.
And that no joy might lack, the king, who knew
The youth was poor, gave him rich Ceffalù
And Cataletta, large and fruitful lands –
Adding much promise when he joined their hands.
At last he said to Lisa, with an air
Gallant yet noble: ''Now we claim our share
From your sweet love, a share which is not small:
For in the sacrament one crumb is all.''
Then taking her small face his hands between,
He kissed her on the brow with kiss serene,
Fit seal to that pure vision her young soul had seen.

Sicilians witnessed that King Pedro kept
His royal promise: Perdicone stept
To many honours honourably won,
Living with Lisa in true union.
Throughout his life the king still took delight
To call himself fair Lisa's faithful knight;
And never wore in field or tournament
A scarf or emblem save by Lisa sent.

Such deeds made subjects loyal in that land:
They joyed that one so worthy to command,
So chivalrous and gentle, had become
The king of Sicily, and filled the room
Of Frenchmen, who abused the Church's trust,
Till, in a righteous vengeance on their lust,
Messina rose, with God, and with the dagger's thrust.

L'ENVOI

Reader, this story pleased me long ago
In the bright pages of Boccaccio,
And where the author of a good we know,
Let us not fail to pay the grateful thanks we owe.

25 January 1869 – 14 February 1869

BROTHER AND SISTER

I

I cannot choose but think upon the time
When our two lives grew like two buds that kiss
At lightest thrill from the bee's swinging chime,
Because the one so near the other is.

He was the elder and a little man
Of forty inches, bound to show no dread,
And I the girl that puppy-like now ran,
Now lagged behind my brother's larger tread.

I held him wise, and when he talked to me
Of snakes and birds, and which God loved the best,
I thought his knowledge marked the boundary
Where men grew blind, though angels knew the rest.

If he said "Hush !" I tried to hold my breath
Wherever he said "Come !" I stepped in faith.

II

Long years have left their writing on my brow,
But yet the freshness and the dew-fed beam
Of those young mornings are about me now,
When we two wandered toward the far-off stream

With rod and line. Our basket held a store
Baked for us only, and I thought with joy
That I should have my share, though he had more,
Because he was the elder and a boy.

The firmaments of daisies since to me
Have had those mornings in their opening eyes,
The bunchèd cowslip's pale transparency
Carries that sunshine of sweet memories,

And wild-rose branches take their finest scent
From those blest hours of infantine content.

III

Our mother bade us keep the trodden ways,
Stroked down my tippet, set my brother's frill,
Then with the benediction of her gaze
Clung to us lessening, and pursued us still

Across the homestead to the rookery elms,
Whose tall old trunks had each a grassy mound,
So rich for us, we counted them as realms
With varied products: here were earth-nuts found,

And here the Lady-fingers in deep shade;
Here sloping toward the Moat the rushes grew,
The large to split for pith, the small to braid;
While over all the dark rooks cawing flew,

And made a happy strange solemnity,
A deep-toned chant from life unknown to me.

IV

Our meadow-path had memorable spots:
One where it bridged a tiny rivulet,
Deep hid my tangled blue Forget-me-nots;
And all along the waving grasses met

My little palm, or nodded to my cheek,
When flowers with upturned faces gazing drew
My wonder downward, seeming all to speak
With eyes of souls that dumbly heard and knew.

Then came the copse, where wild things rushed unseen,
And black-scathed grass betrayed the past abode
Of mystic gypsies, who still lurked between
Me and each hidden distance of the road.

A gypsy once had startled me at play,
Blotting with her dark smile my sunny day.

V

Thus rambling we were schooled in deepest lore,
And learned the meanings that give words a soul,
The fear, the love, the primal passionate store,
Whose shaping impulses make manhood whole.

Those hours were seed to all my after good;
My infant gladness, through eye, ear, and touch,
Took easily as warmth a various food
To nourish the sweet skill of loving much.

For who in age shall roam the earth and find
Reasons for loving that will strike out love
With sudden rod from the hard year-pressed mind ?
Were reasons sown as thick as stars above,

'Tis love must see them, as the eye sees light:
Day is but Number to the darkened sight.

VI

Our brown canal was endless to my thought;
And on its banks I sat in dreamy peace,
Unknowing how the good I loved was wrought,
Untroubled by the fear that it would cease.

Slowly the barges floated into view
Rounding a grassy hill to me sublime
With some Unknown beyond it, whither flew
The parting cuckoo toward a fresh spring time.

The wide-arched bridge, the scented elder-flowers,
The wondrous watery rings that died too soon,
The echoes of the quarry, the still hours
With white robe sweeping-on the shadeless noon,

Were but my growing self, are part of me,
My present Past, my root of piety.

VII

Those long days measured by my little feet
Had chronicles which yield me many a text;
Where irony still finds an image meet
Of full-grown judgments in this world perplext.

One day my brother left me in high charge,
To mind the rod, while he went seeking bait,
And bade me, when I saw a nearing barge,
Snatch out the line, lest he should come too late.

Proud of the task, I watched with all my might
For one whole minute, till my eyes grew wide,
Till sky and earth took on a strange new light
And seemed a dream-world floating on some tide –

A fair pavilioned boat for me alone
Bearing me onward through the vast unknown.

VIII

But sudden came the barge's pitch-black prow,
Nearer and angrier came my brother's cry,
And all my soul was quivering fear, when lo !
Upon the imperilled line, suspended high,

A silver perch ! My guilt that won the prey,
Now turned to merit, had a guerdon rich
Of hugs and praises, and made merry play,
Until my triumph reached its highest pitch

When all at home were told the wondrous feat,
And how the little sister had fished well.
In secret, though my fortune tasted sweet,
I wondered why this happiness befell.

"The little lass had luck," the gardener said:
And so I learned, luck was with glory wed.

IX

We had the self-same world enlarged for each
By loving difference of girl and boy:
The fruit that hung on high beyond my reach
He plucked for me, and oft he must employ

A measuring glance to guide my tiny shoe
Where lay firm stepping-stones, or call to mind
"This thing I like my sister may not do,
For she is little, and I must be kind."

Thus boyish Will the nobler mastery learned
Where inward vision over impulse reigns,
Widening its life with separate life discerned,
A Like unlike, a Self that self restrains.

　　His years with others must the sweeter be
　　For those brief days he spent in loving me.

X

His sorrow was my sorrow, and his joy
Sent little leaps and laughs through all my frame;
My doll seemed lifeless and no girlish toy
Had any reason when my brother came.

I knelt with him at marbles, marked his fling
Cut the ringed stem and make the apple drop,
Or watched him winding close the spiral string
That looped the orbits of the humming top.

Grasped by such fellowship my vagrant thought
Ceased with dream-fruit dream-wishes to fulfil;
My aëry-picturing fantasy was taught
Subjection to the harder, truer skill

　　That seeks with deeds to grave a thought-tracked line,
　　And by "What is," "What will be" to define.

School parted us; we never found again
That childish world where our two spirits mingled
Like scents from varying roses that remain
One sweetness, nor can evermore be singled.

Yet the twin habit of that early time
Lingered for long about the heart and tongue:
We had been natives of one happy clime,
And its dear accent to our utterance clung.

Till the dire years whose awful name is Change
Had grasped our souls still yearning in divorce,
And pitiless shaped them in two forms that range
Two elements which sever their life's course.

But were another childhood-world my share,
I would be born a little sister there.

Summer 1869.

THE LEGEND OF JUBAL

When Cain was driven from Jehovah's land
He wandered eastward, seeking some far strand
Ruled by kind gods who asked no offerings
Save pure field-fruits, as aromatic things,
To feed the subtler sense of frames divine
That lived on fragrance for their food and wine:
Wild joyous gods, who winked at faults and folly,
And could be pitiful and melancholy.
He never had a doubt that such gods were;
He looked within, and saw them mirrored there.
Some think he came at last to Tartary,
And some to Ind; but, howsoe'er it be,
His staff he planted where sweet waters ran.
And in that home of Cain the Arts began.

Man's life was spacious in the early world:
It paused, like some slow ship with sail unfurled
Waiting in seas by scarce a wavelet curled;
Beheld the slow star-paces of the skies,
And grew from strength to strength through centuries;
Saw infant trees fill out their giant limbs,
And heard a thousand times the sweet birds' marriage
    hymns.

In Cain's young city none had heard of Death
Save him, the founder; and it was his faith
That here, away from harsh Jehovah's law,
Man was immortal, since no halt or flaw
In Cain's own flame betrayed six hundred years,
But dark as pines that autumn never sears
His locks thronged backward as he ran, his frame
Rose like the orbèd sun each morn the same,

Lake-mirrored to his gaze; and that red brand,
The scorching impress of Jehovah's hand,
Was still clear-edged to his unwearied eye,
Its secret firm in time-fraught memory.
He said, "My happy offspring shall not know
That the red life from out a man may flow
When smitten by his brother." True, his race
Bore each one stamped upon his new-born face
A copy of the brand no whit less clear;
But every mother held that little copy dear.

Thus generations in glad idlesse throve,
Nor hunted prey, nor with each other strove;
For clearest springs were plenteous in the land,
And gourds for cups; the ripe fruits sought the hand,
Bending the laden boughs with fragrant gold;
And for their roofs and garments wealth untold
Lay everywhere in grasses and broad leaves:
They laboured gently, as a maid who weaves
Her hair in mimic mats, and pauses oft
And strokes across her palm the tresses soft,
Then peeps to watch the poisèd butterfly,
Or little burthened ants that homeward hie.
Time was but leisure to their lingering thought,
There was no need for haste to finish aught;
But sweet beginnings were repeated still
Like infant babblings that no task fulfil;
For love, that loved not change, constrained the simple
    will.

Till, hurling stones in mere athletic joy,
Strong Lamech struck and killed his fairest boy,
And tried to wake him with the tenderest cries,
And fetched and held before the glazèd eyes
The things they best had loved to look upon;

But never glance or smile or sigh he won.
The generations stood around those twain
Helplessly gazing, till their father Cain
Parted the press, and said, "He will not wake;
This is the endless sleep, and we must make
A bed deep down for him beneath the sod;
For know, my sons, there is a mighty God
Angry with all man's race, but most with me.
I fled from out His land in vain ! – 'tis He
Who came and slew the lad, for He has found
This home of ours, and we shall all be bound
By the harsh bands of His most cruel will,
Which any moment may some dear one kill.
Nay, though we live for countless moons, at last
We and all ours shall die like summers past.
This is Jehovah's will, and He is strong;
I thought the way I travelled was too long
For Him to follow me: my thought was vain !
He walks unseen, but leaves a track of pain,
Pale Death His footprint is, and He will come again !"

And a new spirit from that hour came o'er
The race of Cain: soft idlesse was no more,
But even the sunshine had a heart of care,
Smiling with hidden dread – a mother fair
Who folding to her breast a dying child
Beams with feigned joy that but makes sadness mild.
Death was now lord of Life, and at his word
Time, vague as air before, new terrors stirred,
With measured wing now audibly arose
Throbbing through all things to some unknown close.
Now glad Content by clutching Haste was torn,
And Work grew eager, and Device was born.
It seemed the light was never loved before,
Now each man said, " 'Twill go and come no more."

No budding branch, no pebble from the brook,
No form, no shadow, but new dearness took
From the one thought that life must have an end;
And the last parting now began to send
Diffusive dread through love and wedded bliss,
Thrilling them into finer tenderness.
Then Memory disclosed her face divine,
That like the calm nocturnal lights doth shine
Within the soul, and shows the sacred graves,
And shows the presence that no sunlight craves,
No space, no warmth, but moves among them all;
Gone and yet here, and coming at each call,
With ready voice and eyes that understand,
And lips that ask a kiss, and dear responsive hand.
Thus to Cain's race death was tear-watered seed
Of various life and action-shaping need.
But chief the sons of Lamech felt the stings
Of new ambition, and the force that springs
In passion beating on the shores of fate.
They said, "There comes a night when all too late
The mind shall long to prompt the achieving hand,
The eager thought behind closed portals stand,
And the last wishes to the mute lips press
Buried ere death in silent helplessness.
Then while the soul its way with sound can cleave,
And while the arm is strong to strike and heave,
Let soul and arm give shape that will abide
And rule above our graves, and power divide
With that great god of day, whose rays must bend
As we shall make the moving shadows tend.
Come, let us fashion acts that are to be,
When we shall lie in darkness silently,
As our young brother doth, whom yet we see
Fallen and slain, but reigning in our will
By that one image of him pale and still."

For Lamech's sons were heroes of their race:
Jabal, the eldest, bore upon his face
The look of that calm river-god, the Nile,
Mildly secure in power that needs not guile.
But Tubal-Cain was restless as the fire
That glows and spreads and leaps from high to higher
Where'er is aught to seize or to subdue;
Strong as a storm he lifted or o'erthrew,
His urgent limbs like rounded granite grew,
Such granite as the plunging torrent wears
And roaring rolls around through countless years.
But strength that still on movement must be fed,
Inspiring thought of change, devices bred,
And urged his mind through earth and air to rove
For force that he could conquer if he strove,
For lurking forms that might now tasks fulfil
And yield unwilling to his stronger will.
Such Tubal-Cain. But Jubal had a frame
Fashioned to finer senses, which became
A yearning for some hidden soul of things,
Some outward touch complete on inner springs
That vaguely moving bred a lonely pain,
A want that did but stronger grow with gain
Of all good else, as spirits might be sad
For lack of speech to tell us they are glad.

Now Jabal learned to tame the lowing kine,
And from their udders drew the snow-white wine
That stirs the innocent joy, and makes the stream
Of elemental life with fulness teem;
The star-browed calves he nursed with feeding hand,
And sheltered them, till all the little band
Stood mustered gazing at the sunset way
Whence he would come with store at close of day.
He soothed the silly sheep with friendly tone

And reared their staggering lambs that, older grown,
Followed his steps with sense-taught memory;
Till he, their shepherd, could their leader be
And guide them through the pastures as he would,
With sway that grew from ministry of good.
He spread his tents upon the grassy plain
Which, eastward widening like the open main,
Showed the first whiteness 'neath the morning star;
Near him his sister, deft, as women are,
Plied her quick skill in sequence to his thought
Till the hid treasures of the milk she caught
Revealed like pollen 'mid the petals white,
The golden pollen, virgin to the light.
Even the she-wolf with young, on rapine bent,
He caught and tethered in his mat-walled tent,
And cherished all her little sharp-nosed young
Till the small race with hope and terror clung
About his footsteps, till each new-reared brood,
Remoter from the memories of the wood,
More glad discerned their common home with man.
This was the work of Jabal: he began
The pastoral life, and, sire of joys to be,
Spread the sweet ties that bind the family
O'er dear dumb souls that thrilled at man's caress,
And shared his pains with patient helpfulness.

But Tubal-Cain had caught and yoked the fire,
Yoked it with stones that bent the flaming spire
And made it roar in prisoned servitude
Within the furnace, till with force subdued
It changed all forms he willed to work upon,
Till hard from soft, and soft from hard, he won.
The pliant clay he moulded as he would,
And laughed with joy when 'mid the heat it stood
Shaped as his hand had chosen, while the mass

That from his hold, dark, obstinate, would pass,
He drew all glowing from the busy heat,
All breathing as with life that he could beat
With thundering hammer, making it obey
His will creative, like the pale soft clay.
Each day he wrought and better than he planned,
Shape breeding shape beneath his restless hand.
(The soul without still helps the soul within,
And its deft magic ends what we begin.)
Nay, in his dreams his hammer he would wield
And seem to see a myriad types revealed,
Then spring with wondering triumphant cry,
And, lest the inspiring vision should go by,
Would rush to labour with that plastic zeal
Which all the passion of our life can steal
For force to work with. Each day saw the birth
Of various forms which, flung upon the earth,
Seemed harmless toys to cheat the exacting hour.
But were as seeds instinct with hidden power.
The axe, the club, the spikèd wheel, the chain,
Held silently the shrieks and moans of pain;
And near them latent lay in share and spade,
In the strong bar, the saw, and deep-curved blade,
Glad voices of the hearth and harvest-home,
The social good, and all earth's joy to come.
Thus to mixed ends wrought Tubal; and they say,
Some things he made have lasted to this day;
As thirty silver pieces that were found
By Noah's children buried in the ground.
He made them from mere hunger of device,
Those small white discs; but they became the price
The traitor Judas sold his Master for;
And men still handling them in peace and war
Catch foul disease, that comes as appetite,
And lurks and clings as withering, damning blight.

But Tubal-Cain wot not of treachery,
Nor greedy lust, nor any ill to be,
Save the one ill of sinking into nought,
Banished from action and act-shaping thought.
He was the sire of swift-transforming skill,
Which arms for conquest man's ambitious will;
And round him gladly, as his hammer rung,
Gathered the elders and the growing young:
These handled vaguely and those plied the tools,
Till, happy chance begetting conscious rules,
The home of Cain with industry was rife,
And glimpses of a strong persistent life,
Panting through generations as one breath,
And filling with its soul the blank of death.

Jubal, too, watched the hammer, till his eyes,
No longer following its fall or rise,
Seemed glad with something that they could not see,
But only listened to – some melody,
Wherein dumb longings inward speech had found,
Won from the common store of struggling sound.
Then, as the metal shapes more various grew,
And, hurled upon each other, resonance drew,
Each gave new tones, the revelations dim
Of some external soul that spoke for him:
The hollow vessel's clang, the clash, the boom,
Like light that makes wide spiritual room
And skyey spaces in the spaceless thought,
To Jubal such enlargèd passion brought
That love, hope, rage, and all experience,
Were fused in vaster being, fetching thence
Concords and discords, cadences and cries
That seemed from some world-shrouded soul to rise,
Some rapture more intense, some mightier rage,
Some living sea that burst the bounds of man's brief age.

Then with such blissful trouble and glad care
For growth within unborn as mothers bear,
To the far woods he wandered, listening,
And heard the birds their little stories sing
In notes whose rise and fall seemed melted speech –
Melted with tears, smiles, glances – that can reach
More quickly through our frame's deep-winding night,
And without thought raise thought's best fruit, delight.
Pondering, he sought his home again and heard
The fluctuant changes of the spoken word:
The deep remonstrance and the argued want,
Insistent first in close monotonous chant,
Next leaping upward to defiant stand
Or downward beating like the resolute hand;
The mother's call, the children's answering cry,
The laugh's light cataract tumbling from on high;
The suasive repetitions Jabal taught,
That timid browsing cattle homeward brought;
The clear-winged fugue of echoes vanishing;
And through them all the hammer's rhythmic ring.
Jubal sat lonely, all around was dim,
Yet his face glowed with light revealed to him:
For as the delicate stream of odour wakes
The thought-wed sentience and some image makes
From out the mingled fragments of the past,
Finely compact in wholeness that will last,
So streamed as from the body of each sound
Subtler pulsations, swift as warmth, which found
All prisoned germs and all their powers unbound,
Till thought self-luminous flamed from memory,
And in creative vision wandered free.
Then Jubal, standing, rapturous arms upraised,
And on the dark with eager eyes he gazed,
As had some manifested god been there.
It was his thought he saw: the presence fair

Of unachieved achievement, the high task,
The struggling unborn spirit that doth ask
With irresistible cry for blood and breath,
Till feeding its great life we sink in death.

He said, "Were now those mighty tones and cries
That from the giant soul of earth arise,
Those groans of some great travail heard from far,
Some power at wrestle with the things that are,
Those sounds which vary with the varying form
Of clay and metal, and in sightless swarm
Fill the wide space with tremors: were these wed
To human voices with such passion fed
As does but glimmer in our common speech,
But might flame out in tones whose changing reach,
Surpassing meagre need, informs the sense
With fuller union, finer difference –
Were this great vision, now obscurely bright
As morning hills that melt in new-poured light,
Wrought into solid form and living sound,
Moving with ordered throb and sure rebound,
Then – Nay, I Jubal will that work begin !
The generations of our race shall win
New life, that grows from out the heart of this,
As spring from winter, or as lovers' bliss
From out the dull unknown of unwaked energies."

Thus he resolved, and in the soul-fed light
Of coming ages waited through the night,
Watching for that near dawn whose chiller ray
Showed but the unchanged world of yesterday;
Where all the order of his dream divine
Lay like Olympian forms within the mine;
Where fervour that could fill the earthly round
With throngèd joys of form-begotten sound

Must shrink intense within the patient power
That lonely labours through the niggard hour.
Such patience have the heroes who begin,
Sailing the first to lands which others win.
Jubal must dare as great beginners dare,
Strike form's first way in matter rude and bare,
And, yearning vaguely toward the plenteous quire
Of the world's harvest, make one poor small lyre.
He made it, and from out its measured frame
Drew the harmonic soul, whose answers came
With guidance sweet and lessons of delight
Teaching to ear and hand the blissful Right,
Where strictest law is gladness to the sense
And all desire bends toward obedience.

Then Jubal poured his triumph in a song –
The rapturous word that rapturous notes prolong
As radiance streams from smallest things that burn,
Or thought of loving into love doth turn.
And still his lyre gave companionship
In sense-taught concert as of lip with lip.
Alone amid the hills at first he tried
His wingèd song; then with adoring pride
And bridegroom's joy at leading forth his bride,
He said, "This wonder which my soul hath found,
This heart of music in the might of sound,
Shall forthwith be the share of all our race
And like the morning gladden common space:
The song shall spread and swell as rivers do,
And I will teach our youth with skill to woo
This living lyre, to know its secret will,
Its fine division of the good and ill.
So shall men call me sire of harmony,
And where great Song is, there my life shall be."

Thus glorying as a god beneficent,
Forth from his solitary joy he went
To bless mankind. It was at evening,
When shadows lengthen from each westward thing,
When imminence of change makes sense more fine
And light seems holier in its grand decline.
The fruit-trees wore their studded coronal,
Earth and her children were at festival,
Glowing as with one heart and one consent –
Thought, love, trees, rocks, in sweet warm radiance blent.

The tribe of Cain was resting on the ground,
The various ages wreathed in one broad round.
Here lay, while children peeped o'er his huge thighs,
The sinewy man embrowned by centuries;
Here the broad-bosomed mother of the strong
Looked, like Demeter, placid o'er the throng
Of young lithe forms whose rest was movement too –
Tricks, prattle, nods, and laughs that lightly flew,
And swayings as of flower-beds where Love blew.
For all had feasted well upon the flesh
Of juicy fruits, on nuts, and honey fresh,
And now their wine was health-bred merriment,
Which through the generations circling went,
Leaving none sad, for even father Cain
Smiled as a Titan might, despising pain.
Jabal sat climbed on by a playful ring
Of children, lambs and whelps, whose gambolling,
With tiny hoofs, paws, hands, and dimpled feet,
Made barks, bleats, laughs, in pretty hubbub meet.
But Tubal's hammer rang from far away,
Tubal alone would keep no holiday,
His furnace must not slack for any feast,
For of all hardship work he counted least;

He scorned all rest but sleep, where every dream
Made his repose more potent action seem.

Yet with health's nectar some strange thirst was blent,
The fateful growth, the unnamed discontent,
The inward shaping toward some unborn power,
Some deeper-breathing act, the being's flower.
After all gestures, words, and speech of eyes,
The soul had more to tell, and broke in sighs.
Then from the east, with glory on his head
Such as low-slanting beams on corn-waves spread,
Came Jubal with his lyre: there 'mid the throng,
Where the blank space was, poured a solemn song,
Touching his lyre to full harmonic throb
And measured pulse, with cadences that sob,
Exult and cry, and search the inmost deep
Where the dark sources of new passion sleep.
Joy took the air, and took each breathing soul,
Embracing them in one entrancèd whole,
Yet thrilled each varying fmme to various ends,
As Spring new-waking through the creature sends
Or rage or tenderness; more plenteous life
Here breeding dread, and there a fiercer strife.
He who had lived through twice three centuries,
Whose months monotonous, like trees on trees
In hoary forests, stretched a backward maze,
Dreamed himself dimly through the travelled days
Till in clear light he paused, and felt the sun
That warmed him when he was a little one;
Felt that true heaven, the recovered past,
The dear small Known amid the Unknown vast,
And in that heaven wept. But younger limbs
Thrilled toward the future, that bright land which swims
In western glory, isles and streams and bays,
Where hidden pleasures float in golden haze.

And in all these the rhythmic influence,
Sweetly o'ercharging the delighted sense,
Flowed out in movements, little waves that spread
Enlarging, till in tidal union led
The youths and maidens both alike long-tressed,
By grace-inspiring melody possessed,
Rose in slow dance, with beauteous floating swerve
Of limbs and hair, and many a melting curve
Of ringèd feet swayed by each close-linked palm:
Then Jubal poured more rapture in his psalm,
The dance fired music, music fired the dance,
The glow diffusive lit each countenance,
Till all the gazing elders rose and stood
With glad yet awful shock of that mysterious good.

Even Tubal caught the sound, and wondering came,
Urging his sooty bulk like smoke-wrapt flame
Till he could see his brother with the lyre,
The work for which he lent his furnace-fire
And diligent hammer, witting nought of this –
This power in metal shape which made strange bliss,
Entering within him like a dream full-fraught
With new creations finished in a thought.

The sun had sunk, but music still was there,
And when this ceased, still triumph filled the air:
It seemed the stars were shining with delight
And that no night was ever like this night.
All clung with praise to Jubal: some besought
That he would teach them his new skill; some caught,
Swiftly as smiles are caught in looks that meet,
The tone's melodic change and rhythmic beat:
'Twas easy following where invention trod –
All eyes can see when light flows out from God.

And thus did Jubal to his race reveal
Music their larger soul, where woe and weal
Filling the resonant chords, the song, the dance,
Moved with a wider-wingèd utterance.
Now many a lyre was fashioned, many a song
Raised echoes new, old echoes to prolong,
Till things of Jubal's making were so rife,
"Hearing myself," he said, "hems in my life,
And I will get me to some far-off land,
Where higher mountains under heaven stand
And touch the blue at rising of the stars,
Whose song they hear where no rough mingling mars
The great clear voices. Such lands there must be,
Where varying forms make varying symphony –
Where other thunders roll amid the hills,
Some mightier wind a mightier forest fills
With other strains through other-shapen boughs;
Where bees and birds and beasts that hunt or browse
Will teach me songs I know not. Listening there,
My life shall grow like trees both tall and fair
That rise and spread and bloom toward fuller fruit each
    year."

He took a raft, and travelled with the stream
Southward for many a league, till he might deem
He saw at last the pillars of the sky,
Beholding mountains whose white majesty
Rushed through him as new awe, and made new song
That swept with fuller wave the chords along,
Weighting his voice with deep religious chime,
The iteration of slow chant sublime.
It was the region long inhabited
By all the race of Seth; and Jubal said:

" Here have I found my thirsty soul's desire,
Eastward the hills touch heaven, and evening's fire
Flames through deep waters; I will take my rest,
And feed anew from my great mother's breast,
The sky-clasped Earth, whose voices nurture me
As the flowers' sweetness doth the honey-bee."
He lingered wandering for many an age,
And, sowing music, made high heritage
For generations far beyond the Flood –
For the poor late-begotten human brood
Born to life's weary brevity and perilous good.

And ever as he travelled he would climb
The farthest mountain, yet the heavenly chime,
The mighty tolling of the far-off spheres
Beating their pathway, never touched his ears.
But wheresoe'er he rose the heavens rose,
And the far-gazing mountain could disclose
Nought but a wider earth; until one height
Showed him the ocean stretched in liquid light,
And he could hear its multitudinous roar,
Its plunge and hiss upon the pebbled shore:
Then Jubal silent sat, and touched his lyre no more.

He thought, "The world is great, but I am weak,
And where the sky bends is no solid peak
To give me footing, but instead, this main –
Myriads of maddened horses thundering o'er the plain.

"New voices come to me where'er I roam,
My heart too widens with its widening home:
But song grows weaker, and the heart must break
For lack of voice, or fingers that can wake
The lyre's full answer; nay, its chords were all
Too few to meet the growing spirit's call.

The former songs seem little, yet no more
Can soul, hand, voice, with interchanging lore
Tell what the earth is saying unto me:
The secret is too great, I hear confusedly.

"No farther will I travel: once again
My brethren I will see, and that fair plain
Where I and Song were born. There fresh-voiced youth
Will pour my strains with all the early truth
Which now abides not in my voice and hands,
But only in the soul, the will that stands
Helpless to move. My tribe remembering
Will cry ' 'Tis he !' and run to greet me, welcoming."

The way was weary. Many a date-palm grew,
And shook out clustered gold against the blue,
While Jubal, guided by the steadfast spheres,
Sought the dear home of those first eager years,
When, with fresh vision fed, the fuller will
Took living outward shape in pliant skill;
For still he hoped to find the former things,
And the warm gladness recognition brings.
His footsteps erred among the mazy woods
And long illusive sameness of the floods,
Winding and wandering. Through far regions, strange
With Gentile homes and faces, did he range,
And left his music in their memory,
And left at last, when nought besides would free
His homeward steps from clinging hands and cries,
The ancient lyre. And now in ignorant eyes
No sign remained of Jubal, Lamech's son,
That mortal frame wherein was first begun
The immortal life of song. His withered brow
Pressed over eyes that held no lightning now,
His locks streamed whiteness on the hurrying air,

The unresting soul had worn itself quite bare
Of beauteous token, as the outworn might
Of oaks slow dying, gaunt in summer's light.
His full deep voice toward thinnest treble ran:
He was the tune-writ story of a man.

And so at last he neared the well-known land,
Could see the hills in ancient order stand
With friendly faces whose familiar gaze
Looked through the sunshine of his childish days;
Knew the deep-shadowed folds of hanging woods,
And seemed to see the self-same insect broods
Whirling and quivering o'er the flowers − to hear
The self-same cuckoo making distance near.
Yea, the dear Earth, with mother's constancy,
Met and embraced him, and said, "Thou art he !
This was thy cradle, here my breast was thine,
Where feeding, thou didst all thy life entwine
With my sky-wedded life in heritage divine."

But wending ever through the watered plain,
Firm not to rest save in the home of Cain,
He saw dread Change, with dubious face and cold
That never kept a welcome for the old,
Like some strange heir upon the hearth, arise
Saying "This home is mine." He thought his eyes
Mocked all deep memories, as things new made,
Usurping sense, make old things shrink and fade
And seem ashamed to meet the staring day.
His memory saw a small foot-trodden way,
His eyes a broad far-stretching paven road
Bordered with many a tomb and fair abode;
The little city that once nestled low
As buzzing groups about some central glow,
Spread like a murmuring crowd o'er plain and steep,

Or monster huge in heavy-breathing sleep.
His heart grew faint, and tremblingly he sank
Close by the wayside on a weed-grown bank,
Not far from where a new-raised temple stood,
Sky-roofed, and fragrant with wrought cedar wood.
The morning sun was high; his rays fell hot
On this hap-chosen, dusty, common spot,
On the dry-withered grass and withered man:
That wondrous frame where melody began
Lay as a tomb defaced that no eye cared to scan.

But while he sank far music reached his ear.
He listened until wonder silenced fear
And gladness wonder; for the broadening stream
Of sound advancing was his early dream,
Brought like fulfilment of forgotten prayer;
As if his soul, breathed out upon the air,
Had held the invisible seeds of harmony
Quick with the various strains of life to be
He listened: the sweet mingled difference
With charm alternate took the meeting sense;
Then bursting like some shield-broad lily red,
Sudden and near the trumpet's notes out-spread,
And soon his eyes could see the metal flower,
Shining upturned, out on the morning pour
Its incense audible; could see a train
From out the street slow-winding on the plain
With lyres and cymbals, flutes and psalteries,
While men, youths, maids, in concert sang to these
With various throat, or in succession poured,
Or in full volume mingled. But one word
Ruled each recurrent rise and answering fall,
As when the multitudes adoring call
On some great name divine, their common soul,

The common need, love, joy, that knits them in one
    whole.

The word was "Jubal !" . . . "Jubal" filled the air
And seemed to ride aloft, a spirit there,
Creator of the quire, the full-fraught strain
That grateful rolled itself to him again.
The aged man adust upon the bank −
Whom no eye saw − at first with rapture drank
The bliss of music, then, with swelling heart,
Felt, this was his own being's greater part,
The universal joy once born in him.
But when the train, with living face and limb
And vocal breath, came nearer and more near,
The longing grew that they should hold him dear;
Him, Lamech's son, whom all their fathers knew,
The breathing Jubal − him, to whom their love was due.
All was forgotten but the burning need
To claim his fuller self, to claim the deed
That lived away from him, and grew apart,
While he as from a tomb, with lonely heart
Warmed by no meeting glance, no hand that pressed,
Lay chill amid the life his life had blessed.
What though his song should spread from man's small
    race
Out through the myriad worlds that people space,
And make the heavens one joy-diffusing quire ? −
Still 'mid that vast would throb the keen desire
Of this poor aged flesh, this eventide,
This twilight soon in darkness to subside,
This little pulse of self that, having glowed
Through thrice three centuries, and divinely strowed
The light of music through the vague of sound,
Ached with its smallness still in good that had no bound.

For no eye saw him, while with loving pride
Each voice with each in praise of Jubal vied.
Must he in conscious trance, dumb, helpless lie
While all that ardent kindred passed him by ?
His flesh cried out to live with living men
And join that soul which to the inward ken
Of all the hymning train was present there.
Strong passion's daring sees not aught to dare:
The frost-locked starkness of his frame low-bent,
His voice's penury of tones long spent,
He felt not; all his being leaped in flame
To meet his kindred as they onward came
Slackening and wheeling toward the temple's face:
He rushed before them to the glittering space,
And, with a strength that was but strong desire,
Cried, "I am Jubal, I ! . . . I made the lyre !"

The tones amid a lake of silence fell
Broken and strained, as if a feeble bell
Had tuneless pealed the triumph of a land
To listening crowds in expectation spanned.
Sudden came showers of laughter on that lake;
They spread along the train from front to wake
In one great storm of merriment, while he
Shrank doubting whether he could Jubal be,
And not a dream of Jubal, whose rich vein
Of passionate music came with that dream-pain
Wherein the sense slips off from each loved thing
And all appearance is mere vanishing.
But ere the laughter died from out the rear,
Anger in front saw profanation near;
Jubal was but a name in each man's faith
For glorious power untouched by that slow death
Which creeps with creeping time; this too, the spot,
And this the day, it must be crime to blot,

111

Even with scoffing at a madman's lie:
Jubal was not a name to wed with mockery.

Two rushed upon him: two, the most devout
In honour of great Jubal, thrust him out,
And beat him with their flutes. 'Twas little need;
He strove not, cried not, but with tottering speed,
As if the scorn and howls were driving wind
That urged his body, serving so the mind
Which could but shrink and yearn, he sought the screen
Of thorny thickets, and there fell unseen.
The immortal name of Jubal filled the sky,
While Jubal lonely laid him down to die.
He said within his soul, "This is the end:
O'er all the earth to where the heavens bend
And hem men's travel, I have breathed my soul:
I lie here now the remnant of that whole,
The embers of a life, a lonely pain;
As far-off rivers to my thirst were vain,
So of my mighty years nought comes to me again.

"Is the day sinking ? Softest coolness springs
From something round me: dewy shadowy wings
Enclose me all around – no, not above –
Is moonlight there ? I see a face of love,
Fair as sweet music when my heart was strong:
Yea – art thou come again to me, great Song?"

The face bent over him like silver night
In long-remembered summers; that calm light
Of days which shine in firmaments of thought,
That past unchangeable, from change still wrought.
And gentlest tones were with the vision blent:
He knew not if that gaze the music sent,
Or music that calm gaze: to hear, to see,

Was but one undivided ecstasy:
The raptured senses melted into one.
And parting life a moment's freedom won
From in and outer, as a little child
Sits on a bank and sees blue heavens mild
Down in the water, and forgets its limbs,
And knoweth nought save the blue heaven that swims.

"Jubal," the face said, "I am thy loved Past,
The soul that makes thee one from first to last.
I am the angel of thy life and death,
Thy outbreathed being drawing its last breath.
Am I not thine alone, a dear dead bride
Who blest thy lot above all men's beside ?
Thy bride whom thou wouldst never change, nor take
Any bride living, for that dead one's sake ?
Was I not all thy yearning and delight,
Thy chosen search, thy senses' beauteous Right,
Which still had been the hunger of thy frame
In central heaven, hadst thou been still the same ?
Wouldst thou have asked aught else from any god –
Whether with gleaming feet on earth he trod
Or thundered through the skies – aught else for share
Of mortal good, than in thy soul to bear
The growth of song, and feel the sweet unrest
Of the world's spring-tide in thy conscious breast?
No, thou hadst grasped thy lot with all its pain,
Nor loosed it any painless lot to gain
Where music's voice was silent; for thy fate
Was human music's self incorporate:
Thy senses' keenness and thy passionate strife
Were flesh of *her* flesh and her womb of life.
And greatly hast thou lived, for not alone
With hidden raptures were her secrets shown,
Buried within thee, as the purple light

Of gems may sleep in solitary night;
But thy expanding joy was still to give,
And with the generous air in song to live,
Feeding the wave of ever-widening bliss
Where fellowship means equal perfectness.
And on the mountains in thy wandering
Thy feet were beautiful as blossomed spring,
That turns the leafless wood to love's glad home,
For with thy coming Melody was come.
This was thy lot, to feel, create, bestow,
And that immeasurable life to know
From which the fleshly self falls shrivelled, dead,
A seed primeval that has forests bred.
It is the glory of the heritage
Thy life has left, that makes thy outcast age:
Thy limbs shall lie dark, tombless on this sod,
Because thou shinest in man's soul, a god,
Who found and gave new passion and new joy
That nought but Earth's destruction can destroy.
Thy gifts to give was thine of men alone:
'Twas but in giving that thou couldst atone
For too much wealth amid their poverty." –

The words seemed melting into symphony,
The wings upbore him, and the gazing song
Was floating him the heavenly space along,
Where mighty harmonies all gently fell
Through veiling vastness, like the far-off bell,
Till, ever onward through the choral blue,
He heard more faintly and more faintly knew,
Quitting mortality, a quenched sun-wave,
The All-creating Presence for his grave.

5 October 1869 – December 1869/January 1870

ARMGART

SCENE I

A Salon lit with lamps and ornamented with green plants. An open piano, with many scattered sheets of music. Bronze busts of Beethoven and Gluck on pillars opposite each other. A small table spread with supper. To FRÄULEIN WALPURGA, *who advances with a slight lameness of gait from an adjoining room, enters* GRAF DORNBERG *at the opposite door in a travelling dress.*

GRAF. Good morning, Fräulein !

WALPURGA.   What, so soon returned ?
  I feared your mission kept you still at Prague.

GRAF. But now arrived ! You see my travelling dress.
  I hurried from the panting roaring steam
  Like any courier of embassy
  Who hides the fiends of war within his bag.

WALPURGA.
  You know that Armgart sings to-night ?

GRAF.   Has sung !
  'Tis close on half-past nine. The *Orpheus*
  Lasts not so long. Her spirits − were they high ?
  Was Leo confident ?

WALPURGA.   He only feared
  Some tameness at beginning. Let the house
  Once ring, he said, with plaudits, she is safe.

GRAF. And Armgart ?

115

WALPURGA.   She was stiller than her wont.
   But once, at some such trivial word of mine,
   As that the highest prize might yet be won
   By her who took the second – she was roused.
   "For me," she said, "I triumph or I fail.
   I never strove for any second prize."

GRAF. Poor human-hearted singing-bird ! She bears
   Caesar's ambition in her delicate breast,
   And nought to still it with but quivering song !

WALPURGA. I had not for the world been there to-night:
   Unreasonable dread oft chills me more
   Than any reasonable hope can warm.

GRAF. You have a rare affection for your cousin;
   As tender as a sister's.

WALPURGA.   Nay, I fear
   My love is little more than what I felt
   For happy stories when I was a child.
   She fills my life that would lie empty else,
   And lifts my nought to value by her side.

GRAF. She is reason good enough, or seems to be,
   Why all were born whose being ministers
   To her completeness. Is it most her voice
   Subdues us ? or her instinct exquisite,
   Informing each old strain with some new grace
   Which takes our sense like any natural good ?
   Or most her spiritual energy
   That sweeps us in the current of her song ?

WALPURGA. I know not. Losing either, we should lose
   That whole we call our Armgart. For herself,

She often wonders what her life had been
Without that voice for channel to her soul
She says, it must have leaped through all her limbs –
Made her a Maenad – made her snatch a brand
And fire some forest, that her rage might mount
In crashing roaring flames through half a land,
Leaving her still and patient for a while.
"Poor wretch !" she says, of any murderess –
"The world was cruel, and she could not sing:
I carry my revenges in my throat;
I love in singing, and am loved again."

GRAF. Mere mood ! I cannot yet believe it more.
Too much ambition has unwomaned her;
But only for a while. Her nature hides
One half its treasures by its very wealth,
Taxing the hours to show it.

WALPURGA.   Hark ! she comes.

Enter LEO *with a wreath in his hand, holding the
door open for* ARMGART, *who wears a furred mantle
and hood. She is followed by her maid, carrying an
armful of bouquets.*

LEO. Place for the queen of song !

GRAF (*advancing towards* ARMGART, *who throws off her hood
and mantle, and shows a star of brilliants in her hair*).
                              A triumph, then.
You will not be a niggard of your joy
And chide the eagerness that came to share it.

117

ARMGART. O kind! you hastened your return for me.
I would you had been there to hear me sing !
Walpurga, kiss me: never tremble more
Lest Armgart's wing should fail her. She has found
This night the region where her rapture breathes –
Pouring her passion on the air made live
With human heart-throbs. Tell them, Leo, tell them
How I outsang your hope and made you cry
Because Gluck could not hear me. That was folly !
He sang, not listened: every linkèd note
Was his immortal pulse that stirred in mine,
And all my gladness is but part of him.
Give me the wreath.

(She crowns the bust of Gluck.)

LEO *(sardonically)*.   Ay, ay, but mark you this:
It was not part of him – that trill you made
In spite of me and reason !

ARMGART.   You were wrong –
Dear Leo, you were wrong: the house was held
As if a storm were listening with delight
And hushed its thunder.

LEO.   Will you ask the house
To teach you singing ? Quit your *Orpheus* then,
And sing in farces grown to operas,
Where all the prurience of the full-fed mob
Is tickled with melodic impudence:
Jerk forth burlesque bravuras, square your arms
Akimbo with a tavern wench's grace,
And set the splendid compass of your voice
To lyric jigs. Go to ! I thought you meant
To be an artist – lift your audience

To see your vision, not trick forth a show
To please the grossest taste of grossest numbers.

ARMGART (*taking up* LEO's *hand, and kissing it*).
  Pardon, good Leo, I am penitent.
  I will do penance: sing a hundred trills
  Into a deep-dug grave, then burying them
  As one did Midas' secret, rid myself
  Of naughty exultation. O I trilled
  At nature's prompting, like the nightingales.
  Go scold them, dearest Leo.

LEO   I stop my ears.
  Nature in Gluck inspiring Orpheus,
  Has done with nightingales. Are bird-beaks lips?

GRAF. Truce to rebukes ! Tell us – who were not there –
  The double drama: how the expectant house
  Took the first notes.

WALPURGA (*turning from her occupation of decking the room
  with the flowers*).
                        Yes, tell us all, dear Armgart.
  Did you feel tremors? Leo, how did she look ?
  Was there a cheer to greet her ?

LEO.   Not a sound.
  She walked like Orpheus in his solitude
  And seemed to see nought but what no man saw.
  'Twas famous. Not the Schroeder-Devrient
  Had done it better. But your blessed public
  Had never any judgment in cold blood –
  Thinks all perhaps were better otherwise,
  Till rapture brings a reason.

119

ARMGART (*scornfully*).   I knew that !
    The women whispered, "Not a pretty face !"
    The men, "Well, well, a goodly length of limb:
    She bears the chiton." – It were all the same
    Were I the Virgin Mother and my stage
    The opening heavens at the Judgment-day:
    Gossips would peep, jog elbows, rate the price
    Of such a woman in the social mart.
    What were the drama of the world to them,
    Unless they felt the hell-prong ?

LEO.   Peace, now, peace !
    I hate my phrases to be smothered o'er
    With sauce of paraphrase, my sober tune
    Made bass to rambling trebles, showering down
    In endless demi-semi-quavers.

ARMGART (*taking a bon-bon from the table, uplifting it before
    putting it into her mouth, and turning away*).
                              Mum !

GRAF. Yes, tell us all the glory, leave the blame.

WALPURGA. You first, dear Leo – what you saw and heard;
    Then Armgart – she must tell us what she felt.

LEO. Well ! The first notes came clearly firmly forth.
    And I was easy, for behind those rills
    I knew there was a fountain. I could see
    The house was breathing gently, heads were still;
    Parrot opinion was struck meekly mute,
    And human hearts were swelling. Armgart stood
    As if she had been new-created there
    And found her voice which found a melody.
    The minx ! Gluck had not written, nor I taught:

120

Orpheus was Armgart, Armgart Orpheus.
Well, well, all through the *scena* I could feel
The silence tremble now, now poise itself
With added weight of feeling, till at last
Delight o'er toppled it. The final note
Had happy drowning in the unloosed roar
That surged and ebbed and ever surged again,
Till expectation kept it pent awhile
Ere Orpheus returned. Pfui ! He was changed:
My demi-god was pale, had downcast eyes
That quivered like a bride's who fain would send
Backward the rising tear.

ARMGART (*advancing, but then turning away, as if to check
    her speech*).
                            I *was* a bride,
As nuns are at their spousals.

LEO.   Ay, my lady,
    That moment will not come again: applause
    May come and plenty; but the first, first draught !
                        (*Snaps his fingers.*)
    Music has sounds for it – I know no words.
    I felt it once myself when they performed
    My overture to Sintram. Well ! 'tis strange,
    We know not pain from pleasure in such joy

ARMGART (*turning quickly*).
    Oh, pleasure has cramped dwelling in our souls,
    And when full Being comes must call on pain
    To lend it liberal space.

WALPURGA.   I hope the house
    Kept a reserve of plaudits: I am jealous

Lest they had dulled themselves for coming good
That should have seemed the better and the best.

LEO. No, 'twas a revel where they had but quaffed
Their opening cup. I thank the artist's star,
His audience keeps not sober: once afire,
They flame towards climax, though his merit hold
But fairly even.

ARMGART (*her hand on* LEO's *arm*).
                Now, now, confess the truth:
I sang still better to the very end –
All save the trill; I give that up to you,
To bite and growl at. Why, you said yourself,
Each time I sang, it seemed new doors were oped
That you might hear heaven clearer.

LEO (*shaking his finger*).   I was raving.

ARMGART. I am not glad with that mean vanity
Which knows no good beyond its appetite
Full feasting upon praise ! I am only glad,
Being praised for what I know is worth the praise;
Glad of the proof that I myself have part
In what I worship ! At the last applause –
Seeming a roar of tropic winds that tossed
The handkerchiefs and many-coloured flowers,
Falling like shattered rainbows all around –
Think you I felt myself a *prima donna* ?
No, but a happy spiritual star
Such as old Dante saw, wrought in a rose
Of light in Paradise, whose only self
Was consciousness of glory wide-diffused,
Music, life, power – I moving in the midst
With a sublime necessity of good.

LEO (*with a shrug*).
   I thought it was a *prima donna* came
   Within the side-scenes; ay, and she was proud
   To find the bouquet from the royal box
   Enclosed a jewel-case, and proud to wear
   A star of brilliants, quite an earthly star,
   Valued by thalers. Come, my lady, own
   Ambition has five senses, and a self
   That gives it good warm lodging when it sinks
   Plump down from ecstasy.

ARMGART.   Own it ? why not ?
   Am I a sage whose words must fall like seed
   Silently buried toward a far off spring ?
   I sing to living men and my effect
   Is like the summer's sun, that ripens corn
   Or now or never. If the world brings me gifts,
   Gold, incense, myrrh – 'twill be the needful sign
   That I have stirred it as the high year stirs
   Before I sink to winter.

GRAF.   Ecstasies
   Are short – most happily ! We should but lose
   Were Armgart borne too commonly and long
   Out of the self that charms us. Could I choose,
   She were less apt to soar beyond the reach
   Of woman's foibles, innocent vanities,
   Fondness for trifles like that pretty star
   Twinkling beside her cloud of ebon hair.

ARMGART (*taking out the gem and looking at it*).
   This little star ! I would it were the seed
   Of a whole Milky Way, if such bright shimmer
   Were the sole speech men told their rapture with
   At Armgart's music. Shall I turn aside

123

From splendours which flash out the glow I make,
And live to make, in all the chosen breasts
Of half a Continent ? No, may it come,
That splendour ! May the day be near when men
Think much to let my horses draw me home,
And new lands welcome me upon their beach,
Loving me for my fame. That is the truth
Of what I wish, nay, yearn for. Shall I lie ?
Pretend to seek obscurity – to sing
In hope of disregard ? A vile pretence !
And blasphemy besides. For what is fame
But the benignant strength of One, transformed
To joy of Many ? Tributes, plaudits come
As necessary breathing of such joy;
And may they come to me !

GRAF.   The auguries
Point clearly that way. Is it no offence
To wish the eagle's wing may find repose,
As feebler wings do, in a quiet nest?
Or has the taste of fame already turned
The Woman to a Muse . . .

LEO (*going to the table*).
                                    Who needs no supper.
I am her priest, ready to eat her share
Of good Walpurga's offerings.

WALPURGA.   Armgart, come.
Graf, will you come ?

GRAF.   Thanks, I play truant here,
And must retrieve my self-indulged delay.
But will the Muse receive a votary
At any hour tomorrow ?

ARMGART.   Any hour
    After rehearsal, after twelve at noon.

                        SCENE II

The same Salon, morning. ARMGART *seated, in her bonnet
and walking dress. The* GRAF *standing near her against
the piano.*

GRAF. Armgart, to many minds the first success
    Is reason for desisting. I have known
    A man so versatile, he tried all arts,
    But when in each by turns he had achieved
    Just so much mastery as made men say,
    "He could be king here if he would," he threw
    The lauded skill aside. He hates, said one,
    The level of achieved pre-eminence,
    He must be conquering still – but others said –

ARMGART. The truth, I hope: he had a meagre soul,
    Holding no depth where love could root itself.
    "Could if he would ?" True greatness ever wills –
    It lives in wholeness if it live at all,
    And all its strength is knit with constancy

GRAF. He used to say himself he was too sane
    To give his life away for excellence
    Which yet must stand, an ivory statuette
    Wrought to perfection through long lonely years,
    Huddled in the mart of mediocrities.
    He said, the very finest doing wins
    The admiring only; but to leave undone,
    Promise and not fulfil, like buried youth,
    Wins all the envious, makes them sigh your name

                        125

As that fair Absent, blameless Possible,
Which could alone impassion them; and thus,
Serene negation has free gift of all,
Panting achievement struggles, is denied,
Or wins to lose again. What say you, Armgart ?
Truth has rough flavours if we bite it through;
I think this sarcasm came from out its core
Of bitter irony.

ARMGART.   It is the truth
Mean souls select to feed upon. What then ?
Their meanness is a truth, which I will spurn.
The praise I seek lives not in envious breath
Using my name to blight another's deed.
I sing for love of song and that renown
Which is the spreading act, the world-wide share,
Of good that I was born with. Had I failed –
Well, that had been a truth most pitiable
I cannot bear to think what life would be
With high hope shrunk to endurance, stunted aims
Like broken lances ground to eating-knives,
A self sunk down to look with level eyes
At low achievement, doomed from day to day
To distaste of its consciousness. But I –

GRAF. Have won, not lost, in your decisive throw.
And I too glory in this issue; yet,
The public verdict has no potency
To sway my judgment of what Armgart is:
My pure delight in her would be but sullied,
If it o'erflowed with mixture of men's praise.
And had she failed, I should have said, "The pearl
Remains a pearl for me, reflects the light
With the same fitness that first charmed my gaze –
Is worth as fine a setting now as then."

126

ARMGART (*rising*).

    Oh, you are good ! But why will you rehearse
    The talk of cynics, who with insect eyes
    Explore the secrets of the rubbish-heap ?
    I hate your epigrams and pointed saws
    Whose narrow truth is but broad falsity.
    Confess your friend was shallow.

GRAF.   I confess

    Life is not rounded in an epigram,
    And saying aught, we leave a world unsaid.
    I quoted, merely to shape forth my thought
    That high success has terrors when achieved –
    Like preternatural spouses whose dire love
    Hangs perilous on slight observances:
    Whence it were possible that Armgart crowned
    Might turn and listen to a pleading voice,
    Though Armgart striving in the race was deaf.
    You said you dared not think what life had been
    Without the stamp of eminence; have you thought
    How you will bear the poise of eminence
    With dread of sliding ? Paint the future out
    As an unchecked and glorious career,
    'Twill grow more strenuous by the very love
    You bear to excellence, the very fate
    Of human powers, which tread at every step
    On possible verges.

ARMGART.   I accept the peril.

    I choose to walk high with sublimer dread
    Rather than crawl in safety. And, besides,
    I am an artist as you are a noble:
    I ought to bear the burthen of my rank.

GRAF. Such parallels, dear Armgart, are but snares
     To catch the mind with seeming argument –
     Small baits of likeness 'mid disparity.
     Men rise the higher as their task is high,
     The task being well achieved. A woman's rank
     Lies in the fulness of her womanhood:
     Therein alone she is royal.

ARMGART.   Yes, I know
     The oft-taught Gospel: "Woman, thy desire
     Shall be that all superlatives on earth
     Belong to men, save the one highest kind –
     To be a mother. Thou shalt not desire
     To do aught best save pure subservience:
     Nature has willed it so !" O blessed Nature !
     Let her be arbitress; she gave me voice
     Such as she only gives a woman child,
     Best of its kind, gave me ambition too,
     That sense transcendent which can taste the joy
     Of swaying multitudes, of being adored
     For such achievement, needed excellence,
     As man's best art must wait for, or be dumb.
     Men did not say, when I had sung last night,
     " 'Twas good, nay, wonderful, considering
     She is a woman" – and then turn to add,
     "Tenor or baritone had sung her songs
     Better, of course: she's but a woman spoiled."
     I beg your pardon, Graf, you said it.

GRAF.   No !
     How should I say it, Armgart ? I who own
     The magic of your nature-given art
     As sweetest effluence of your womanhood
     Which, being to my choice the best, must find
     The best of utterance. But this I say:

128

Your fervid youth beguiles you; you mistake
A strain of lyric passion for a life
Which in the spending is a chronicle
With ugly pages. Trust me, Armgart, trust me;
Ambition exquisite as yours which soars
Toward something quintessential you call fame,
Is not robust enough for this gross world
Whose fame is dense with false and foolish breath.
Ardour, a-twin with nice refining thought,
Prepares a double pain. Pain had been saved,
Nay, purer glory reached, had you been throned
As woman only, holding all your art
As attribute to that dear sovereignty –
Concentering your power in home delights
Which penetrate and purify the world.

ARMGART. What ! leave the opera with my part ill-sung
While I was warbling in a drawing-room ?
Sing in the chimney-corner to inspire
My husband reading news ? Let the world hear
My music only in his morning speech
Less stammering than most honourable men's ?
No ! tell me that my song is poor, my art
The piteous feat of weakness aping strength –
That were fit proem to your argument.
Till then, I am an artist by my birth –
By the same warrant that I am a woman:
Nay, in the added rarer gift I see
Supreme vocation: if a conflict comes,
Perish – no, not the woman, but the joys
Which men make narrow by their narrowness.
Oh, I am happy ! The great masters write
For women's voices, and great Music wants me !
I need not crush myself within a mould

Of theory called Nature: I have room
To breathe and grow unstunted.

GRAF.   Armgart, hear me.
I meant not that our talk should hurry on
To such collision. Foresight of the ills
Thick shadowing your path, drew on my speech
Beyond intention. True, I came to ask
A great renunciation, but not this
Towards which my words at first perversely strayed,
As if in memory of their earlier suit,
Forgetful . . . .
Armgart, do you remember too ? the suit
Had but postponement, was not quite disdained –
Was told to wait and learn – what it has learned –
A more submissive speech.

ARMGART (*with some agitation*).
                                    Then it forgot
Its lesson cruelly. As I remember,
'Twas not to speak save to the artist crowned,
Nor speak to her of casting off her crown.

GRAF. Nor will it, Armgart. I come not to seek
Any renunciation save the wife's,
Which turns away from other possible love
Future and worthier, to take his love
Who asks the name of husband. He who sought
Armgart obscure, and heard her answer, "Wait" –
May come without suspicion now to seek
Armgart applauded.

ARMGART (*turning towards him*).
                                    Yes, without suspicion
Of aught save what consists with faithfulness

In all expressed intent. Forgive me, Graf –
I am ungrateful to no soul that loves me –
To you most grateful. Yet the best intent
Grasps but a living present which may grow
Like any unfledged bird. You are a noble,
And have a high career; just now you said
'Twas higher far than aught a woman seeks
Beyond mere womanhood. You claim to be
More than a husband, but could not rejoice
That I were more than wife. What follows, then ?
You choosing me with such persistency
As is but stretched-out rashness, soon must find
Our marriage asks concessions, asks resolve
To share renunciation or demand it.
Either we both renounce a mutual ease,
As in a nation's need both man and wife
Do public services, or one of us
Must yield that something else for which each lives
Besides the other. Men are reasoners:
That premiss of superior claims perforce
Urges conclusion – "Armgart, it is you."

GRAF. But if I say I have considered this
    With strict prevision, counted all the cost
    Which that great good of loving you demands –
    Questioned my stores of patience, half resolved
    To live resigned without a bliss whose threat
    Touched you as well as me – and finally,
    With impetus of undivided will
    Returned to say, "You shall be free as now;
    Only accept the refuge, shelter, guard,
    My love will give your freedom" – then your words
    Are hard accusal.

131

ARMGART.   Well, I accuse myself.
  My love would be accomplice of your will.

GRAF. Again – my will ?

ARMGART.   Oh, your unspoken will.
  Your silent tolerance would torture me,
  And on that rack I should deny the good
  I yet believed in.

GRAF.   Then I am the man
  Whom you would love ?

ARMGART.   Whom I refuse to love !
  No; I will live alone and pour my pain
  With passion into music, where it turns
  To what is best within my better self.
  I will not take for husband one who deems
  The thing my soul acknowledges as good –
  The thing I hold worth striving, suffering for,
  To be a thing dispensed with easily,
  Or else the idol of a mind infirm.

GRAF. Armgart, you are ungenerous; you strain
  My thought beyond its mark. Our difference
  Lies not so deep as love – as union
  Through a mysterious fitness that transcends
  Formal agreement.

ARMGART   It lies deep enough
  To chafe the union. If many a man
  Refrains, degraded, from the utmost right,
  Because the pleadings of his wife's small fears
  Are little serpents biting at his heel, –
  How shall a woman keep her steadfastness

132

Beneath a frost within her husband's eyes
Where coldness scorches ? Graf, it is your sorrow
That you love Armgart. Nay, it is her sorrow
That she may not love you.

GRAF.   Woman, it seems,
Has enviable power to love or not
According to her will.

ARMGART.   She has the will –
I have – who am one woman – not to take
Disloyal pledges that divide her will.
The man who marries me must wed my Art –
Honour and cherish it, not tolerate.

GRAF. The man is yet to come whose theory
Will weigh as nought with you against his love.

ARMGART. Whose theory will plead beside his love.

GRAF. Himself a singer, then ? who knows no life
Out of the opera books, where tenor parts
Are found to suit him ?

ARMGART.   You are bitter, Graf.
Forgive me; seek the woman you deserve,
All grace, all goodness, who has not yet found
A meaning in her life, nor any end
Beyond fulfilling yours. The type abounds.

GRAF. And happily, for the world.

ARMGART.   Yes, happily.
Let it excuse me that my kind is rare:
Commonness is its own security.

GRAF. Armgart, I would with all my soul I knew
   The man so rare that he could make your life
   As woman sweet to you, as artist safe.

ARMGART. Oh, I can live unmated, but not live
   Without the bliss of singing to the world,
   And feeling all my world respond to me.

GRAF. May it be lasting. Then, we two must part?

ARMGART. I thank you from my heart for all. Farewell !

SCENE III

A Year Later

The same Salon. WALPURGA *is standing looking towards
the window with an air of uneasiness.* DOCTOR GRAHN.

DOCTOR. Where is my patient, Fräulein ?

WALPURGA.   Fled ! escaped !
   Gone to rehearsal. Is it dangerous ?

DOCTOR. No, no; her throat is cured. I only came
   To hear her try her voice. Had she yet sung ?

WALPURGA. No; she had meant to wait for you. She said,
   "The Doctor has a right to my first song."
   Her gratitude was full of little plans,
   But all were swept away like gathered flowers
   By sudden storm. She saw this opera bill –
   It was a wasp to sting her: she turnd pale,
   Snatched up her hat and mufflers, said in haste,

"I go to Leo – to rehearsal – none
Shall sing Fidelio to-night but me !"
Then rushed down-stairs.

DOCTOR (*looking at his watch*).

And this, not long ago ?

WALPURGA.   Barely an hour.

DOCTOR.   I will come again,
  Returning from Charlottenburg at one.

WALPURGA.   Doctor, I feel a strange presentiment.
  Are you quite easy ?

DOCTOR.   She can take no harm.
  'Twas time for her to sing: her throat is well.
  It was a fierce attack and dangerous;
  I had to use strong remedies, but – well !
  At one, dear Fräulein, we shall meet again.

SCENE IV

Two Hours Later

WALPURGA *starts up, looking towards the door.* ARMGART
enters, followed by LEO. *She throws herself on a chair
which stands with its back towards the door, speechless,
not seeming to see anything.* WALPURGA *casts a questioning
terrified look at* LEO. *He shrugs his shoulders, and lifts
up his hands behind* ARMGART, *who sits like a helpless
image while* WALPURGA *takes off her hat and mantle.*

WALPURGA.   Armgart, dear Armgart (*kneeling and taking her*

135

hands), only speak to me,
Your poor Walpurga. Oh, your hands are cold.
Clasp mine, and warm them ! I will kiss them warm.

(ARMGART *looks at her an instant, then draws away
her hands, and, turning aside, buries her face
against the back of the chair*, WALPURGA *rising and
standing near*.)

(DOCTOR GRAHN *enters*.)

DOCTOR. News ! stirring news to-day ! wonders come thick.

ARMGART. (*starting up at the first sound of his voice, and
speaking vehemently*).
Yes, thick, thick, thick ! and you have murdered it !
Murdered my voice – poisoned the soul in me,
And kept me living.
You never told me that your cruel cures
Were clogging films – a mouldy, dead'ning blight –
A lava-mud to crust and bury me,
Yet hold me living in a deep, deep tomb,
Crying unheard for ever ! Oh, your cures
Are devil's triumphs: you can rob, maim, slay,
And keep a hell on the other side your cure
Where you can see your victim quivering
Between the teeth of torture – see a soul
Made keen by loss – all anguish with a good
Once known and gone !
   (*Turns and sinks back on her chair.*)
                              O misery, misery !
You might have killed me, might have let me sleep
After my happy day and wake – not here !
In some new unremembered world, – not here,
Where all is faded, flat – a feast broke off –

136

Banners all meaningless – exulting words
Dull, dull – a drum that lingers in the air
Beating to melody which no man hears.

DOCTOR (*after a moment's silence*).
A sudden check has shaken you, poor child !
All things seem livid, tottering to your sense,
From inward tumult. Stricken by a threat
You see your terrors only. Tell me, Leo:
'Tis not such utter loss.
    (LEO, *with a shrug, goes quietly out*.)
        The freshest bloom
Merely, has left the fruit; the fruit itself . . .

ARMGART. Is ruined, withered, is a thing to hide
Away from scorn or pity. Oh, you stand
And look compassionate now, but when Death came
With mercy in his hands, you hindered him.
I did not choose to live and have your pity.
You never told me, never gave me choice
To die a singer, lightning-struck, unmaimed,
Or live what you would make me with your cures –
A self accursed with consciousness of change,
A mind that lives in nought but members lopped,
A power turned to pain – as meaningless
As letters fallen asunder that once made
A hymn of rapture. Oh, I had meaning once,
Like day and sweetest air. What am I now ?
The millionth woman in superfluous herds.
Why should I be, do, think ? 'Tis thistle-seed,
That grows and grows to feed the rubbish-heap.
Leave me alone !

DOCTOR.   Well, I will come again;
    Send for me when you will, though but to rate me.
    That is medicinal – a letting blood.

ARMGART. Oh, there is one physician, only one,
    Who cures and never spoils. Him I shall send for;
    He comes readily.

DOCTOR (*to* WALPURGA).
                        One word, dear Fräulein.

                        SCENE V

                    ARMGART, WALPURGA.

ARMGART. Walpurga, have you walked this morning ?

WALPURGA.   No.

ARMGART. Go, then, and walk; I wish to be alone.

WALPURGA. I will not leave you. .

ARMGART.   Will not, at my wish ?

WALPURGA. Will not, because you wish it. Say no more,
    But take this draught.

ARMGART.   The Doctor gave it you ?
    It is an anodyne. Put it away.
    He cured me of my voice, and now he wants
    To cure me of my vision and resolve –
    Drug me to sleep that I may wake again
    Without a purpose, abject as the rest

                        138

To bear the yoke of life. He shall not cheat me
Of that fresh strength which anguish gives the soul,
The inspiration of revolt, ere rage
Slackens to faltering. Now I see the truth.

WALPURGA (*setting down the glass*),
    Then you must see a future in your reach,
    With happiness enough to make a dower
    For two of modest claims.

ARMGART.   Oh, you intone
    That chant of consolation wherewith ease
    Makes itself easier in the sight of pain.

WALPURGA. No; I would not console you, but rebuke.

ARMGART. That is more bearable. Forgive me, dear.
    Say what you will. But now I want to write.
                (She rises and moves towards a table.)

WALPURGA. I say then, you are simply fevered, mad;
    You cry aloud at horrors that would vanish
    If you would change the light, throw into shade
    The loss you aggrandise, and let day fall
    On good remaining, nay on good refused
    Which may be gain now. Did you not reject
    A woman's lot more brilliant, as some held,
    Than any singer's ? It may still be yours.
    Graf Dornberg loved you well.

ARMGART.   Not me, not me.
    He loved one well who was like me in all
    Save in a voice which made that All unlike
    As diamond is to charcoal. Oh, a man's love !
    Think you he loves a woman's inner self

Aching with loss of loveliness ? – as mothers
Cleave to the palpitating pain that dwells
Within their misformed offspring ?

WALPURGA.   But the Graf
Chose you as simple Armgart – had preferred
That you should never seek for any fame
But such as matrons have who rear great sons.
And therefore you rejected him; but now –

ARMGART. Ay, now – now he would see me as I am,
                    (*She takes up a hand-mirror*.)
Russet and songless as a missel-thrush.
An ordinary girl – a plain brown girl,
Who, if some meaning flash from out her words,
Shocks as a disproportioned thing – a Will
That, like an arm astretch and broken off,
Has nought to hurl – the torso of a soul.
I sang him into love of me: my song
Was consecration, lifted me apart
From the crowd chiselled like me, sister forms,
But empty of divineness. Nay, my charm
Was half that I could win fame yet renounce !
A wife with glory possible absorbed
Into her husband's actual.

WALPURGA.   For shame !
Armgart, you slander him. What would you say
If now he came to you and asked again
That you would be his wife ?

ARMGART.   No, and thrice no !
It would be pitying constancy, not love,
That brought him to me now. I will not be
A pensioner in marriage. Sacraments

140

Are not to feed the paupers of the world.
If he were generous – I am generous too.

WALPURGA. Proud, Armgart, but not generous.

ARMGART.   Say no more.
He will not know until –

WALPURGA.   He knows already.

ARMGART (*quickly*).
Is he come back ?

WALPURGA.   Yes, and will soon be here.
The Doctor had twice seen him and would go
From hence again to see him.

ARMGART.   Well, he knows.
It is all one.

WALPURGA.   What if he were outside ?
I hear a footstep in the ante-room.

ARMGART (*raising herself and assuming calmness*).
Why let him come, of course. I shall behave
Like what I am, a common personage
Who looks for nothing but civility.
I shall not play the fallen heroine,
Assume a tragic part and throw out cues
For a beseeching lover.

WALPURGA.   Some one raps.
                (*Goes to the door*).
A letter – from the Graf.

141

ARMGART.   Then open it.
           (WALPURGA *still offers it*.)
Nay, my head swims. Read it. I cannot see.
        (WALPURGA *opens it, reads and pauses*.)
Read it. Have done ! No matter what it is.

WALPURGA (*reads in a low, hesitating voice*).
"I am deeply moved − my heart is rent, to hear of your
illness and its cruel result, just now communicated to me
by Dr Grahn. But surely it is possible that this result
may not lie permanent. For youth such as yours, Time
may hold in store something more than resignation: who
shall say that it does not hold renewal ? I have not
dared to ask admission to you in the hours of a recent
shock, but I cannot depart on a long mission without
tendering my sympathy and my farewell. I start this
evening for the Caucasus, and thence I proceed to India,
where I am intrusted by the Government with business
which may be of long duration."
           (WALPURGA *sits down dejectedly*.)

ARMGART (*after a slight shudder, bitterly*).
The Graf has much discretion. I am glad.
He spares us both a pain, not seeing me.
What I like least is that consoling hope −
That empty cup, so neatly ciphered "Time,"
Handed me as a cordial for despair.
           (*Slowly and dreamily*)
Time − what a word to fling as charity !
Bland neutral word for slow, dull-beating pain −
Days, months, and years ! − If I would wait for them
     (*She takes up her hat and puts it on, then wraps
     her mantle round her.* WALPURGA *leaves the room.*)
Why, this is but beginning. (WALPURGA *re-enters*.)
           Kiss me, dear.

I am going now – alone – out – for a walk.
Say you will never wound me any more
With such cajolery as nurses use
To patients amorous of a crippled life.
Flatter the blind: I see.

WALPURGA.   Well, I was wrong.
In haste to soothe, I snatched at flickers merely.
Believe me, I will flatter you no more.

ARMGART. Bear witness, I am calm. I read my lot
Writ by a creeping feuilletonist and called
"The Woman's Lot: a Tale of Everyday:"
A middling woman's, to impress the world
With high superfluousness; her thoughts a crop
Of chick-weed errors or of pot-herb facts,
Smiled at like some child's drawing on a slate.
"Genteel?" "O yes, gives lessons; not so good
As any man's would be, but cheaper far."
"Pretty ?" "No; yet she makes a figure fit
For good society. Poor thing, she sews
Both late and early, turns and alters all
To suit the changing mode. Some widower
Might do well, marrying her; but in these days ! . . .
Well, she can somewhat eke her narrow gains
By writing, just to furnish her with gloves
And droschkies in the rain. They print her things
Often for charity." – Oh, a dog's life !
A harnessed dog's, that draws a little cart
Voted a nuisance ! I am going now.

WALPURGA. Not now, the door is locked.

ARMGART.   Give me the key!

WALPURGA. Locked on the outside. Gretchen has the key:
  She is gone on errands.

ARMGART.   What, you dare to keep me
  Your prisoner ?

WALPURGA.   And have I not been yours ?
  Your wish has been a bolt to keep me in.
  Perhaps that middling woman whom you paint
  With far-off scorn . . . . .

ARMGART.   I paint what I must be !
  What is my soul to me without the voice
  That gave it freedom ? – gave it one grand touch
  And made it nobly human ? – Prisoned now,
  Prisoned in all the petty mimicries
  Called woman's knowledge, that will fit the world
  As doll-clothes fit a man. I can do nought
  Better than what a million women do –
  Must drudge among the crowd and feel my life
  Beating upon the world without response,
  Beating with passion through an insect's horn
  That moves a millet-seed laboriously –
  If I *would* do it !

WALPURGA (*coldly*).   And why should you not?

ARMGART (*turning quickly*).
  Because Heaven made me royal – wrought me out
  With subtle finish towards pre-eminence,
  Made every channel of my soul converge
  To one high function, and then flung me down,
  That breaking I might turn to subtlest pain.
  An inborn passion gives a rebel's right:
  I would rebel and die in twenty worlds

Sooner than bear the yoke of thwarted life,
Each keenest sense turned into keen distaste,
Hunger not satisfied but kept alive
Breathing in languor half a century.
All the world now is but a rack of threads
To twist and dwarf me into pettiness
And basely feigned content, the placid mask
Of women's misery.

WALPURGA (*indignantly*). Ay, such a mask
As the few born like you to easy joy,
Cradled in privilege, take for natural
On all the lowly faces that must look
Upward to you ! What revelation now
Shows you the mask or gives presentiment
Of sadness hidden ? You who every day
These five years saw me limp to wait on you,
And thought the order perfect which gave *me*,
The girl without pretension to be aught,
A splendid cousin for my happiness:
To watch the night through when her brain was fired
With too much gladness – listen, always listen
To what *she* felt, who having power had right
To feel exorbitantly, and submerge
The souls around her with the poured-out flood
Of what must be ere she were satisfied !
That was feigned patience, was it ? Why not love,
Love nurtured even with that strength of self
Which found no room save in another's life ?
Oh, such as I know joy by negatives,
And all their deepest passion is a pang
Till they accept their pauper's heritage,
And meekly live from out the general store
Of joy they were born stripped of. I accept –
Nay, now would sooner choose it than the wealth

Of natures you call royal, who can live
In mere mock knowledge of their fellows' woe,
Thinking their smiles may heal it.

ARMGART (*tremulously*).   Nay, Walpurga,
I did not make a palace of my joy
To shut the world's truth from me. All my good
Was that I touched the world and made a part
In the world's dower of beauty, strength, and bliss;
Now I am fallen dark; I sit in gloom,
Remembering bitterly. Yet you speak truth;
I wearied you it seems; took all your help
As cushioned nobles use a weary serf,
Not looking at his face.

WALPURGA.   Oh, I but stand
As a small symbol for the mighty sum
Of claims unpaid to needy myriads;
I think you never set your loss beside
That mighty deficit. Is your work gone –
The prouder queenly work that paid itself
And yet was overpaid with men's applause ?
Are you no longer chartered, privileged,
But sunk to simple woman's penury,
To ruthless Nature's chary average –
Where is the rebel's right for you alone ?
Noble rebellion lifts a common load;
But what is he who flings his own load off
And leaves his fellows toiling ? Rebel's right ?
Say rather, the deserter's. Oh, you smiled
From your clear height on all the million lots
Which yet you brand as abject.

ARMGART.   I was blind
With too much happiness: true vision comes

146

Only, it seems, with sorrow. Were there one
This moment near me, suffering what I feel,
And needing me for comfort in her pang –
Then it were worth the while to live; not else.

WALPURGA. One – near you – why, they throng ! you
    hardly stir
But your act touches them. We touch afar.
For did not swarthy slaves of yesterday
Leap in their bondage at the Hebrews' flight,
Which touched them through the thrice millennial dark ?
But you can find the sufferer you need
With touch less subtle.

ARMGART.   Who has need of me ?

WALPURGA. Love finds the need it fills. But you are hard.

ARMGART. Is it not you, Walpurga, who are hard ?
    You humoured all my wishes till to-day,
    When fate has blighted me.

WALPURGA.   You would not hear
    The "chant of consolation:" words of hope
    Only embittered you. Then hear the truth –
    A lame girl's truth, whom no one ever praised
    For being cheerful. "It is well," they said:
    "Were she cross-grained she could not be endured."
    A word of truth from her had startled you;
    But you – you claimed the universe; nought less
    Than all existence working in sure tracks
    Towards your supremacy. The wheels might scathe
    A myriad destinies – nay, must perforce;
    But yours they must keep clear of; just for you
    The seething atoms through the firmament

Must bear a human heart — which you had not !
For what is it to you that women, men,
Plod, faint, are weary, and espouse despair
Of aught but fellowship ? Save that you spurn
To be among them? Now, then, you are lame —
Maimed, as you said, and levelled with the crowd:
Call it new birth — birth from that monstrous Self
Which, smiling down upon a race oppressed,
Says, "All is good, for I am throned at ease."
Dear Armgart — nay, you tremble — I am cruel.

ARMGART.
    O no! hark ! Some one knocks. Come in ! — come in !
                      (*Enter* LEO.)

LEO. See, Gretchen let me in. I could not rest
Longer away from you.

ARMGART.   Sit down, dear Leo.
Walpurga, I would speak with him alone.
            (WALPURGA *goes out*.)

LEO (*hesitatingly*).
    You mean to walk ?

ARMGART.   No, I shall stay within.
    (*She takes off her hat and mantle, and sits down
    immediately. After a pause, speaking in a subdued
    tone to* LEO.)
How old are you ?

LEO.   Threescore and five.

ARMGART.   That's old.
I never thought till now how you have lived.

They hardly ever play your music ?

LEO (*raising his eyebrows and throwing out his lip*).
                                        No !
Schubert too wrote for silence: half his work
Lay like a frozen Rhine till summers came
That warmed the grass above him. Even so !
His music lives now with a mighty youth.

ARMGART. Do you think yours will live when you are dead ?

LEO. Pfui ! The time was, I drank that home-brewed wine
And found it heady, while my blood was young:
Now it scarce warms me. Tipple it as I may,
I am sober still, and say: "My old friend Leo,
Much grain is wasted in the world and rots;
Why not thy handful ?"

ARMGART   Strange ! since I have known you
Till now I never wondered how you lived.
When I sang well – that was your jubilee.
But you were old already.

LEO.   Yes, child, yes:
Youth thinks itself the goal of each old life;
Age has but travelled from a far-off time
Just to be ready for youth's service. Well !
It was my chief delight to perfect you.

ARMGART.   Good Leo ! You have lived on little joys.
But your delight in me is crushed for ever
Your pains, where are they now? They shaped intent
Which action frustrates; shaped an inward sense
Which is but keen despair, the agony
Of highest vision in the lowest pit.

149

LEO. Nay, nay, I have a thought: keep to the stage,
   To drama without song; for you can act –
   Who knows how well, when all the soul is poured
   Into that sluice alone ?

ARMGART.   I know, and you:
   The second or third best in tragedies
   That cease to touch the fibre of the time.
   No; song is gone, but nature's other gift,
   Self-judgment, is not gone. Song was my speech,
   And with its impulse only, action came:
   Song was the battle's onset, when cool purpose
   Glows into rage, becomes a warring god
   And moves the limbs with miracle. But now –
   Oh, I should stand hemmed in with thoughts and rules–
   Say "This way passion acts," yet never feel
   The might of passion. How should I declaim ?
   As monsters write with feet instead of hands.
   I will not feed on doing great tasks ill,
   Dull the world's sense with mediocrity,
   And live by trash that smothers excellence.
   One gift I had that ranked me with the best –
   The secret of my frame – and that is gone.
   For all life now I am a broken thing.
   But silence there ! Good Leo, advise me now.
   I would take humble work and do it well –
   Teach music, singing – what I can – not here,
   But in some smaller town where I may bring
   The method you have taught me, pass your gift
   To others who can use it for delight.
   You think I can do that ?
           (She pauses with a sob in her voice.)

LEO.   Yes, yes, dear child !

And it were well, perhaps, to change the place –
Begin afresh as I did when I left
Vienna with a heart half broken.

ARMGART (*roused by surprise*).   You ?

LEO. Well, it is long ago. But I had lost –
No matter ! We must bury our dead joys
And live above them with a living world.
But whither, think you, you would like to go ?

ARMGART. To Freiburg.

LEO.   In the Breisgau ? And why there ?
It is too small.

ARMGART.   Walpurga was born there,
And loves the place. She quitted it for me
These five years past. Now I will take her there.
Dear Leo, I will bury my dead joy.

LEO. Mothers do so, bereaved; then learn to love
Another's living child.

ARMGART.   Oh, it is hard
To take the little corpse, and lay it low,
And say, "None misses it but me."
She sings . . .
I mean Paulina sings Fidelio,
And they will welcome her to-night.

LEO.   Well, well,
'Tis better that our griefs should not spread far.

4 August – September 1870

ARION

(HEROD. I. 24.)

Arion, whose melodic soul
Taught the dithyramb to roll
    Like forest fires, and sing
    Olympian suffering,

Had carried his diviner lore
From Corinth to the sister shore
    Where Greece could largelier be,
    Branching o'er Italy.

Then weighted with his glorious name
And bags of gold, aboard he came
    'Mid harsh seafaring men
    To Corinth bound again.

The sailors eyed the bags and thought:
"The gold is good, the man is nought −
    And who shall track the wave
    That opens for his grave ?"

With brawny arms and cruel eyes
They press around him where he lies
    In sleep beside his lyre,
    Hearing the Muses quire.

He waked and saw this wolf-faced Death
Breaking the dream that filled his breath
    With inspiration strong
    Of yet unchanted song.

"Take, take my gold and let me live !"
He prayed, as kings do when they give
     Their all with royal will,
     Holding born kingship still.

To rob the living they refuse,
One death or other he must choose,
     Either the watery pall
     Or wounds and burial.

"My solemn robe then let me don,
Give me high space to stand upon,
     That dying I may pour
     A song unsung before."

It pleased them well to grant this prayer,
To hear for nought how it might fare
     With men who paid their gold
     For what a poet sold.

In flowing stole, his eyes aglow
With inward fire, he neared the prow
     And took his god-like stand,
     The cithara in hand.

The wolfish men all shrank aloof,
And feared this singer might be proof
     Against their murderous power,
     After his lyric hour.

But he, in liberty of song,
Fearless of death or other wrong,
     With full spondaic toll
     Poured forth his mighty soul:

Poured forth the strain his dream had taught,
A nome with lofty passion fraught
　　Such as makes battles won
　　On fields of Marathon.

The last long vowels trembled then
As awe within those wolfish men:
　　They said, with mutual stare,
　　Some god was present there.

But lo ! Arion leaped on high
Ready, his descant done, to die;
　　Not asking, "Is it well ?"
　　Like a pierced eagle fell.

April 1873

Your soul was lifted by the wings to-day
Hearing the master of the violin:
You praised him, praised the great Sebastian too
Who made that fine Chaconne; but did you think
Of old Antonio Stradivari ? – him
Who a good century and half ago
Put his true work in that brown instrument
And by the nice adjustment of its frame
Gave it responsive life, continuous
With the master's finger-tips and perfected
Like them by delicate rectitude of use.
Not Bach alone, helped by fine precedent
Of genius gone before, nor Joachim
Who holds the strain afresh incorporate
By inward hearing and notation strict
Of nerve and muscle, made our joy to-day:
Another soul was living in the air
And swaying it to true deliverance
Of high invention and responsive skill: –
That plain white-aproned man who stood at work
Patient and accurate full fourscore years,
Cherished his sight and touch by temperance,
And since keen sense is love of perfectness
Made perfect violins, the needed paths
For inspiration and high mastery.

No simpler man than he: he never cried,
"Why was I born to this monotonous task
Of making violins ?" or flung them down
To suit with hurling act a well-hurled curse
At labour on such perishable stuff.
Hence neighbours in Cremona held him dull,

155

Called him a slave, a mill-horse, a machine,
Begged him to tell his motives or to lend
A few gold pieces to a loftier mind.
Yet he had pithy words full fed by fact;
For Fact, well-trusted, reasons and persuades,
Is gnomic, cutting, or ironical,
Draws tears, or is a tocsin to arouse —
Can hold all figures of the orator
In one plain sentence; has her pauses too —
Eloquent silence at the chasm abrupt
Where knowledge ceases. Thus Antonio
Made answers as Fact willed, and made them strong.

Naldo, a painter of eclectic school,
Taking his dicers, candlelight and grins
From Caravaggio, and in holier groups
Combining Flemish flesh with martyrdom —
Knowing all tricks of style at thirty-one,
And weary of them, while Antonio
At sixty-nine wrought placidly his best
Making the violin you heard to-day —
Naldo would tease him oft to tell his aims.

"Perhaps thou hast some pleasant vice to feed —
The love of louis d'ors in heaps of four,
Each violin a heap — I've nought to blame;
My vices waste such heaps. But then, why work
With painful nicety ? Since fame once earned
By luck or merit — oftenest by luck —
(Else why do I put Bonifazio's name
To work that 'pinxit Naldo' would not sell ?)
Is welcome index to the wealthy mob
Where they should pay their gold, and where they pay
There they find merit — take your tow for flax,

And hold the flax unlabelled with your name,
Too coarse for sufferance."

Antonio then:

"I like the gold – well, yes – but not for meals.
And as my stomach, so my eye and hand,
And inward sense that works along with both,
Have hunger that can never feed on coin.
Who draws a line and satisfies his soul,
Making it crooked where it should be straight ?
An idiot with an oyster-shell may draw
His lines along the sand, all wavering,
Fixing no point or pathway to a point;
An idiot one remove may choose his line,
Straggle and be content; but God be praised,
Antonio Stradivari has an eye
That winces at false work and loves the true,
With hand and arm that play upon the tool
As willingly as any singing bird
Sets him to sing his morning roundelay,
Because he likes to sing and likes the song."

Then Naldo: " 'Tis a petty kind of fame
At best, that comes of making violins;
And saves no masses, either. Thou wilt go
To purgatory none the less."

But he:

" 'Twere purgatory here to make them ill;
And for my fame – when any master holds
'Twixt chin and hand a violin of mine,
He will be glad that Stradivari lived,
Made violins, and made them of the best.
The masters only know whose work is good:
They will choose mine, and while God gives them skill

I give them instruments to play upon,
God choosing me to help Him."

                        "What ! were God
At fault for violins, thou absent ?"

                              " Yes;
He were at fault for Stradivari's work."

"Why, many hold Giuseppe's violins
As good as thine."

                "May be: they are different.
His quality declines: he spoils his hand
With over-drinking. But were his the best,
He could not work for two. My work is mine,
And, heresy or not, if my hand slacked
I should rob God – since He is fullest good –
Leaving a blank instead of violins.
I say, not God Himself can make man's best
Without best men to help Him. I am one best
Here in Cremona, using sunlight well
To fashion finest maple till it serves
More cunningly than throats, for harmony.
'Tis rare delight: I would not change my skill
To be the Emperor with bungling hands,
And lose my work, which comes as natural
As self at waking."

                "Thou art little more
Than a deft potter's wheel, Antonio;
Turning out work by mere necessity
And lack of varied function. Higher arts
Subsist on freedom – eccentricity –
Uncounted inspirations – influence
That comes with drinking, gambling, talk turned wild,
Then moody misery and lack of food –
With every dithyrambic fine excess:
These make at last a storm which flashes out

In lightning revelations. Steady work
Turns genius to a loom; the soul must lie
Like grapes beneath the sun till ripeness comes
And mellow vintage. I could paint you now
The finest Crucifixion; yesternight
Returning home I saw it on a sky
Blue-black, thick-starred. I want two louis d'ors
To buy the canvas and the costly blues –
Trust me a fortnight."

       "Where are those last two
I lent thee for thy Judith ? – her thou saw'st
In saffron gown, with Holofernes' head
And beauty all complete ?"

       "She is but sketched:
I lack the proper model – and the mood.
A great idea is an eagle's egg,
Craves time for hatching; while the eagle sits
Feed her."

    "If thou wilt call thy pictures eggs
I call the hatching, Work. 'Tis God gives skill,
But not without men's hands: He could not make
Antonio Stradivari's violins
Without Antonio. Get thee to thy easel."

September 1873

Young Hamlet, not the hesitating Dane,
But one named after him, who lately strove
For honours at our English Wittenberg, –
Blond, metaphysical, and sensuous,
Questioning all things and yet half convinced
Credulity were better; held inert
'Twixt fascinations of all opposites,
And half suspecting that the mightiest soul
(Perhaps his own ?) was union of extremes,
Having no choice but choice of everything:
As, drinking deep to-day for love of wine,
To-morrow half a Brahmin, scorning life
As mere illusion, yearning for that True
Which has no qualities; another day
Finding the fount of grace in sacraments,
And purest reflex of the light divine
In gem-bossed pyx and broidered chasuble,
Resolved to wear no stockings and to fast
With arms extended, waiting ecstasy;
But getting cramps instead, and needing change,
A would-be pagan next: –

                Young Hamlet sat
A guest with five of somewhat riper age
At breakfast with Horatio, a friend
With few opinions, but of faithful heart,
Quick to detect the fibrous spreading roots
Of character that feed men's theories,
Yet cloaking weaknesses with charity
And ready in all service save rebuke.

With ebb of breakfast and the cider-cup
Came high debate: the others seated there

Were Osric, spinner of fine sentences,
A delicate insect creeping over life
Feeding on molecules of floral breath,
And weaving gossamer to trap the sun;
Laertes ardent, rash, and radical;
Discursive Rosencranz, grave Guildenstern,
And he for whom the social meal was made –
The polished priest, a tolerant listener,
Disposed to give a hearing to the lost,
And breakfast with them ere they went below.

From alpine metaphysic glaciers first
The talk sprang copious; the themes were old,
But so is human breath, so infant eyes,
The daily nurslings of creative light.
Small words held mighty meanings: Matter, Force,
Self, Not-self, Being, Seeming, Space and Time –
Plebeian toilers on the dusty road
Of daily traffic, turned to Genii
And cloudy giants darkening sun and moon.
Creation was reversed in human talk:
None said, "Let Darkness be," but Darkness was;
And in it weltered with Teutonic ease,
An argumentative Leviathan,
Blowing cascades from out his element,
The thunderous Rosencranz, till

                              "Truce, I beg !"
Said Osric, with nice accent. "I abhor
That battling of the ghosts, that strife of terms
For utmost lack of colour, form, and breath,
That tasteless squabbling called Philosophy:
As if a blue-winged butterfly afloat
For just three days above the Italian fields,
Instead of sipping at the heart of flowers,
Poising in sunshine, fluttering towards its bride,

161

Should fast and speculate, considering
What were if it were not ? or what now is
Instead of that which seems to be itself ?
Its deepest wisdom surely were to be
A sipping, marrying, blue-winged butterfly;
Since utmost speculation on itself
Were but a three days' living of worse sort –
A bruising struggle all within the bounds
Of butterfly existence."

                         "I protest,"
Burst in Laertes, "against arguments
That start with calling me a butterfly,
A bubble, spark, or other metaphor
Which carries your conclusions as a phrase
In quibbling law will carry property.
Put a thin sucker for my human lips
Fed at a mother's breast, who now needs food
That I will earn for her; put bubbles blown
From frothy thinking, for the joy, the love,
The wants, the pity, and the fellowship
(The ocean deeps I might say, were I bent
On bandying metaphors) that make a man –
Why, rhetoric brings within your easy reach
Conclusions worthy of – a butterfly.
The universe, I hold, is no charade,
No acted pun unriddled by a word,
Nor pain a decimal diminishing
With hocus-pocus of a dot or nought.
For those who know it, pain is solely pain:
Not any letters of the alphabet
Wrought syllogistically pattern-wise,
Nor any cluster of fine images,
Nor any missing of their figured dance
By blundering molecules. Analysis
May show you the right physic for the ill,

Teaching the molecules to find their dance,
But spare me your analogies, that hold
Such insight as the figure of a crow
And bar of music put to signify
A crowbar."

        Said the Priest, "There I agree –
Would add that sacramental grace is grace
Which to be known must first be felt, with all
The strengthening influxes that come by prayer.
I note this passingly – would not delay
The conversation's tenor, save to hint
That taking stand with Rosencranz one sees
Final equivalence of all we name
Our Good and Ill – their difference meanwhile
Being inborn prejudice that plumps you down
An Ego, brings a weight into your scale
Forcing a standard. That resistless weight
Obstinate, irremovable by thought,
Persisting through disproof, an ache, a need
That spaceless stays where sharp analysis
Has shown a plenum filled without it – what
If this, to use your phrase, were just that Being
Not looking solely, grasping from the dark,
Weighing the difference you call Ego ? This
Gives you persistence, regulates the flux
With strict relation rooted in the All.
Who is he of your late philosophers
Takes the true name of Being to be Will ?
I – nay, the Church objects nought, is content:
Reason has reached its utmost negative,
Physic and metaphysic meet in the inane
And backward shrink to intense prejudice,
Making their absolute and homogene
A loaded relative, a choice to be
Whatever is – supposed: a What is not.

The Church demands no more, has standing room
And basis for her doctrine: this (no more) –
That the strong bias which we name the Soul,
Though fed and clad by dissoluble waves,
Has antecedent quality, and rules
By veto or consent the strife of thought,
Making arbitrament that we call faith."

Here was brief silence, till young Hamlet spoke.
"I crave direction, Father, how to know
The sign of that imperative whose right
To sway my act in face of thronging doubts
Were an oracular gem in price beyond
Urim and Thummim lost to Israel.
That bias of the soul, that conquering die
Loaded with golden emphasis of Will –
How find it where resolve, once made, becomes
The rash exclusion of an opposite
Which draws the stronger as I turn aloof."

"I think I hear a bias in your words,"
The Priest said mildly, – "that strong natural bent
Which we call hunger. What more positive
Than appetite ? – of spirit or of flesh,
I care not – 'sense of need' were truer phrase.
You hunger for authoritative right,
And yet discern no difference of tones,
No weight of rod that marks imperial rule ?
Laertes granting, I will put your case
In analogic form: the doctors hold
Hunger which gives no relish – save caprice
That tasting venison fancies mellow pears –
A symptom of disorder, and prescribe
Strict discipline. Were I physician here
I would prescribe that exercise of soul

164

Which lies in full obedience: you ask,
Obedience to what ? The answer lies
Within the word itself; for how obey
What has no rule, asserts no absolute claim ?
Take inclination, taste – why, that is you,
No rule above you. Science, reasoning
On nature's order – they exist and move
Solely by disputation, hold no pledge
Of final consequence, but push the swing
Where Epicurus and the Stoic sit
In endless see-saw. One authority,
And only one, says simply this, Obey:
Place yourself in that current (test it so !)
Of spiritual order where at least
Lies promise of a high communion
A Head informing members, Life that breathes
With gift of forces over and above
The *plus* of arithmetic interchange.
'The Church too has a body,' you object,
'Can be dissected, put beneath the lens
And shown the merest continuity
Of all existence else beneath the sun.'
I grant you; but the lens will not disprove
A presence which eludes it. Take your wit,
Your highest passion, widest-reaching thought:
Show their conditions if you will or can,
But though you saw the final atom-dance
Making each molecule that stands for sign
Of love being present, where is still your love ?
How measure that, how certify its weight ?
And so I say, the body of the Church
Carries a Presence, promises and gifts
Never disproved – whose argument is found
In lasting failure of the search elsewhere
For what it holds to satisfy man's need.

But I grow lengthy: my excuse must be
Your question, Hamlet, which has probed right through
To the pith of our belief. And I have robbed
Myself of pleasure as a listener.
'Tis noon, I see; and my appointment stands
For half-past twelve with Voltimand. Good-bye.''

Brief parting, brief regret – sincere, but quenched
In fumes of best Havannah, which consoles
For lack of other certitude. Then said,
Mildly sarcastic, quiet Guildenstern:
"I marvel how the Father gave new charm
To weak conclusions: I was half convinced
The poorest reasoner made the finest man,
And held his logic lovelier for its limp."

"I fain would hear," said Hamlet, "how you find
A stronger footing than the Father gave.
How base your self-resistance save on faith
In some invisible Order, higher Right
Than changing impulse. What does Reason bid ?
To take a fullest rationality
What offers best solution: so the Church.
Science, detecting hydrogen aflame
Outside our firmament, leaves mystery
Whole and untouched beyond; nay, in our blood
And in the potent atoms of each germ
The Secret lives – envelops, penetrates
Whatever sense perceives or thought divines.
Science, whose soul is explanation, halts
With hostile front at mystery. The Church
Takes mystery as her empire, brings its wealth
Of possibility to fill the void
'Twixt contradictions – warrants so a faith
Defying sense and all its ruthless train

Of arrogant 'Therefores.' Science with her lens
Dissolves the Forms that made the other half
Of all our love, which thenceforth widowed lives
To gaze with maniac stare at what is not.
The Church explains not, governs – feeds resolve
By vision fraught with heart-experience
And human yearning."

                    "Ay," said Guildenstern.
With friendly nod, "the Father, I can see,
Has caught you up in his air-chariot.
His thought takes rainbow-bridges, out of reach
By solid obstacles, evaporates
The coarse and common into subtilties,
Insists that what is real in the Church
Is something out of evidence, and begs
(Just in parenthesis) you'll never mind
What stares you in the face and bruises you.
Why, by his method I could justify
Each superstition and each tyranny
That ever rode upon the back of man,
Pretending fitness for his sole defence
Against life's evil. How can aught subsist
That holds no theory of gain or good ?
Despots with terror in their red right hand
Must argue good to helpers and themselves,
Must let submission hold a core of gain
To make their slaves choose life. Their theory,
Abstracting inconvenience of racks,
Whip-lashes, dragonnades and all things coarse
Inherent in the fact or concrete mass,
Presents the pure idea – utmost good
Secured by Order only to be found
In strict subordination, hierarchy
Of forces where, by nature's law, the strong
Has rightful empire, rule of weaker proved

Mere dissolution. What can you object?
The Inquisition – if you turn away
From narrow notice how the scent of gold
Has guided sense of damning heresy –
The Inquisition is sublime, is love
Hindering the spread of poison in men's souls:
The flames are nothing: only smaller pain
To hinder greater, or the pain of one
To save the many, such as throbs at heart
Of every system born into the world.
So of the Church as high communion
Of Head with members, fount of spirit force
Beyond the calculus, and carrying proof
In her sole power to satisfy man's need:
That seems ideal truth as clear as lines
That, necessary though invisible, trace
The balance of the planets and the sun –
Until I find a hitch in that last claim.
'To satisfy man's need.' Sir, that depends:
We settle first the measure of man's need
Before we grant capacity to fill.
John, James, or Thomas, you may satisfy:
But since you choose ideals I demand
Your Church shall satisfy ideal man,
His utmost reason and his utmost love.
And say these rest a-hungered – find no scheme
Content them both, but hold the world accursed,
A Calvary where Reason mocks at Love,
And Love forsaken sends out orphan cries
Hopeless of answer; still the soul remains
Larger, diviner than your half-way Church,
Which racks your reason into false consent,
And soothes your Love with sops of selfishness.''

"There I am with you," cried Laertes. "What
To me are any dictates, though they came
With thunders from the Mount, if still within
I see a higher Right, a higher Good
Compelling love and worship ? Though the earth
Held force electric to discern and kill
Each thinking rebel – what is martyrdom
But death-defying utterance of belief,
Which being mine remains my truth supreme
Though solitary as the throb of pain
Lying outside the pulses of the world ?
Obedience is good: ay, but to what ?
And for what ends ? For say that I rebel
Against your rule as devilish, or as rule
Of thunder-guiding powers that deny
Man's highest benefit: rebellion then
Were strict obedience to another rule
Which bids me flout your thunder."

                              "Lo you now !"
Said Osric, delicately, "how you come,
Laertes mine, with all your warring zeal
As Python-slayer of the present age –
Cleansing all social swamps by darting rays
Of dubious doctrine, hot with energy
Of private judgment and disgust for doubt –
To state my thesis, which you most abhor
When sung in Daphnis-notes beneath the pines
To gentle rush of waters. Your belief –
In essence what is it but simply Taste ?
I urge with you exemption from all claims
That come from other than my proper will,
An Ultimate within to balance yours,
A solid meeting you, excluding you,
Till you show fuller force by entering
My spiritual space and crushing Me

169

To a subordinate complement of You:
Such ultimate must stand alike for all.
Preach your crusade, then: all will join who like
The hurly-burly of aggressive creeds;
Still your unpleasant Ought, your itch to choose
What grates upon the sense, is simply Taste,
Differs, I think, from mine (permit the word,
Discussion forces it) in being bad."

The tone was too polite to breed offence,
Showing a tolerance of what was "bad"
Becoming courtiers. Louder Rosencranz
Took up the ball with rougher movement, wont
To show contempt for doting reasoners
Who hugged some reasons with a preference,
As warm Laertes did: he gave five puffs
Intolerantly sceptical, then said,
"Your human good, which you would make supreme,
How do you know it ? Has it shown its face
In adamantine type, with features clear,
As this republic, or that monarchy ?
As federal grouping, or municipal ?
Equality, or finely shaded lines
Of social difference ? ecstatic whirl
And draught intense of passionate joy and pain,
Or sober self-control that starves its youth
And lives to wonder what the world calls joy ?
Is it in sympathy that shares men's pangs
Or in cool brains that can explain them well ?
Is it in labour or in laziness ?
In training for the tug of rivalry
To be admired, or in the admiring soul ?
In risk or certitude ? In battling rage
And hardy challenges of Protean luck,
Or in a sleek and rural apathy

Full fed with sameness ? Pray define your Good
Beyond rejection by majority;
Next, how it may subsist without the Ill
Which seems its only outline. Show a world
Of pleasure not resisted; or a world
Of pressure equalised, yet various
In action formative; for that will serve
As illustration of your human good —
Which at its perfecting (your goal of hope)
Will not be straight extinct, or fall to sleep
In the deep bosom of the Unchangeable.
What will you work for, then, and call it good
With full and certain vision — good for aught
Save partial ends which happen to be yours ?
How will you get your stringency to bind
Thought or desire in demonstrated tracks
Which are but waves within a balanced whole ?
Is 'relative' the magic word that turns
Your flux mercurial of good to gold ?
Why, that analysis at which you rage
As anti-social force that sweeps you down
The world in one cascade of molecules,
Is brother 'relative' — and grins at you
Like any convict whom you thought to send
Outside society, till this enlarged
And meant New England and Australia too.
The Absolute is your shadow, and the space
Which you say might be real were you milled
To curves pellicular, the thinnest thin,
Equation of no thickness, is still you."

"Abstracting all that makes him clubbable,"
Horatio interposed. But Rosencranz,
Deaf as the angry turkey-cock whose ears
Are plugged by swollen tissues when he scolds

At men's pretensions: "Pooh, your 'Relative'
Shuts you in, hopeless, with your progeny
As in a Hunger-tower; your social good,
Like other deities by turn supreme,
Is transient reflex of a prejudice,
Anthology of causes and effects
To suit the mood of fanatics who lead
The mood of tribes or nations. I admit
If you could show a sword, nay, chance of sword
Hanging conspicuous to their inward eyes
With edge so constant threatening as to sway
All greed and lust by terror; and a law
Clear-writ and proven as the law supreme
Which that dread sword enforces – then your Right,
Duty, or social Good, were it once brought
To common measure with the potent law,
Would dip the scale, would put unchanging marks
Of wisdom or of folly on each deed,
And warrant exhortation. Until then,
Where is your standard or criterion ?
'What always, everywhere, by all men' – why,
That were but Custom, and your system needs
Ideals never yet incorporate,
The imminent doom of Custom. Can you find
Appeal beyond the sentience in each man ?
Frighten the blind with scarecrows ? raise an awe
Of things unseen where appetite commands
Chambers of imagery in the soul
At all its avenues ? – You chant your hymns
To Evolution, on your altar lay
A sacred egg called Progress: have you proved
A Best unique where all is relative,
And where each change is loss as well as gain ?
The age of healthy Saurians, well supplied
With heat and prey, will balance well enough

A human age where maladies are strong
And pleasures feeble; wealth a monster gorged
Mid hungry populations; intellect
Aproned in laboratories, bent on proof
That *this* is *that* and both are good for nought
Save feeding error through a weary life;
While Art and Poesy struggle like poor ghosts
To hinder cock-crow and the dreadful light,
Lurking in darkness and the charnel-house,
Or like two stalwart greybeards, imbecile
With limbs still active, playing at belief
That hunt the slipper, foot-ball, hide-and-seek,
Are sweetly merry, donning pinafores
And lisping emulously in their speech.
O human race ! Is this then all thy gain ? –
Working at disproof, playing at belief,
Debate on causes, distaste of effects,
Power to transmute all elements, and lack
Of any power to sway the fatal skill
And make thy lot aught else than rigid doom ?
The Saurians were better. – Guildenstern,
Pass me the taper. Still the human curse
Has mitigation in the best cigars."

Then swift Laertes, not without a glare
Of leonine wrath, "I thank thee for that word:
That one confession, were I Socrates,
Should force you onward till you ran your head
At your own image – flatly gave the lie
To all your blasphemy of that human good
Which bred and nourished you to sit at ease
And learnedly deny it. Say the world
Groans ever with the pangs of doubtful births:
Say, life's a poor donation at the best –
Wisdom a yearning after nothingness –

Nature's great vision and the thrill supreme
Of thought-fed passion but a weary play –
I argue not against you. Who can prove
Wit to be witty when with deeper ground
Dulness intuitive declares wit dull ?
If life is worthless to you – why, it is.
You only know how little love you feel
To give you fellowship, how little force
Responsive to the quality of things.
Then end your life, throw off the unsought yoke.
If not – if you remain to taste cigars,
Choose racy diction, perorate at large
With tacit scorn of meaner men who win
No wreath or tripos – then admit at least
A possible Better in the seeds of earth;
Acknowledge debt to that laborious life
Which, sifting evermore the mingled seeds,
Testing the Possible with patient skill,
And daring ill in presence of a good
For futures to inherit, made your lot
One you would choose rather than end it, nay,
Rather than, say, some twenty million lots
Of fellow-Britons toiling all to make
That nation, that community, whereon
You feed and thrive and talk philosophy.
I am no optimist whose faith must hang
On hard pretence that pain is beautiful
And agony explained for men at ease
By virtue's exercise in pitying it.
But this I hold: that he who takes one gift
Made for him by the hopeful work of man,
Who tastes sweet bread, walks where he will unarmed,
His shield and warrant the invisible law,
Who owns a hearth and household charities,
Who clothes his body and his sentient soul

With skill and thoughts of men, and yet denies
A human good worth toiling for, is cursed
With worse negation than the poet feigned
In Mephistopheles. The Devil spins
His wire-drawn argument against all good
With sense of brimstone as his private lot,
And never drew a solace from the Earth."

Laertes fuming paused, and Guildenstern
Took up with cooler skill the fusillade:
"I meet your deadliest challenge, Rosencranz: –
Where get, you say, a binding law, a rule
Enforced by sanction, an Ideal throned
With thunder in its hand ? I answer, there
Whence every faith and rule has drawn its force
Since human consciousness awaking owned
An Outward, whose unconquerable sway
Resisted first and then subdued desire
By pressure of the dire Impossible
Urging to possible ends the active soul
And shaping so its terror and its love.
Why, you have said it – threats and promises
Depend on each man's sentience for their force:
All sacred rules, imagined or revealed,
Can have no form or potency apart
From the percipient and emotive mind.
God, duty, love, submission, fellowship,
Must first be framed in man, as music is,
Before they live outside him as a law.
And still they grow and shape themselves anew,
With fuller concentration in their life
Of inward and of outward energies
Blending to make the last result called Man,
Which means, not this or that philosopher
Looking through beauty into blankness, not

The swindler who has sent his fruitful lie
By the last telegram: it means the tide
Of needs reciprocal, toil, trust, and love –
The surging multitude of human claims
Which make 'a presence not to be put by'
Above the horizon of the general soul.
Is inward Reason shrunk to subtleties,
And inward wisdom pining passion-starved ? –
The outward Reason has the world in store,
Regenerates passion with the stress of want,
Regenerates knowledge with discovery,
Shows sly rapacious Self a blunderer,
Widens dependence, knits the social whole
In sensible relation more defined.
Do Boards and dirty-handed millionaires
Govern the planetary system ? – sway
The pressure of the Universe ? – decide
That man henceforth shall retrogress to ape,
Emptied of every sympathetic thrill
The All has wrought in him? dam up henceforth
The flood of human claims as private force
To turn their wheels and make a private hell
For fish-pond to their mercantile domain ?
What are they but a parasitic growth
On the vast real and ideal world
Of man and nature blent in one divine ?
Why, take your closing dirge – say evil grows
And good is dwindling; science mere decay,
Mere dissolution of ideal wholes
Which through the ages past alone have made
The earth and firmament of human faith;
Say, the small arc of Being we call man
Is near its mergence, what seems growing life
Nought but a hurrying change towards lower types,
The ready rankness of degeneracy.

Well, they who mourn for the world's dying good
May take their common sorrows for a rock,
On it erect religion and a church,
A worship, rites, and passionate piety –
The worship of the Best though crucified
And God-forsaken in its dying pangs;
The sacramental rites of fellowship
In common woe; visions that purify
Through admiration and despairing love
Which keep their spiritual life intact
Beneath the murderous clutches of disproof
And feed a martyr-strength."

                              "Religion high !"
(Rosencranz here) "but with communicants
Few as the cedars upon Lebanon –
A child might count them. What the world demands
Is faith coercive of the multitude."

"Tush, Guildenstern, you granted him too much,"
Burst in Laertes; "I will never grant
One inch of law to feeble blasphemies
Which hold no higher ratio to life –
Full vigorous human life that peopled earth
And wrought and fought and loved and bravely died –
Than the sick morning glooms of debauchees.
Old nations breed old children, wizened babes
Whose youth is languid and incredulous,
Weary of life without the will to die;
Their passions visionary appetites
Of bloodless spectres wailing that the world
For lack of substance slips from out their grasp;
Their thoughts the withered husks of all things dead,
Holding no force of germs instinct with life,
Which never hesitates but moves and grows.

Yet hear them boast in screams their godlike ill,
Excess of knowing ! Fie on you, Rosencranz !
You lend your brains and fine-dividing tongue
For bass-notes to this shrivelled crudity,
This immature decrepitude that strains
To fill our ears and claim the prize of strength
For mere unmanliness. Out on them all ! –
Wits, puling minstrels, and philosophers,
Who living softly prate of suicide,
And suck the commonwealth to feed their ease
While they vent epigrams and threnodies,
Mocking or wailing all the eager work
Which makes that public store whereon they feed.
Is wisdom flattened sense and mere distaste ?
Why, any superstition warm with love,
Inspired with purpose, wild with energy
That streams resistless through its ready frame,
Has more of human truth within its life
Than souls that look through colour into nought, –
Whose brain, too unimpassioned for delight,
Has feeble ticklings of a vanity
Which finds the universe beneath its mark,
And scorning the blue heavens as merely blue
Can only say, 'What then ?' – pre-eminent
In wondrous want of likeness to their kind,
Founding that worship of sterility
Whose one supreme is vacillating Will
Which makes the Light, then says ' 'Twere better not.' "

Here rash Laertes brought his Handel-strain
As of some angry Polypheme, to pause;
And Osric, shocked at ardours out of taste,
Relieved the audience with a tenor voice
And delicate delivery.

"For me,
I range myself in line with Rosencranz
Against all schemes, religious or profane,
That flaunt a Good as pretext for a lash
To flog us all who have the better taste,
Into conformity, requiring me
At peril of the thong and sharp disgrace
To care how mere Philistines pass their lives;
Whether the English pauper-total grows
From one to two before the noughts; how far
Teuton will outbreed Roman; if the class
Of proletaires will make a federal band
To bind all Europe and America,
Throw, in their wrestling, every government,
Snatch the world's purse and keep the guillotine:
Or else (admitting these are casualties)
Driving my soul with scientific hail
That shuts the landscape out with particles;
Insisting that the Palingenesis
Means telegraphs and measure of the rate
At which the stars move – nobody knows where.
So far, my Rosencranz, we are at one.
But not when you blaspheme the life of Art,
The sweet perennial youth of Poesy,
Which asks no logic but its sensuous growth,
No right but loveliness; which fearless strolls
Betwixt the burning mountain and the sea,
Reckless of earthquake and the lava stream,
Filling its hour with beauty. It knows nought
Of bitter strife, denial, grim resolve,
Sour resignation, busy emphasis
Of fresh illusions named the new-born True,
Old Error's latest child; but as a lake
Images all things, yet within its depths
Dreams them all lovelier – thrills with sound

And makes a harp of plenteous liquid chords –
So Art or Poesy: we its votaries
Are the Olympians, fortunately born
From the elemental mixture; 'tis our lot
To pass more swiftly than the Delian God,
But still the earth breaks into flowers for us,
And mortal sorrows when they reach our ears
Are dying falls to melody divine.
Hatred, war, vice, crime, sin, those human storms,
Cyclones, floods, what you will – outbursts of force –
Feed art with contrast, give the grander touch
To the master's pencil and the poet's song,
Serve as Vesuvian fires or navies tossed
On yawning waters, which when viewed afar
Deepen the calm sublime of those choice souls
Who keep the heights of poesy and turn
A fleckless mirror to the various world,
Giving its many-named and fitful flux
An imaged, harmless, spiritual life,
With pure selection, native to art's frame,
Of beauty only, save its minor scale
Of ill and pain to give the ideal joy
A keener edge. This is a mongrel globe;
All finer being wrought from its coarse earth
Is but accepted privilege: what else
Your boasted virtue, which proclaims itself
A good above the average consciousness ?
Nature exists by partiality
(Each planet's poise must carry two extremes
With verging breadths of minor wretchedness):
We are her favourites and accept our wings.
For your accusal, Rosencranz, that art
Shares in the dread and weakness of the time,
I hold it null; since art or poesy pure,
Being blameless by all standards save her own,

Takes no account of modern or antique
In morals, science, or philosophy:
No dull elenchus makes a yoke for her,
Whose law and measure are the sweet consent
Of sensibilities that move apart
From rise or fall of systems, states or creeds –
Apart from what Philistines call man's weal."

"Ay, we all know those votaries of the Muse
Ravished with singing till they quite forgot
Their manhood, sang, and gaped, and took no food,
Then died of emptiness, and for reward
Lived on as grasshoppers " – Laertes thus:
But then he checked himself as one who feels
His muscles dangerous, and Guildenstern
Filled up the pause with calmer confidence.

"You use your wings, my Osric, poise yourself
Safely outside all reach of argument,
Then dogmatise at will (a method known
To ancient women and philosophers,
Nay, to Philistines whom you most abhor);
Else, could an arrow reach you, I should ask
Whence came taste, beauty, sensibilities
Refined to preference infallible ?
Doubtless, ye're gods – these odours ye inhale,
A sacrificial scent. But how, I pray,
Are odours made, if not by gradual change
Of sense or substance ? Is your beautiful
A seedless, rootless flower, or has it grown
With human growth, which means the rising sum
Of human struggle, order, knowledge ? – sense
Trained to a fuller record, more exact –
To truer guidance of each passionate force ?
Get me your roseate flesh without the blood;

Get fine aromas without structure wrought
From simpler being into manifold:
Then and then only flaunt your Beautiful
As what can live apart from thought, creeds, states,
Which mean life's structure. Osric, I beseech –
The infallible should be more catholic –
Join in a war-dance with the cannibals,
Hear Chinese music, love a face tattooed,
Give adoration to a pointed skull,
And think the Hindu Siva looks divine:
'Tis art, 'tis poesy. Say, you object:
How came you by that lofty dissidence,
If not through changes in the social man
Widening his consciousness from Here and Now
To larger wholes beyond the reach of sense;
Controlling to a fuller harmony
The thrill of passion and the rule of fact;
And paling false ideals in the light
Of full-rayed sensibilities which blend
Truth and desire ? Taste, beauty, what are they
But the soul's choice towards perfect bias wrought
By finer balance of a fuller growth –
Sense brought to subtlest metamorphosis
Through love, thought, joy – the general human store
Which grows from all life's functions ? As the plant
Holds its corolla, purple, delicate,
Solely as outflush of that energy
Which moves transformingly in root and branch."

Guildenstern paused, and Hamlet quivering
Since Osric spoke, in transit imminent
From catholic striving into laxity,
Ventured his word. "Seems to me, Guildenstern,
Your argument, though shattering Osric's point
That sensibilities can move apart

From social order, yet has not annulled
His thesis that the life of poesy
(Admitting it must grow from out the whole)
Has separate functions, a transfigured realm
Freed from the rigours of the practical,
Where what is hidden from the grosser world –
Stormed down by roar of engines and the shouts
Of eager concourse – rises beauteous
As voice of water-drops in sapphire caves;
A realm where finest spirits have free sway
In exquisite selection, uncontrolled
By hard material necessity
Of cause and consequence. For you will grant
The Ideal has discoveries which ask
No test, no faith, save that we joy in them:
A new-found continent, with spreading lands
Where pleasure charters all, where virtue, rank,
Use, right, and truth have but one name, Delight.
Thus Art's creations, when etherealised
To least admixture of the grosser fact
Delight may stamp as highest."

                              "Possible !"
Said Guildenstern, with touch of weariness,
"But then we might dispute of what is gross,
What high, what low."

                         "Nay," said Laertes, "ask
The mightiest makers who have reigned, still reign
Within the ideal realm. See if their thought
Be drained of practice and the thick warm blood
Of hearts that beat in action various
Through the wide drama of the struggling world.
Good-bye, Horatio."

                         Each now said "Good-bye."
Such breakfast, such beginning of the day

Is more than half the whole. The sun was hot
On southward branches of the meadow elms,
The shadows slowly farther crept and veered
Like changing memories, and Hamlet strolled
Alone and dubious on the empurpled path
Between the waving grasses of new June
Close by the stream where well-compacted boats
Were moored or moving with a lazy creak
To the soft dip of oars. All sounds were light
As tiny silver bells upon the robes
Of hovering silence. Birds made twitterings
That seemed but Silence self o'erfull of love.
'Twas invitation all to sweet repose;
And Hamlet, drowsy with the mingled draughts
Of cider and conflicting sentiments,
Chose a green couch and watched with half-closed eyes
The meadow-road, the stream and dreamy lights,
Until they merged themselves in sequence strange
With undulating ether, time, the soul,
The will supreme, the individual claim,
The social Ought, the lyrist's liberty,
Democritus, Pythagoras, in talk
With Anselm, Darwin, Comte, and Schopenhauer,
The poets rising slow from out their tombs
Summoned as arbiters – that border-world
Of dozing, ere the sense is fully locked.

And then he dreamed a dream so luminous
He woke (he says) convinced; but what it taught
Withholds as yet. Perhaps those graver shades
Admonished him that visions told in haste
Part with their virtues to the squandering lips
And leave the soul in wider emptiness.

March – April 1874

"I grant you ample leave
To use the hoary formula 'I am'
Naming the emptiness where thought is not;
But fill the void with definition, 'I'
Will be no more a datum than the words
You link false inference with, the 'Since' and 'so'
That, true or not, make up the atom-whirl.
Resolve your 'Ego', it is all one web
With vibrant ether clotted into worlds:
Your subject, self, or self-assertive 'I'
Turns nought but object, melts to molecules,
Is stripped from naked Being with the rest
Of those rag-garments named the Universe.
Or if, in strife to keep your 'Ego' strong
You make it weaver of the etherial light,
Space, motion, solids and the dream of Time –
Why, still 'tis Being looking from the dark,
The core, the centre of your consciousness,
That notes your bubble-world: sense, pleasure, pain,
What are they but a shifting otherness,
Phantasmal flux of moments ? –"

(*1874*)

ERINNA

"Erinna died in early youth when chained by her mother to the spinning-wheel. She had as yet known the charm of existence in imagination alone. Her poem called 'The Spindle' – 'Ηλακάτη – containing only 300 hexameter verses, in which she probably expressed the restless and aspiring thoughts which crowded on her youthful mind as she pursued her monotonous work, has been deemed by many of the ancients of such high poetic merit as to entitle it to a place beside the epics of Homer." *Müller, Hist. Gr. Lit.* Four lines of the ἡλακάτη are extant. The dialect is a mixture of Doric and Æolic spoken at Rhodes where Erinna was born; the date about B. C. 612:

Τούτω κῆς 'Αΐδαν κενεα διανήχεται ἀχω.
σιγᾷ δ' ἐν νεκύεσσι τὸ δὲ σκότος ὕσσε κατέρρει.

Stob. Flor. cxviii,4

. . . .

πομπῖλε, ναύταισιν πέμπων πλόον εὔπλοον ἰχθύ,
πομπεύσαις πρύμναθεν ἐμὰν ἀδεῖαν ἕταιραν.

Athanaeus, vii. 283

1

'Twas in the isle that Helios saw
  Uprising from the sea a flower-tressed bride
To meet his kisses – Rhodes, the filial pride
    Of god-taught craftsmen who gave Art its law:
    She held the spindle as she sat,
    Erinna with the thick-coiled mat
    Of raven hair and deepest agate eyes,
    Gazing with a sad surprise
    At surging visions of her destiny
    To spin the byssus drearily
  In insect labour, while the throng
Of Gods and men wrought deeds that poets wrought in song.

Visions of ocean-wreathed Earth
Shone through with light of epic rhapsody
Where Zeus looked with Olympus and the sea
    Smiled back with Aphrodite's birth;
    Where heroes sailed on daring quests
    In ships that knew and loved their guests;
    Where the deep-bosomed matron and sweet maid
    Died for others unafraid;
    Where Pindus echoed to the Ionian shore
    Songs fed with action and the love
    Of primal work, where Themis saw
Brute Fear beneath her rod ennobled into awe.

3

    Hark, the passion in her eyes
    Changes to melodic cries
    Lone she pours her lonely pain.
    Song unheard is not in vain:
    The god within us plies
His shaping power and moulds in speech
Harmonious a statue of our sorrow,
Till suffering turn beholding and we borrow,
Gazing on Self apart, the wider reach
    Of solemn souls that contemplate
And slay with full-beamed thought the darling Dragon Hate.

4

    "Great Cybele, whose ear doth love
The piercing flute, why is my maiden wail

Like hers, the loved twice lost, whose dear hands pale
    Yearning, severed seemed to move
    Thin phantoms on the night-black air ?
    But thou art deaf to human care:
    Thy breasts impartial cherish with their food
    Strength alike of ill and good.
    The dragon and the hero, friend and foe,
    Who makes the city's weal, and who its woe,
    All draw their strength from thee; and what I draw
  Is rage divine in limbs fast bound by narrow law.

5

But Pallas, thou dost choose and bless
The nobler cause, thy maiden height
And terrible beauty marshalling the fight
Inspire weak limbs with stedfastness.
    Thy virgin breast uplifts
   The direful aegis, but thy hand
Wielded its weapon with benign command
  In Rivalry of highest gifts
With strong Poseidon whose earth-shaking roll
Matched not the delicate tremors of thy spear
  Piercing Athenian land and drawing thence
    With conquering beneficence
    Thy subtly chosen dole
The sacred olive fraught with light and plenteous cheer.
What, though thou pliest the distaff and the loom ?
    Counsel is thine, to sway the doubtful doom
    Of cities with a leaguer at their gate;
    Thine the device that snares the hulk elate
Of purblind force and saves the hero or the State."

SELF. Changeful comrade, Life of mine,
　　Before we two must part,
　I will tell thee, thou shalt say,
　　What thou hast been and art.
　Ere I lose my hold of thee
　Justify thyself to me.

LIFE. I was thy warmth upon thy mother's knee
　　When light and love within her eyes were one;
　We laughed together by the laurel-tree,
　　Culling warm daisies 'neath the sloping sun;
　　　We heard the chickens' lazy croon,
　　　　Where the trellised woodbines grew,
　　　And all the summer afternoon
　　　　Mystic gladness o'er thee threw.
　　　　　Was it person ? Was it thing ?
　　　　　Was it touch or whispering ?
　　　　　It was bliss and it was I:
　　　　　Bliss was what thou knew'st me by.

SELF. Soon I knew thee more by Fear
　　And sense of what was not,
　Haunting all I held most dear
　　I had a double lot:
　Ardour, cheated with alloy,
　Wept the more for dreams of joy.

LIFE. Remember how thy ardour's magic sense
    Made poor things rich to thee and small things great;
How hearth and garden, field and bushy fence,
    Were thy own eager love incorporate;
        And how the solemn, splendid Past
        O'er thy early widened earth
        Made grandeur, as on sunset cast
        Dark elms near take mighty girth.
            Hands and feet were tiny still
            When we knew the historic thrill,
            Breathed deep breath in heroes dead,
            Tasted the immortals' bread.

SELF. Seeing what I might have been
    Reproved the thing I was,
Smoke on heaven's clearest sheen,
    The speck within the rose.
By revered ones' frailties stung
Reverence was with anguish wrung.

LIFE. But all thy anguish and thy discontent
    Was growth of mine, the elemental strife
Towards feeling manifold with vision blent
    To wider thought: I was no vulgar life
        That, like the water-mirrored ape,
        Not discerns the thing it sees,
        Nor knows its own in others' shape,
        Railing, scorning, at its ease.
            Half man's truth must hidden lie
            If unlit by Sorrow's eye.
            I by Sorrow wrought in thee
            Willing pain of ministry.

SELF. Slowly was the lesson taught
       Through passion, error, care;
    Insight was with loathing fraught
       And effort with despair.
    Written on the wall I saw
    "Bow !" I knew, not loved, the law.

LIFE. But then I brought a love that wrote within
       The law of gratitude, and made thy heart
    Beat to the heavenly tune of seraphin
       Whose only joy in having is, to impart:
          Till thou, poor Self – despite thy ire,
             Wrestling 'gainst my mingled share,
          Thy faults, hard falls, and vain desire
             Still to be what others were –
                Filled, o'erflowed with tenderness
                Seeming more as thou wert less,
                Knew me through that anguish past
                As a fellowship more vast.

SELF. Yea, I embrace thee, changeful Life !
       Far-sent, unchosen mate !
    Self and thou, no more at strife,
       Shall wed in hallowed state.
    Willing spousals now shall prove
    Life is justified by love.

' SWEET EVENINGS COME AND GO, LOVE.'

> " La noche buena se viene,
>   La noche buena se va,
> Y nosotros nos iremos
>   Y no volveremos mas."

– Old *Villancico*.

Sweet evenings come and go, love,
  They came and went of yore:
This evening of our life, love,
  Shall go and come no more.

When we have passed away, love,
  All things will keep their name;
But yet no life on earth, love,
  With ours will be the same.

The daisies will be there, love,
  The stars in heaven will shine:
I shall not feel thy wish, love,
  Nor thou my hand in thine.

A better time will come, love,
  And better souls be born:
I would not be the best, love,
  To leave thee now forlorn.

(FIVE FRAGMENTS FROM THE NOTEBOOK)

I would not have your beauties in exchange
For the sweet thoughts your beauty breeds in me.

(Suggested by Sappho, Fr. 17)

For shaken creeds are as the tottering poles,
The Earth reels madly to the maddened sense
And men, because they numbered falsely, hold
All number false.

Mercy haunts lazar-houses, sighs and weeps
O'er famished clowns, but opes its nostrils wide
To scent the blood of nobles.

The ocean-meadow where the dark flocks play
Of wandering clouds whose shepherd is the day.

Master in loving ! till we met
I lacked the pattern thy sweet love hath set:
I hear Death's footstep – must we then forget ? –
Stay, stay – not yet !

(' 'MID MY GOLD-BROWN CURLS')

'Mid my gold-brown curls
  There twined a silver hair:
I plucked it idly out
And scarcely knew 'twas there.
Coiled in my velvet sleeve it lay
And like a serpent hissed:
"Me thou canst pluck and fling away,
  One hair is lightly missed;
But how on that near day
When all the wintry army muster in array ?"

(1875)

"Away from me the garment of forgetfulness,
Withering the heart;
The oil and wine from presses of the Goyim,
Poisoned with scorn.
Solitude is on the sides of Mount Nebo,
In its heart a tomb:
There the buried ark and golden cherubim
Make hidden light:
There the solemn faces gaze unchanged,
The wings are spread unbroken:
Shut beneath in silent awful speech
The Law lies graven.
Solitude and darkness are my covering,
And my heart a tomb;
Smite and shatter it, O Gabriel !
Shatter it as the clay of the founder
Around the golden image."

From Daniel Deronda, *Book V, Chapter 38.*

(December 1875)

THE DEATH OF MOSES

Moses, who spake with God as with his friend,
And ruled his people with the twofold power
Of wisdom that can dare and still be meek,
Was writing his last word, the sacred name
Unutterable of that Eternal Will
Which was and is and evermore shall be.
Yet was his task not finished, for the flock
Needed its shepherd and the life-taught sage
Leaves no successor; but to chosen men,
The rescuers and guides of Israel,
A death was given called the Death of Grace,
Which freed them from the burden of the flesh
But left them rulers of the multitude
And loved companions of the lonely. This
Was God's last gift to Moses, this the hour
When soul must part from self and be but soul.

God spake to Gabriel, the messenger
Of mildest death that draws the parting life
Gently, as when a little rosy child
Lifts up its lips from off the bowl of milk
And so draws forth a curl that dipped its gold
In the soft white – thus Gabriel draws the soul.
"Go bring the soul of Moses unto me !"
And the awe-stricken angel answered, " Lord,
How shall I dare to take his life who lives
Sole of his kind, not to be likened once
In all the generations of the earth ?"

Then God called Michaël, him of pensive brow
Snow-vest and flaming sword, who knows and acts:
"Go bring the spirit of Moses unto me !"

196

But Michaël with such grief as angels feel,
Loving the mortals whom they succour, pled:
"Almighty, spare me; it was I who taught
Thy servant Moses; he is part of me
As I of thy deep secrets, knowing them."

Then God called Zamaël, the terrible,
The angel of fierce death, of agony
That comes in battle and in pestilence
Remorseless, sudden or with lingering throes.
And Zamaël, his raiment and broad wings
Blood-tinctured, the dark lustre of his eyes
Shrouding the red, fell like the gathering night
Before the prophet. But that radiance
Won from the heavenly presence in the mount
Gleamed on the prophet's brow and dazzling pierced
Its conscious opposite: the angel turned
His murky gaze aloof and inly said:
"An angel this, deathless to angel's stroke."

But Moses felt the subtly nearing dark: −
"Who art thou ? and what wilt thou ?" Zamaël then:
"I am God's reaper; through the fields of life
I gather ripened and unripened souls
Both willing and unwilling. And I come
Now to reap thee." But Moses cried,
Firm as a seer who waits the trusted sign:
"Reap thou the fruitless plant and common herb −
Not him who from the womb was sanctified
To teach the law of purity and love."
And Zamaël baffled from his errand fled.

But Moses, pausing, in the air serene
Heard now that mystic whisper, far yet near,
The all-penetrating Voice, that said to him,

"Moses, the hour is come and thou must die."
"Lord, I obey; but thou rememberest
How thou, Ineffable, didst take me once
Within thy orb of light untouched by death."
Then the voice answered, "Be no more afraid:
With me shall be thy death and burial."
So Moses waited, ready now to die.

And the Lord came, invisible as a thought,
Three angels gleaming on his secret track,
Prince Michaël, Zamaël, Gabriel, charged to guard
The soul-forsaken body as it fell
And bear it to the hidden sepulchre
Denied for ever to the search of man.
And the Voice said to Moses: "Close thine eyes."
He closed them. "Lay thine hand upon thine heart,
And draw thy feet together." He obeyed.
And the Lord said, " O spirit ! child of mine !
A hundred years and twenty thou hast dwelt
Within this tabernacle wrought of clay.
This is the end: come forth and flee to heaven."

But the grieved soul with plaintive pleading cried,
"I love this body with a clinging love:
The courage fails me, Lord, to part from it."

"O child, come forth ! for thou shalt dwell with me
About the immortal throne where seraphs joy
In growing vision and in growing love."

Yet hesitating, fluttering, like the bird
With young wing weak and dubious, the soul
Stayed. But behold ! upon the death-dewed lips
A kiss descended, pure, unspeakable –
The bodiless Love without embracing Love

That lingered in the body, drew it forth
With heavenly strength and carried it to heaven.

But now beneath the sky the watchers all,
Angels that keep the homes of Israel
Or on high purpose wander o'er the world
Leading the Gentiles, felt a dark eclipse:
The greatest ruler among men was gone.
And from the westward sea was heard a wail,
A dirge as from the isles of Javanim,
Crying, "Who now is left upon the earth
Like him to teach the right and smite the wrong ?"
And from the East, far o'er the Syrian waste,
Came slowlier, sadlier, the answering dirge:
"No prophet like him lives or shall arise
In Israel or the world for evermore."

But Israel waited, looking toward the mount,
Till with the deepening eve the elders came
Saying, "His burial is hid with God.
We stood far off and saw the angels lift
His corpse aloft until they seemed a star
That burnt itself away within the sky."

The people answered with mute orphaned gaze
Looking for what had vanished evermore.
Then through the gloom without them and within
The spirit's shaping light, mysterious speech,
Invisible Will wrought clear in sculptured sound,
The thought-begotten daughter of the voice,
Thrilled on their listening sense: "He has no tomb.
He dwells not with you dead, but lives as Law."

(*December 1875*)

THE SPANISH GYPSY

(AUTHOR'S PREFACE)

This Work was originally written in the winter of 1864-65; after a visit to Spain in 1867 it was rewritten and amplified. The reader conversant with Spanish poetry will see that in two of the Lyrics an attempt has been made to imitate the trochaic measure and assonance of the Spanish Ballad.

May 1868.

BOOK I

'Tis the warm South, where Europe spreads her lands
Like fretted leaflets, breathing on the deep:
Broad-breasted Spain, leaning with equal love
On the Mid Sea that moans with memories,
And on the untravelled Ocean's restless tides.
This river, shadowed by the battlements
And gleaming silvery towards the northern sky,
Feeds the famed stream that waters Andalus
And loiters, amorous of the fragrant air,
By Córdova and Seville to the bay
Fronting Algarva and the wandering flood
Of Guadiana. This deep mountain gorge
Slopes widening on the olive-pluméd plains
Of fair Granáda: one far-stretching arm
Points to Elvira, one to eastward heights
Of Alpujarras where the new-bathed Day
With oriflamme uplifted o'er the peaks
Saddens the breasts of northward-looking snows
That loved the night, and soared with soaring stars;
Flashing the signals of his nearing swiftness
From Almería's purple-shadowed bay
On to the far-off rocks that gaze and glow –
On to Alhambra, strong and ruddy heart
Of glorious Morisma, gasping now,
A maiméd giant in his agony.
This town that dips its feet within the stream,
And seems to sit a tower-crowned Cybele,
Spreading her ample robe adown the rocks,
Is rich Bedmár: 'twas Moorish long ago,
But now the Cross is sparkling on the Mosque,
And bells make Catholic the trembling air.
The fortress gleams in Spanish sunshine now

('Tis south a mile before the rays are Moorish) –
Hereditary jewel, agraffe bright
On all the many-titled privilege
Of young Duke Silva. No Castilian knight
That serves Queen Isabel has higher charge;
For near this frontier sits the Moorish king,
Not Boabdil the waverer, who usurps
A throne he trembles in, and fawning licks
The feet of conquerors, but that fierce lion
Grisly El Zagal, who has made his lair
In Guadix' fort, and rushing thence with strength
Half his own fierceness, half the untainted heart
Of mountain bands that fight for holiday,
Wastes the fair lands that lie by Alcalá,
Wreathing his horse's neck with Christian heads.

To keep the Christian frontier – such high trust
Is young Duke Silva's; and the time is great.
(What times are little ? To the sentinel
That hour is regal when he mounts on guard.)
The fifteenth century since the Man Divine
Taught and was hated in Capernaum
Is near its end – is falling as a husk
Away from all the fruit its years have riped.
The Moslem faith, now flickering like a torch
In a night struggle on this shore of Spain,
Glares, a broad column of advancing flame,
Along the Danube and the Illyrian shore
Far into Italy, where eager monks,
Who watch in dreams and dream the while they watch,
See Christ grow paler in the baleful light,
Crying again the cry of the forsaken.
But faith, the stronger for extremity,
Becomes prophetic, hears the far-off tread
Of western chivalry, sees downward sweep

The archangel Michael with the gleaming sword,
And listens for the shriek of hurrying fiends
Chased from their revels in God's sanctuary.
So trusts the monk, and lifts appealing eyes
To the high dome, the Church's firmament,
Where the blue light-pierced curtain, rolled away,
Reveals the throne and Him who sits thereon.
So trust the men whose best hope for the world
Is ever that the world is near its end:
Impatient of the stars that keep their course
And make no pathway for the coming Judge.

But other futures stir the world's great heart.
The West now enters on the heritage
Won from the tombs of mighty ancestors,
The seeds, the gold, the gems, the silent harps
That lay deep buried with the memories
Of old renown.
No more, as once in sunny Avignon,
The poet-scholar spreads the Homeric page,
And gazes sadly, like the deaf at song;
For now the old epic voices ring again
And vibrate with the beat and melody
Stirred by the warmth of old Ionian days.
The martyred sage, the Attic orator,
Immortally incarnate, like the gods,
In spiritual bodies, wingéd words
Holding a universe impalpable,
Find a new audience. For evermore,
With grander resurrection than was feigned
Of Attila's fierce Huns, the soul of Greece
Conquers the bulk of Persia. The maimed form
Of calmly-joyous beauty, marble-limbed,
Yet breathing with the thought that shaped its lips,
Looks mild reproach from out its opened grave

At creeds of terror; and the vine-wreathed god
Fronts the pierced Image with the crown of thorns.
The soul of man is widening towards the past:
No longer hanging at the breast of life
Feeding in blindness to his parentage –
Quenching all wonder with Omnipotence,
Praising a name with indolent piety –
He spells the record of his long descent,
More largely conscious of the life that was.
And from the height that shows where morning shone
On far-off summits pale and gloomy now,
The horizon widens round him, and the west
Looks vast with untracked waves whereon his gaze
Follows the flight of the swift-vanished bird
That like the sunken sun is mirrored still
Upon the yearning soul within the eye.
And so in Córdova through patient nights
Columbus watches, or he sails in dreams
Between the setting stars and finds new day;
Then wakes again to the old weary days,
Girds on the cord and frock of pale Saint Francis,
And like him zealous pleads with foolish men.
"I ask but for a million maravedis:
Give me three caravels to find a world,
New shores, new realms, new soldiers for the Cross.
Son cosas grandes !" Thus he pleads in vain;
Yet faints not utterly, but pleads anew,
Thinking, "God means it, and has chosen me."
For this man is the pulse of all mankind
Feeding an embryo future, offspring strange
Of the fond Present, that with mother-prayers
And mother-fancies looks for championship
Of all her loved beliefs and old-world ways
From that young Time she bears within her womb.
The sacred places shall be purged again,

The Turk converted, and the Holy Church,
Like the mild Virgin with the outspread robe,
Shall fold all tongues and nations lovingly.

But since God works by armies, who shall be
The modern Cyrus ? Is it France most Christian,
Who with his lilies and brocaded knights,
French oaths, French vices, and the newest style
Of out-puffed sleeve, shall pass from west to east,
A winnowing fan to purify the seed
For fair millennial harvests soon to come ?
Or is not Spain the land of chosen warriors ? —
Crusaders consecrated from the womb,
Carrying the sword-cross stamped upon their souls
By the long yearnings of a nation's life,
Through all the seven patient centuries
Since first Pelayo and his resolute band
Trusted the God within their Gothic hearts
At Covadunga, and defied Mahound;
Beginning so the Holy War of Spain
That now is panting with the eagerness
Of labour near its end. The silver cross
Glitters o'er Malaga and streams dread light
On Moslem galleys, turning all their stores
From threats to gifts. What Spanish knight is he
Who, living now, holds it not shame to live
Apart from that hereditary battle
Which needs his sword ? Castilian gentlemen
Choose not their task — they choose to do it well.

The time is great, and greater no man's trust
Than his who keeps the fortress for his king,
Wearing great honours as some delicate robe
Brocaded o'er with names 'twere sin to tarnish.
Born de la Cerda, Calatravan knight,

Count of Segura, fourth Duke of Bedmár,
Offshoot from that high stock of old Castile
Whose topmost branch is proud Medina Celi –
Such titles with their blazonry are his
Who keeps this fortress, its sworn governor,
Lord of the valley, master of the town,
Commanding whom he will, himself commanded
By Christ his Lord who sees him from the Cross
And from bright heaven where the Mother pleads; –
By good Saint James upon the milk-white steed,
Who leaves his bliss to fight for chosen Spain; –
By the dead gaze of all his ancestors; –
And by the mystery of his Spanish blood
Charged with the awe and glories of the past.

See now with soldiers in his front and rear
He winds at evening through the narrow streets
That toward the Castle gate climb devious:
His charger, of fine Andalusian stock,
An Indian beauty, black but delicate,
Is conscious of the herald trumpet note,
The gathering glances, and familiar ways
That lead fast homeward: she forgets fatigue,
And at the light touch of the master's spur
Thrills with the zeal to bear him royally,
Arches her neck and clambers up the stones
As if disdainful of the difficult steep.
Night-black the charger, black the rider's plume,
But all between is bright with morning hues –
Seems ivory and gold and deep blue gems,
And starry flashing steel and pale vermilion,
All set in jasper: on his surcoat white
Glitter the sword-belt and the jewelled hilt,
Red on the back and breast the holy cross,
And 'twixt the helmet and the soft-spun white

Thick tawny wavelets like the lion's mane
Turn backward from his brow, pale, wide, erect,
Shadowing blue eyes – blue as the rain-washed sky
That braced the early stem of Gothic kings
He claims for ancestry. A goodly knight,
A noble caballero, broad of chest
And long of limb. So much the August sun,
Now in the west but shooting half its beams
Past a dark rocky profile toward the plain,
At windings of the path across the slope
Makes suddenly luminous for all who see:
For women smiling from the terraced roofs;
For boys that prone on trucks with head up-propped
Lazy and curious, stare irreverent;
For men who make obeisance with degrees
Of good-will shading towards servility,
Where good-will ends and secret fear begins
And curses, too, low-muttered through the teeth,
Explanatory to the god of Shem.

Five, grouped within a whitened tavern court
Of Moorish fashion, where the trellised vines
Purpling above their heads make odorous shade,
Note through the open door the passers-by,
Getting some rills of novelty to speed
The lagging stream of talk and help the wine.
'Tis Christian to drink wine: whoso denies
His flesh at bidding save of Holy Church,
Let him beware and take to Christian sins
Lest he be taxed with Moslem sanctity.

The souls are five, the talkers only three.
(No time, most tainted by wrong faith and rule,
But holds some listeners and dumb animals.)
MINE HOST is one: he with the well-arched nose,

Soft-eyed, fat-handed, loving men for nought
But his own humour, patting old and young
Upon the back, and mentioning the cost
With confidential blandness, as a tax
That he collected much against his will
From Spaniards who were all his bosom friends:
Warranted Christian — else how keep an inn,
Which calling asks true faith ? though like his wine
Of cheaper sort, a trifle over-new.
His father was a convert, chose the chrism
As men choose physic, kept his chimney warm
With smokiest wood upon a Saturday,
Counted his gains and grudges on a chaplet,
And crossed himself asleep for fear of spies;
Trusting the God of Israel would see
'Twas Christian tyranny that made him base.
Our host his son was born ten years too soon,
Had heard his mother call him Ephraim,
Knew holy things from common, thought it sin
To feast on days when Israel's children mourned,
So had to be converted with his sire,
To doff the awe he learned as Ephraim,
And suit his manners to a Christian name.
But infant awe, that unborn moving thing,
Dies with what nourished it, can never rise
From the dead womb and walk and seek new pasture.
Thus baptism seemed to him a merry game
Not tried before, all sacraments a mode
Of doing homage for one's property,
And all religions a queer human whim
Or else a vice, according to degrees:
As, 'tis a whim to like your chestnuts hot,
Burn your own mouth and draw your face awry,
A vice to pelt frogs with them — animals
Content to take life coolly. And Lorenzo

Would have all lives made easy, even lives
Of spiders and inquisitors, yet still
Wishing so well to flies and Moors and Jews
He rather wished the others easy death;
For loving all men clearly was deferred
Till all men loved each other. Such mine Host,
With chiselled smile caressing Seneca,
The solemn mastiff leaning on his knee.

His right-hand guest is solemn as the dog,
Square-faced and massive: BLASCO is his name,
A prosperous silversmith from Aragon;
In speech not silvery, rather tuned as notes
From a deep vessel made of plenteous iron,
Or some great bell of slow but certain swing
That, if you only wait, will tell the hour
As well as flippant clocks that strike in haste
And set off chiming a superfluous tune –
Like JUAN there, the spare man with the lute,
Who makes you dizzy with his rapid tongue,
Whirring athwart your mind with comment swift
On speech you would have finished by-and-by,
Shooting your bird for you while you are loading,
Cheapening your wisdom as a pattern known,
Woven by any shuttle on demand.
Can never sit quite still, too: sees a wasp
And kills it with a movement like a flash;
Whistles low notes or seems to thrum his lute
As a mere hyphen 'twixt two syllables
Of any steadier man; walks up and down
And snuffs the orange flowers and shoots a pea
To hit a streak of light let through the awning.
Has a queer face: eyes large as plums, a nose
Small, round, uneven, like a bit of wax
Melted and cooled by chance. Thin-fingered, lithe,

And as a squirrel noiseless, startling men
Only by quickness. In his speech and look
A touch of graceful wildness, as of things
Not trained or tamed for uses of the world;
Most like the Fauns that roamed in days of old
About the listening whispering woods, and shared
The subtler sense of sylvan ears and eyes
Undulled by scheming thought, yet joined the rout
Of men and women on the festal days,
And played the syrinx too, and knew love's pains,
Turning their anguish into melody.
For Juan was a minstrel still, in times
When minstrelsy was held a thing outworn.
Spirits seem buried and their epitaph
Is writ in Latin by severest pens,
Yet still they flit above the trodden grave
And find new bodies, animating them
In quaint and ghostly way with antique souls.
So Juan was a troubadour revived,
Freshening life's dusty road with babbling rills
Of wit and song, living 'mid harnessed men
With limbs ungalled by armour, ready so
To soothe them weary, and to cheer them sad.
Guest at the board, companion in the camp,
A crystal mirror to the life around,
Flashing the comment keen of simple fact
Defined in words; lending brief lyric voice
To grief and sadness; hardly taking note
Of difference betwixt his own and others';
But rather singing as a listener
To the deep moans, the cries, the wild strong joys
Of universal Nature, old yet young.
Such Juan, the third talker, shimmering bright
As butterfly or bird with quickest life.
The silent ROLDAN has his brightness too,

But only in his spangles and rosettes.
His parti-coloured vest and crimson hose
Are dulled with old Valencian dust, his eyes
With straining fifty years at gilded balls
To catch them dancing, or with brazen looks
At men and women as he made his jests
Some thousand times and watched to count the
  pence
His wife was gathering. His olive face
Has an old writing in it, characters
Stamped deep by grins that had no merriment,
The soul's rude mark proclaiming all its blank;
As on some faces that have long grown old
In lifting tapers up to forms obscene
On ancient walls and chuckling with false zest
To please my lord, who gives the larger fee
For that hard industry in apishness.
Roldan would gladly never laugh again;
Pensioned, he would be grave as any ox,
And having beans and crumbs and oil secured
Would borrow no man's jokes for evermore.
'Tis harder now because his wife is gone,
Who had quick feet, and danced to ravishment
Of every ring jewelled with Spanish eyes,
But died and left this boy, lame from his birth,
And sad and obstinate, though when he will
He sings God-taught such marrow-thrilling strains
As seem the very voice of dying Spring,
A flute-like wail that mourns the blossoms gone,
And sinks, and is not, like their fragrant breath,
With fine transition on the trembling air.
He sits as if imprisoned by some fear,
Motionless, with wide eyes that seem not made
For hungry glancing of a twelve-year'd boy
To mark the living thing that he could teaze,

213

But for the gaze of some primeval sadness
Dark twin with light in the creative ray.
This little PABLO has his spangles too,
And large rosettes to hide his poor left foot
Rounded like any hoof (his mother thought
God willed it so to punish all her sins).

I said the souls were five – besides the dog.
But there was still a sixth, with wrinkled face,
Grave and disgusted with all merriment
Not less than Roldan. It is ANNIBAL,
The experienced monkey who performs the tricks,
Jumps through the hoops, and carries round the hat.
Once full of sallies and impromptu feats,
Now cautious not to light on aught that's new,
Lest he be whipped to do it o'er again
From A to Z, and make the gentry laugh:
A misanthropic monkey, grey and grim,
Bearing a lot that has no remedy
For want of concert in the monkey tribe.

We see the company, above their heads
The braided matting, golden as ripe corn,
Stretched in a curving strip close by the grapes,
Elsewhere rolled back to greet the cooler sky;
A fountain near, vase-shapen and broad-lipped,
Where timorous birds alight with tiny feet,
And hesitate and bend wise listening ears,
And fly away again with undipped beak.
On the stone floor the juggler's heaped-up goods,
Carpet and hoops, viol and tambourine,
Where Annibal sits perched with brows severe,
A serious ape whom none take seriously,
Obliged in this fool's world to earn his nuts
By hard buffoonery. We see them all,

And hear their talk – the talk of Spanish men,
With Southern intonation, vowels turned
Caressingly between the consonants,
Persuasive, willing, with such intervals
As music borrows from the wooing birds,
That plead with subtly curving, sweet descent –
And yet can quarrel, as these Spaniards can.

JUAN *(near the doorway).*
    You hear the trumpet ? There's old Ramon's blast.
    No bray but his can shake the air so well.
    He takes his trumpeting as solemnly
    As angel charged to wake the dead; thinks war
    Was made for trumpeters, and their great art
    Made solely for themselves who understand it.
    His features all have shaped themselves to blowing,
    And when his trumpet's bagged or left at home
    He seems a chattel in a broker's booth,
    A spoutless watering-can, a promise to pay
    No sum particular. O fine old Ramon !
    The blasts get louder and the clattering hoofs;
    They crack the ear as well as heaven's thunder
    For owls that listen blinking. There's the banner.

HOST *(joining him: the others follow to the door).*
    The Duke has finished reconnoitring, then ?
    We shall hear news. They say he means a sally –
    Would strike El Zagal's Moors as they push home
    Like ants with booty heavier than themselves;
    Then, joined by other nobles with their bands,
    Lay siege to Guadix. Juan, you're a bird
    That nest within the Castle. What say you ?

JUAN. Nought, I say nought. 'Tis but a toilsome game
    To bet upon that feather Policy,

And guess where after twice a hundred puffs
'Twill catch another feather crossing it:
Guess how the Pope will blow and how the king;
What force my lady's fan has; how a cough
Seizing the Padre's throat may raise a gust,
And how the queen may sigh the feather down.
Such catching at imaginary threads,
Such spinning twisted air, is not for me.
If I should want a game, I'll rather bet
On racing snails, two large, slow, lingering snails –
No spurring, equal weights – a chance sublime,
Nothing to guess at, pure uncertainty.
Here comes the Duke. They give but feeble shouts.
And some look sour.

HOST.   That spoils a fair occasion.
    Civility brings no conclusions with it,
    And cheerful *Vivas* make the moments glide
    Instead of grating like a rusty wheel.

JUAN. O they are dullards, kick because they're stung,
    And bruise a friend to show they hate a wasp.

HOST. Best treat your wasp with delicate regard;
    When the right moment comes say, "By your leave,"
    Use your heel – so ! and make an end of him.
    That's if we talked of wasps; but our young Duke –
    Spain holds not a more gallant gentleman.
    Live, live, Duke Silva ! 'Tis a rare smile he has,
    But seldom seen.

JUAN.   A true hidalgo's smile,
    That gives much favour, but beseeches none.
    His smile is sweetened by his gravity:
    It comes like dawn upon Sierra snows,

Seeming more generous for the coldness gone;
Breaks from the calm – a sudden opening flower
On dark deep waters: now a chalice shut,
A mystic shrine, the next a full-rayed star,
Thrilling, pulse-quickening as a living word.
I'll make a song of that.

HOST.   Prithee, not now.
You'll fall to staring like a wooden saint,
And wag your head as it were set on wires.
Here's fresh sherbét. Sit, be good company.
(*To* BLASCO) You are a stranger, sir, and cannot know
How our Duke's nature suits his princely frame.

BLASCO. Nay, but I marked his spurs – chased cunningly !
A duke should know good gold and silver plate;
Then he will know the quality of mine.
I've ware for tables and for altars too,
Our Lady in all sizes, crosses, bells:
He'll need such weapons full as much as swords
If he would capture any Moorish town.
For, let me tell you, when a mosque is cleansed . . .

JUAN. The demons fly so thick from sound of bells
And smell of incense, you may see the air
Streaked with them as with smoke. Why, they are spirits:
You may well think how crowded they must be
To make a sort of haze.

BLASCO.   I knew not that.
Still, they're of smoky nature, demons are;
And since you say so – well, it proves the more
The need of bells and censers. Ay, your Duke
Sat well: a true hidalgo. I can judge –
Of harness specially. I saw the camp,

217

The royal camp at Velez Malaga.
'Twas like the court of heaven – such liveries !
And torches carried by the score at night
Before the nobles. Sirs, I made a dish
To set an emerald in would fit a crown,
For Don Alonzo, lord of Aguilar.
Your Duke's no whit behind him in his mien
Or harness either. But you seem to say
The people love him not.

HOST.   They've nought against him.
But certain winds will make men's temper bad
When the Solano blows hot venomed breath
It acts upon men's knives: steel takes to stabbing
Which else, with cooler winds, were honest steel
Cutting but garlick. There's a wind just now
Blows right from Seville –

BLASCO.   Ay, you mean the wind . . .
Yes, yes, a wind that's rather hot . . .

HOST.   With faggots.

JUAN. A wind that suits not with our townsmen's blood.
Abram, 'tis said, objected to be scorched,
And, as the learned Arabs vouch, he gave
The antipathy in full to Ishmaël.
'Tis true, these patriarchs had their oddities.

BLASCO. Their oddities ? I'm of their mind, I know.
Though, as to Abraham and Ishmaël,
I'm an old Christian, and owe nought to them
Or any Jew among them. But I know
We made a stir in Saragossa – we:
The men of Aragon ring hard – true metal.

Sirs, I'm no friend to heresy, but then
A Christian's money is not safe. As how ?
A lapsing Jew or any heretic
May owe me twenty ounces: suddenly
He's prisoned, suffers penalties − 'tis well:
If men will not believe, 'tis good to make them,
But let the penalties fall on them alone.
The Jew is stripped, his goods are confiscate;
Now, where, I pray you, go my twenty ounces ?
God knows, and perhaps the King may, but not I.
And more, my son may lose his young wife's dower
Because 'twas promised since her father's soul
Fell to wrong thinking. How was I to know ?
I could but use my sense and cross myself.
Christian is Christian − I give in − but still
Taxing is taxing, though you call it holy.
We Saragossans liked not this new tax
They call the − nonsense, I'm from Aragon !
I speak too bluntly. But, for Holy Church,
No man believes more.

HOST.   Nay, sir, never fear.
　　Good Master Roldan here is no delator.

ROLDAN   (*starting from a reverie*).
　　You speak to me, sirs ? I perform to-night −
　　The Plaça Santiago. Twenty tricks,
　　All different. I dance, too. And the boy
　　Sings like a bird. I crave your patronage.

BLASCO. Faith, you shall have it, sir. In travelling
　　I take a little freedom, and am gay.
　　You marked not what I said just now ?

219

ROLDAN.   I ? no.
    I pray your pardon. I've a twinging knee,
    That makes it hard to listen. You were saying ?

BLASCO.
    Nay, it was nought. (*Aside to* HOST) Is it his deepness ?

HOST.   No.
    He's deep in nothing but his poverty.

BLASCO. But 'twas his poverty that made me think . . .

HOST. His piety might wish to keep the feasts
    As well as fasts. No fear; he hears not.

BLASCO.   Good.
    I speak my mind about the penalties,
    But, look you, I'm against assassination.
    You know my meaning – Master Arbués,
    The grand Inquisitor in Aragon.
    I knew nought – paid no copper towards the deed.
    But I was there, at prayers, within the church.
    How could I help it ? Why, the saints were there,
    And looked straight on above the altars. I . . .

JUAN. Looked carefully another way.

BLASCO.   Why, at my beads.
    'Twas after midnight, and the canons all
    Were chanting matins. I was not in church
    To gape and stare. I saw the martyr kneel:
    I never liked the look of him alive –
    He was no martyr then. I thought he made
    An ugly shadow as he crept athwart
    The bands of light, then passed within the gloom

By the broad pillar. 'Twas in our great Seo,
At Saragossa. The pillars tower so large
You cross yourself to see them, lest white Death
Should hide behind their dark. And so it was.
I looked away again and told my beads
Unthinkingly; but still a man has ears;
And right across the chanting came a sound
As if a tree had crashed above the roar
Of some great torrent. So it seemed to me;
For when you listen long and shut your eyes
Small sounds get thunderous. He had a shell
Like any lobster: a good iron suit
From top to toe beneath the innocent serge.
That made the tell-tale sound. But then came shrieks.
The chanting stopped and turned to rushing feet,
And in the midst lay Master Arbués,
Felled like an ox. 'Twas wicked butchery.
Some honest men had hoped it would have scared
The Inquisition out of Aragon.
'Twas money thrown away – I would say, crime –
Clean thrown away.

HOST.   That was a pity now.
Next to a missing thrust, what irks me most
Is a neat well-aimed stroke that kills your man,
Yet ends in mischief – as in Aragon.
It was a lesson to our people here.
Else there's a monk within our city walls,
A holy, high-born, stern Dominican,
They might have made the great mistake to kill.

BLASCO. What ! is he ? . . .

HOST.   Yes; a Master Arbués
Of finer quality. The Prior here

221

And uncle to our Duke.

BLASCO.   He will want plate:
A holy pillar or a crucifix.
But, did you say, he was like Arbués ?

JUAN. As a black eagle with gold beak and claws
Is like a raven. Even in his cowl,
Covered from head to foot, the Prior is known
From all the black herd round. When he uncovers
And stands white-frocked, with ivory face, his eyes
Black-gleaming, black his coronal of hair
Like shredded jasper, he seems less a man
With struggling aims, than pure incarnate Will,
Fit to subdue rebellious nations, nay,
That human flesh he breathes in, charged with passion
Which quivers in his nostril and his lip,
But disciplined by long in-dwelling will
To silent labour in the yoke of law.
A truce to thy comparisons, Lorenzo !
Thine is no subtle nose for difference;
'Tis dulled by feigning and civility.

HOST. Pooh, thou'rt a poet, crazed with finding words
May stick to things and seem like qualities.
No pebble is a pebble in thy hands:
'Tis a moon out of work, a barren egg,
Or twenty things that no man sees but thee.
Our Father Isidor's – a living saint,
And that is heresy, some townsmen think:
Saints should be dead, according to the Church.
My mind is this: the Father is so holy
'Twere sin to wish his soul detained from bliss.
Easy translation to the realms above,

The shortest journey to the seventh heaven,
Is what I'd never grudge him.

BLASCO.   Piously said.
  Look you, I'm dutiful, obey the Church
  When there's no help for it: I mean to say,
  When Pope and Bishop and all customers
  Order alike. But there be bishops now,
  And were aforetime, who have held it wrong,
  This hurry to convert the Jews. As how ?
  Your Jew pays tribute to the bishop, say.
  That's good, and must please God, to see the Church
  Maintained in ways that ease the Christian's purse.
  Convert the Jew, and where's the tribute, pray ?
  He lapses, too: 'tis slippery work, conversion:
  And then the holy taxing carries off
  His money at one sweep. No tribute more !
  He's penitent or burnt, and there's an end
  Now guess which pleases God . . .

JUAN.   Whether he likes
  A well-burnt Jew or well-fed bishop best.

[While Juan put this problem theologic
Entered, with resonant step, another guest –
A soldier: all his keenness in his sword,
His eloquence in scars upon his cheek,
His virtue in much slaying of the Moor:
With brow well-creased in horizontal folds
To save the space, as having nought to do:
Lips prone to whistle whisperingly – no tune,
But trotting rhythm: meditative eyes,
Most often fixed upon his legs and spurs:
Styled Captain Lopez.]

LOPEZ.   At your service, sirs.

JUAN. Ha, Lopez ? Why, thou hast a face full-charged
　As any herald's. What news of the wars ?

LOPEZ. Such news as is most bitter on my tongue.

JUAN. Then spit it forth.

HOST.   Sit, Captain: here's a cup,
　Fresh-filled. What news ?

LOPEZ.   'Tis bad. We make no sally:
　We sit still here and wait whate'er the Moor
　Shall please to do.

HOST.   Some townsmen will be glad.

LOPEZ. Glad, will they be ? But I'm not glad, not I,
　Nor any Spanish soldier of clean blood.
　But the Duke's wisdom is to wait a siege
　Instead of laying one. Therefore − meantime −
　He will be married straightway.

HOST.   Ha, ha, ha !
　Thy speech is like an hourglass; turn it down
　The other way, 'twill stand as well, and say
　The Duke will wed, therefore he waits a siege.
　But what say Don Diego and the Prior ?
　The holy uncle and the fiery Don ?

LOPEZ. O there be sayings running all abroad
　As thick as nuts o'erturned. No man need lack.
　Some say, 'twas letters changed the Duke's intent:
　From Malaga, says Blas. From Rome, says Quintin.

From spies at Guadix, says Sebastian.
Some say, 'tis all a pretext – say, the Duke
Is but a lapdog hanging on a skirt,
Turning his eyeballs upward like a monk:
'Twas Don Diego said that – so says Blas;
Last week, he said . . .

JUAN.   O do without the "said !"
Open thy mouth and pause in lieu of it.
I had as lief be pelted with a pea
Irregularly in the self-same spot
As hear such iteration without rule,
Such torture of uncertain certainty.

LOPEZ. Santiago ! Juan, thou art hard to please.
I speak not for my own delighting, I.
I can be silent, I.

BLASCO.   Nay, sir, speak on !
I like your matter well. I deal in plate.
This wedding touches me. Who is the bride ?

LOPEZ. One that some say the Duke does ill to wed.
One that his mother reared – God rest her soul ! –
Duchess Diana – she who died last year.
A bird picked up away from any nest.
Her name – the Duchess gave it – is Fedalma.
No harm in that. But the Duke stoops, they say,
In wedding her. And that's the simple truth.

JUAN. Thy simple truth is but a false opinion:
The simple truth of asses who believe
Their thistle is the very best of food.
Fie, Lopez, thou a Spaniard with a sword
Dreamest a Spanish noble ever stoops

By doing honour to the maid he loves !
He stoops alone when he dishonours her.

LOPEZ.   Nay, I said nought against her.

JUAN.   Better not.
   Else I would challenge thee to fight with wits,
   And spear thee through and through ere thou couldst
     draw
   The bluntest word. Yes, yes, consult thy spurs:
   Spurs are a sign of knighthood, and should tell thee
   That knightly love is blent with reverence
   As heavenly air is blent with heavenly blue.
   Don Silva's heart beats to a loyal tune:
   He wills no highest-born Castilian dame,
   Betrothed to highest noble, should be held
   More sacred than Fedalma. He enshrines
   Her virgin image for the general awe
   And for his own – will guard her from the world,
   Nay, his profaner self, lest he should lose
   The place of his religion. He does well.
   Nought can come closer to the poet's strain.

HOST. Or farther from his practice, Juan, eh ?
   If thou'rt a sample ?

JUAN.   Wrong there, my Lorenzo !
   Touching Fedalma the poor poet plays
   A finer part even than the noble Duke.

LOPEZ. By making ditties, singing with round mouth
   Likest a crowing cock ? Thou meanest that ?

JUAN. Lopez, take physic, thou art getting ill,
   Growing descriptive; 'tis unnatural.

I mean, Don Silva's love expects reward,
Kneels with a heaven to come; but the poor poet
Worships without reward, nor hopes to find
A heaven save in his worship. He adores
The sweetest woman for her sweetness' sake,
Joys in the love that was not born for him,
Because 'tis lovingness, as beggars joy,
Warming their naked limbs on wayside walls,
To hear a tale of princes and their glory.
There's a poor poet (poor, I mean, in coin)
Worships Fedalma with so true a love
That if her silken robe were changed for rags,
And she were driven out to stony wilds
Barefoot, a scornéd wanderer, he would kiss
Her ragged garment's edge, and only ask
For leave to be her slave. Digest that, friend,
Or let it lie upon thee as a weight
To check light thinking of Fedalma.

LOPEZ.   I ?

I think no harm of her; I thank the saints
I wear a sword and peddle not in thinking.
'Tis Father Marcos says she'll not confess
And loves not holy water; says her blood
Is infidel; says the Duke's wedding her
Is union of light with darkness.

JUAN.   Tush !

[Now Juan – who by snatches touched his lute
With soft arpeggio, like a whispered dream
Of sleeping music, while he spoke of love –
In jesting anger at the soldier's talk
Thrummed loud and fast, then faster and more loud,
Till, as he answered "Tush !" he struck a chord

Sudden as whip-crack close by Lopez' ear.
Mine host and Blasco smiled, the mastiff barked,
Roldan looked up and Annibal looked down,
Cautiously neutral in so new a case;
The boy raised longing, listening eyes that seemed
An exiled spirit's waiting in strained hope
Of voices coming from the distant land.
But Lopez bore the assault like any rock:
That was not what he drew his sword at – he !
He spoke with neck erect.]

LOPEZ.   If that's a hint
   The company should ask thee for a song,
   Sing, then !

HOST.   Ay, Juan, sing, and jar no more.
   Something brand new. Thou'rt wont to make my ear
   A test of novelties. Hast thou aught fresh ?

JUAN. As fresh as rain-drops. Here's a Cancion
   Springs like a tiny mushroom delicate
   Out of the priest's foul scandal of Fedalma.

[He preluded with querying intervals,
Rising, then falling just a semitone,
In minor cadence – sound with poiséd wing
Hovering and quivering towards the needed fall.
Then in a voice that shook the willing air
With masculine vibration sang this song.

     Should I long that dark were fair ?
     Say, O song !
     Lacks my love aught, that I should long ?

Dark the night, with breath all flow'rs,
And tender broken voice that fills
With ravishment the listening hours:
Whisperings, wooings,
Liquid ripples and soft ring-dove cooings
In low-toned rhythm that love's aching stills.
Dark the night,
Yet is she bright,
For in her dark she brings the mystic star,
Trembling yet strong, as is the voice of love,
From some unknown afar.
O radiant Dark ! O darkly-fostered ray !
Thou hast a joy too deep for shallow Day.

While Juan sang, all round the tavern court
Gathered a constellation of black eyes.
Fat Lola leaned upon the balcony
With arms that might have pillowed Hercules
(Who built, 'tis known, the mightiest Spanish towns);
Thin Alda's face, sad as a wasted passion,
Leaned o'er the nodding baby's; 'twixt the rails
The little Pepe showed his two black beads,
His flat-ringed hair and small Semitic nose,
Complete and tiny as a new-born minnow;
Patting his head and holding in her arms
The baby senior, stood Lorenzo's wife
All negligent, her kerchief discomposed
By little clutches, woman's coquetry
Quite turned to mother's cares and sweet content.
These on the balcony, while at the door
Gazed the lank boys and lazy-shouldered men.
'Tis likely too the rats and insects peeped,
Being southern Spanish ready for a lounge.
The singer smiled, as doubtless Orpheus smiled,
To see the animals both great and small,

The mountainous elephant and scampering mouse,
Held by the ears in decent audience;
Then, when mine host desired the strain once more,
He fell to preluding with rhythmic change
Of notes recurrent, soft as pattering drops
That fall from off the eaves in faëry dance
When clouds are breaking; till at measured pause
He struck with strength, in rare responsive chords.]

HOST. Come, then, a gayer ballad, if thou wilt:
    I quarrel not with change. What say you, Captain ?

LOPEZ. All's one to me. I note no change of tune,
    Not I, save in the ring of horses' hoofs,
    Or in the drums and trumpets when they call
    To action or retreat. I ne'er could see
    The good of singing.

BLASCO.　　　　　　　Why, it passes time –
    Saves you from getting over-wise: that's good.
    For, look you, fools are merry here below,
    Yet they will go to heaven all the same,
    Having the sacraments; and, look you, heaven
    Is a long holiday, and solid men,
    Used to much business, might be ill at ease
    Not liking play. And so, in travelling,
    I shape myself betimes to idleness
    And take fools' pleasures . . .

HOST.　　　　　　　　　Hark, the song begins !

JUAN *(sings)*.

> *Maiden, crowned with glossy blackness,*
> *Lithe as panther forest-roaming,*
> *Long-armed naiad, when she dances,*
> *On a stream of ether floating –*
> *Bright, O bright Fedalma !*
>
> *Form all curves like softness drifted,*
> *Wave-kissed marble roundly dimpling,*
> *Far-off music slowly wingéd,*
> *Gently rising, gently sinking –*
> *Bright, O bright Fedalma !*
>
> *Pure as rain-tear on a rose-leaf*
> *Cloud high-born in noonday spotless,*
> *Sudden perfect as the dew-bead,*
> *Gem of earth and sky begotten –*
> *Bright, O bright Fedalma !*
>
> *Beauty has no mortal father,*
> *Holy light her form engendered*
> *Out of tremor, yearning, gladness,*
> *Presage sweet and joy remembered –*
> *Child of Light, Fedalma !*

BLASCO. Faith, a good song, sung to a stirring tune.
I like the words returning in a round;
It gives a sort of sense. Another such !

ROLDAN *(rising)*. Sirs, you will hear my boy. 'Tis very hard
When gentles sing for nought to all the town.
How can a poor man live ? And now 'tis time
I go to the Plaça – who will give me pence
When he can hear hidalgos and give nought ?

JUAN. True, friend. Be pacified. I'll sing no more.
Go thou, and we will follow. Never fear.
My voice is common as the ivy-leaves,
Plucked in all seasons – bears no price; thy boy's
Is like the almond blossoms. Ah, he's lame !

HOST. Load him not heavily. Here, Pedro ! help.
Go with them to the Plaça, take the hoops.
The sights will pay thee.

BLASCO.   I'll be there anon,
And set the fashion with a good white coin.
But let us see as well as hear.

HOST.   Ay, prithee.
Some tricks, a dance.

BLASCO.   Yes, 'tis more rational.

ROLDAN (*turning round with the bundle and monkey on his
shoulders*).
You shall see all, sirs. There's no man in Spain
Knows his art better. I've a twinging knee
Oft hinders dancing, and the boy is lame.
But no man's monkey has more tricks than mine.

[At this high praise the gloomy Annibal,
Mournful professor of high drollery,
Seemed to look gloomier, and the little troop
Went slowly out, escorted from the door
By all the idlers. From the balcony
Slowly subsided the black radiance
Of agate eyes, and broke in chattering sounds,
Coaxings and trampings, and the small hoarse squeak
Of Pepe's reed. And our group talked again.]

232

Host. I'll get this juggler, if he quits him well,
    An audience here as choice as can be lured.
    For me, when a poor devil does his best,
    'Tis my delight to soothe his soul with praise.
    What though the best be bad ? remains the good
    Of throwing food to a lean hungry dog.
    I'd give up the best jugglery in life
    To see a miserable juggler pleased.
    But that's my humour. Crowds are malcontent
    And cruel as the Holy . . . . Shall we go ?
    All of us now together ?

Lopez.   Well, not I.
    I may be there anon, but first I go
    To the lower prison. There is strict command
    That all our gypsy prisoners shall to-night
    Be lodged within the fort. They've forged enough
    Of balls and bullets – used up all the metal.
    At morn to-morrow they must carry stones
    Up the south tower. 'Tis a fine stalwart band,
    Fit for the hardest tasks. Some say, the queen
    Would have the Gypsies banished with the Jews.
    Some say, 'twere better harness them for work.
    They'd feed on any filth and save the Spaniard.
    Some say – but I must go. 'Twill soon be time
    To head the escort. We shall meet again.

Blasco. Go, sir, with God. (*exit* Lopez). A very proper man,
    And soldierly. But, for this banishment
    Some men are hot on, it ill pleases me.
    The Jews, now (sirs, if any Christian here
    Had Jews for ancestors, I blame him not;
    We cannot all be Goths of Aragon) –
    Jews are not fit for heaven, but on earth
    They are most useful. 'Tis the same with mules,

233

Horses, or oxen, or with any pig
Except Saint Anthony's. They are useful here
(The Jews, I mean) though they may go to hell.
And, look you, useful sins – why Providence
Sends Jews to do 'em, saving Christian souls.
The very Gypsies, curbed and harnessed well,
Would make draught cattle, feed on vermin too,
Cost less than grazing brutes, and turn bad food
To handsome carcasses; sweat at the forge
For little wages, and well drilled and flogged
Might work like slaves, some Spaniards looking on.
I deal in plate, and am no priest to say
What God may mean, save when he means plain sense;
But when he sent the Gypsies wandering
In punishment because they sheltered not
Our Lady and Saint Joseph (and no doubt
Stole the small ass they fled with into Egypt),
Why send them here ? 'Tis plain he saw the use
They'd be to Spaniards. Shall we banish them,
And tell God we know better ? 'Tis a sin.
They talk of vermin; but, sirs, vermin large
Were made to eat the small, or else to eat
The noxious rubbish, and picked Gypsy men
Might serve in war to climb, be killed, and fall
To make an easy ladder. Once I saw
A Gypsy sorcerer, at a spring and grasp
Kill one who came to seize him: talk of strength !
Nay, swiftness too, for while we crossed ourselves
He vanished like – say, like . . .

JUAN.   A swift black snake,
    Or like a living arrow fledged with will.

BLASCO. Why, did you see him, pray ?

234

JUAN.   Not then, but now,
    As painters see the many in the one.
    We have a Gypsy in Bedmár whose frame
    Nature compacted with such fine selection,
    'Twould yield a dozen types: all Spanish knights,
    From him who slew Rolando at the pass
    Up to the mighty Cid; all deities,
    Thronging Olympus in fine attitudes;
    Or all hell's heroes whom the poet saw
    Tremble like lions, writhe like demigods.

HOST. Pause not yet, Juan — more hyperbole !
    Shoot upward still and flare in meteors
    Before thou sink to earth in dull brown fact.

BLASCO. Nay, give me fact, high shooting suits not me,
    I never stare to look for soaring larks.
    What is this Gypsy ?

HOST.   Chieftain of a band,
    The Moor's allies, whom full a month ago
    Our Duke suprised and brought as captives home.
    He needed smiths, and doubtless the brave Moor
    Has missed some useful scouts and archers too.
    Juan's fantastic pleasure is to watch
    These Gypsies forging, and to hold discourse
    With this great chief, whom he transforms at will
    To sage or warrior, and like the sun
    Plays daily at fallacious alchemy,
    Turns sand to gold and dewy spider-webs
    To myriad rainbows. Still the sand is sand,
    And still in sober shade you see the web.
    'Tis so, I'll wager, with his Gypsy chief —
    A piece of stalwart cunning, nothing more.

JUAN. No ! My invention had been all too poor
     To frame this Zarca as I saw him first.
     'Twas when they stripped him. In his chieftain's gear,
     Amidst his men he seemed a royal barb
     Followed by wild-maned Andalusian colts.
     He had a necklace of a strange device
     In finest gold of unknown workmanship,
     But delicate as Moorish, fit to kiss
     Fedalma's neck, and play in shadows there.
     He wore fine mail, a rich-wrought sword and belt,
     And on his surcoat black a broidered torch,
     A pine-branch flaming, grasped by two dark hands.
     But when they stripped him of his ornaments
     It was the baubles lost their grace, not he.
     His eyes, his mouth, his nostril, all inspired
     With scorn that mastered utterance of scorn,
     With power to check all rage until it turned
     To ordered force, unleashed on chosen prey –
     It seemed the soul within him made his limbs
     And made them grand. The baubles were well gone.
     He stood the more a king, when bared to man.

BLASCO. Maybe. But nakedness is bad for trade,
     And is not decent. Well-wrought metal, sir,
     Is not a bauble. Had you seen the camp,
     The royal camp at Velez Malaga,
     Ponce de Leon and the other dukes,
     The king himself and all his thousand knights
     For bodyguard, 'twould not have left you breath
     To praise a Gypsy thus. A man's a man;
     But when you see a king, you see the work
     Of many thousand men. King Ferdinand
     Bears a fine presence, and hath proper limbs;
     But what though he were shrunken as a relic ?
     You'd see the gold and gems that cased him o'er,

236

And all the pages round him in brocade,
And all the lords, themselves a sort of kings,
Doing him reverence. That strikes an awe
Into a common man – especially
A judge of plate.

HOST.   Faith, very wisely said.
  Purge thy speech, Juan. It is over-full
  Of this same Gypsy. Praise the Catholic King.
  And come now, let us see the juggler's skill.

The Plaça Santiago

'Tis daylight still, but now the golden cross
Uplifted by the angel on the dome
Stands rayless in calm colour clear-defined
Against the northern blue; from turrets high
The flitting splendour sinks with folded wing
Dark-hid till morning, and the battlements
Wear soft relenting whiteness mellowed o'er
By summers generous and winters bland.
Now in the east the distance casts its veil
And gazes with a deepening earnestness.
The old rain-fretted mountains in their robes
Of shadow-broken grey; the rounded hills
Reddened with blood of Titans, whose huge limbs,
Entombed within, feed full the hardy flesh
Of cactus green and blue broad-sworded aloes;
The cypress soaring black above the lines
Of white court-walls; the jointed sugar-canes
Pale-golden with their feathers motionless
In the warm quiet: – all thought-teaching form
Utters itself in firm unshimmering hues.
For the great rock has screened the westering sun

That still on plains beyond streams vaporous gold
Among the branches; and within Bedmár
Has come the time of sweet serenity
When colour glows unglittering, and the soul
Of visible things shows silent happiness,
As that of lovers trusting though apart.
The ripe-cheeked fruits, the crimson-petalled flowers;
The wingéd life that pausing seems a gem
Cunningly carven on the dark green leaf;
The face of man with hues supremely blent
To difference fine as of a voice 'mid sounds: –
Each lovely light-dipped thing seems to emerge
Flushed gravely from baptismal sacrament.
All beauteous existence rests, yet wakes,
Lies still, yet conscious, with clear open eyes
And gentle breath and mild suffuséd joy.
'Tis day, but day that falls like melody
Repeated on a string with graver tones –
Tones such as linger in a long farewell.

The Plaça widens in the passive air –
The Plaça Santiago, where the church,
A mosque converted, shows an eyeless face
Red-checkered, faded, doing penance still –
Bearing with Moorish arch the imaged saint,
Apostle, baron, Spanish warrior,
Whose charger's hoofs trample the turbaned dead,
Whose banner with the Cross, the bloody sword
Flashes athwart the Moslem's glazing eye,
And mocks his trust in Allah who forsakes.
Up to the church the Plaça gently slopes,
In shape most like the pious palmer's shell,
Girdled with low white houses; high above
Tower the strong fortress and sharp-angled wall
And well-flanked castle gate. From o'er the roofs,

238

And from the shadowed pátios cool, there spreads
The breath of flowers and aromatic leaves
Soothing the sense with bliss indefinite –
A baseless hope, a glad presentiment,
That curves the lip more softly, fills the eye
With more indulgent beam. And so it soothes,
So gently sways the pulses of the crowd
Who make a zone about the central spot
Chosen by Roldan for his theatre.
Maids with arched eyebrows, delicate-pencilled, dark,
Fold their round arms below the kerchief full;
Men shoulder little girls; and grandames grey,
But muscular still, hold babies on their arms;
While mothers keep the stout-legged boys in front
Against their skirts, as old Greek pictures show
The Glorious Mother with the Boy divine.
Youths keep the places for themselves, and roll
Large lazy eyes, and call recumbent dogs
(For reasons deep below the reach of thought).
The old men cough with purpose, wish to hint
Wisdom within that cheapens jugglery,
Maintain a neutral air, and knit their brows
In observation. None are quarrelsome,
Noisy, or very merry; for their blood
Moves slowly into fervour – they rejoice
Like those dark birds that sweep with heavy wing,
Cheering their mates with melancholy cries.

But now the gilded balls begin to play
In rhythmic numbers, ruled by practice fine
Of eye and muscle: all the juggler's form
Consents harmonious in swift-gliding change,
Easily forward stretched or backward bent
With lightest step and movement circular
Round a fixed point: 'tis not the old Roldan now,

The dull, hard, weary, miserable man,
The soul all parched to languid appetite
And memory of desire: 'tis wondrous force
That moves in combination multiform
Towards conscious ends: 'tis Roldan glorious,
Holding all eyes like any meteor,
King of the moment save when Annibal
Divides the scene and plays the comic part,
Gazing with blinking glances up and down
Dancing and throwing nought and catching it,
With mimicry as merry as the tasks
Of penance-working shades in Tartarus.

Pablo stands passive, and a space apart,
Holding a viol, waiting for command.
Music must not be wasted, but must rise
As needed climax; and the audience
Is growing with late comers. Juan now,
And the familiar Host, with Blasco broad,
Find way made gladly to the inmost round
Studded with heads. Lorenzo knits the crowd
Into one family by showing all
Good-will and recognition. Juan casts
His large and rapid-measuring glance around;
But – with faint quivering, transient as a breath
Shaking a flame – his eyes make sudden pause
Where by the jutting angle of a street
Castle-ward leading, stands a female form,
A kerchief pale square-drooping o'er the brow,
About her shoulders dim brown serge – in garb
Most like a peasant woman from the vale,
Who might have lingered after marketing
To see the show. What thrill mysterious,
Ray-borne from orb to orb of conscious eyes,
The swift observing sweep of Juan's glance

Arrests an instant, then with prompting fresh
Diverts it lastingly ? He turns at once
To watch the gilded balls, and nod and smile
At little round Pepíta, blondest maid
In all Bedmár − Pepíta, fair yet flecked,
Saucy of lip and nose, of hair as red
As breasts of robins stepping on the snow −
Who stands in front with little tapping feet,
And baby-dimpled hands that hide enclosed
Those sleeping crickets, the dark castanets.
But soon the gilded balls have ceased to play
And Annibal is leaping through the hoops,
That turn to twelve, meeting him as he flies
In the swift circle. Shuddering he leaps,
But with each spring flies swift and swifter still
To loud and louder shouts, while the great hoops
Are changed to smaller. Now the crowd is fired.
The motion swift, the living victim urged,
The imminent failure and repeated scape
Hurry all pulses and intoxicate
With subtle wine of passion many-mixt.
'Tis all about a monkey leaping hard
Till near to gasping; but it serves as well
As the great circus or arena dire,
Where these are lacking. Roldan cautiously
Slackens the leaps and lays the hoops to rest,
And Annibal retires with reeling brain
And backward stagger − pity, he could not smile !

Now Roldan spreads his carpet, now he shows
Strange metamorphoses: the pebble black
Changes to whitest egg within his hand;
A staring rabbit, with retreating ears,
Is swallowed by the air and vanishes;
He tells men's thoughts about the shaken dice,

241

Their secret choosings; makes the white beans pass
With causeless act sublime from cup to cup
Turned empty on the ground – diablerie
That pales the girls and puzzles all the boys:
These tricks are samples, hinting to the town
Roldan's great mastery. He tumbles next,
And Annibal is called to mock each feat
With arduous comicality and save
By rule romantic the great public mind
(And Roldan's body) from too serious strain.

But with the tumbling, lest the feats should fail,
And so need veiling in a haze of sound,
Pablo awakes the viol and the bow –
The masculine bow that draws the woman's heart
From out the strings and makes them cry, yearn, plead,
Tremble, exult, with mystic union
Of joy acute and tender suffering.
To play the viol and discreetly mix
Alternate with the bow's keen biting tones
The throb responsive to the finger's touch,
Was rarest skill that Pablo half had caught
From an old blind and wandering Catalan;
The other half was rather heritage
From treasure stored by generations past
In winding chambers of receptive sense.

The wingéd sounds exalt the thick-pressed crowd
With a new pulse in common, blending all
The gazing life into one larger soul
With dimly widened consciousness: as waves
In heightened movement tell of waves far off.
And the light changes; westward stationed clouds,
The sun's ranged outposts, luminous message spread,
Rousing quiescent things to doff their shade

And show themselves as added audience.
Now Pablo, letting fall the eager bow,
Solicits softer murmurs from the strings,
And now above them pours a wondrous voice
(Such as Greek reapers heard in Sicily)
With wounding rapture in it, like love's arrows;
And clear upon clear air as coloured gems
Dropped in a crystal cup of water pure,
Fall words of sadness, simple, lyrical:

> Spring comes hither,
>   Buds the rose;
> Roses wither,
>   Sweet spring goes.
> Ojalà, would she carry me !
>
> Summer soars –
>   Wide-winged day
> White light pours,
>   Flies away.
> Ojalà, would he carry me !
>
> Soft winds blow,
>   Westward born,
> Onward go
>   Toward the morn.
> Ojalà, would they carry me !
>
> Sweet birds sing
>   O'er the graves,
> Then take wing
>   O'er the waves.
> Ojalà, would they carry me !

When the voice paused and left the viol's note
To plead forsaken, 'twas as when a cloud
Hiding the sun, makes all the leaves and flowers
Shiver. But when with measured change the strings
Had taught regret new longing, clear again,
Welcome as hope recovered, flowed the voice.

> *Warm whispering through the slender olive leaves*
> > *Came to me a gentle sound,*
> > *Whispering of a secret found*
> *In the clear sunshine 'mid the golden sheaves:*
> *Said it was sleeping for me in the morn,*
> > *Called it gladness, called it joy,*
> > *Drew me on − "Come hither, boy" −*
> *To where the blue wings rested on the corn.*
> *I thought the gentle sound had whispered true −*
> > *Thought the little heaven mine,*
> > *Leaned to clutch the thing divine,*
> *And saw the blue wings melt within the blue.*

The long notes linger on the trembling air,
With subtle penetration enter all
The myriad corridors of the passionate soul,
Message-like spread, and answering action rouse
Not angular jigs that warm the chilly limbs
In hoary northern mists, but action curved
To soft andante strains pitched plaintively.
Vibrations sympathetic stir all limbs:
Old men live backward in their dancing prime,
And move in memory; small legs and arms
With pleasant agitation purposeless
Go up and down like pretty fruits in gales.
All long in common for the expressive act
Yet wait for it; as in the olden time
Men waited for the bard to tell their thought.

"The dance ! the dance !" is shouted all around.
How Pablo lifts the bow, Pepíta now,
Ready as bird that sees the sprinkled corn,
When Juan nods and smiles, puts forth her foot
And lifts her arm to wake the castanets.
Juan advances, too, from out the ring
And bends to quit his lute; for now the scene
Is empty; Roldan weary, gathers pence,
Followed by Annibal with purse and stick.
The carpet lies a coloured isle untrod,
Inviting feet: "The dance, the dance," resounds,
The bow entreats with slow melodic strain,
And all the air with expectation yearns.

Sudden, with gliding motion like a flame
That through dim vapour makes a path of glory,
A figure lithe, all white and saffron-robed,
Flashed right across the circle, and now stood
With ripened arms uplift and regal head,
Like some tall flower whose dark and intense heart
Lies half within a tulip-tinted cup.

Juan stood fixed and pale; Pepíta stepped
Backward within the ring: the voices fell
From shouts insistent to more passive tones
Half meaning welcome, half astonishment.
"Lady Fedalma ! – will she dance for us ?"

But she, sole swayed by impulse passionate,
Feeling all life was music and all eyes
The warming quickening light that music makes,
Moved as, in dance religious, Miriam,
When on the Red Sea shore she raised her voice
And led the chorus of the people's joy;
Or as the Trojan maids that reverent sang

Watching the sorrow-crownéd Hecuba:
Moved in slow curves voluminous, gradual,
Feeling and action flowing into one,
In Eden's natural taintless marriage-bond;
Ardently modest, sensuously pure,
With young delight that wonders at itself
And throbs as innocent as opening flowers
Knowing not comment – soilless, beautiful.
The spirit in her gravely glowing face
With sweet community informs her limbs,
Filling their fine gradation with the breath
Of virgin majesty; as full vowelled words
Are new impregnate with the master's thought.
Even the chance-strayed delicate tendrils black,
That backward 'scape from out her wreathing hair –
Even the pliant folds that cling transverse
When with obliquely-soaring bend altern
She seems a goddess quitting earth again –
Gather expression – a soft undertone
And resonance exquisite from the grand chord
Of her harmoniously bodied soul.

At first a reverential silence guards
The eager senses of the gazing crowd:
They hold their breath, and live by seeing her.
But soon the admiring tension finds relief –
Sighs of delight, applausive murmurs low,
And stirrings gentle as of earéd corn
Or seed-bent grasses, when the ocean's breath
Spreads landward. Even Juan is impelled
By the swift-travelling movement: fear and doubt
Give way before the hurrying energy;
He takes his lute and strikes in fellowship,
Filling more full the rill of melody
Raised ever and anon to clearest flood

By Pablo's voice, that dies away too soon
Like the sweet blackbird's fragmentary chant,
Yet wakes again, with varying rise and fall,
In songs that seem emergent memories
Prompting brief utterance – little canciόns
And villancicos, Andalusia-born.

PABLO (*sings*).
> *It was in the prime*
> *Of the sweet Spring-time.*
>> *In the linnet's throat*
>> *Trembled the love-note,*
> *And the love-stirred air*
> *Thrilled the blossoms there.*
>> *Little shadows danced*
>>> *Each a tiny elf,*
>> *Happy in large light*
>> *And the thinnest self.*

> *It was but a minute*
>> *In a far-off Spring,*
>> *But each gentle thing,*
> *Sweetly-wooing linnet,*
> *Soft-thrilled hawthorn tree,*
>> *Happy shadowy elf*
>>> *With the thinnest self,*
>> *Live still on in me.*
> *O the sweet, sweet prime*
> *Of the past Spring-time !*

And still the light is changing: high above
Float soft pink clouds; others with deeper flush
Stretch like flamingos bending toward the south.
Comes a more solemn brilliance o'er the sky,
A meaning more intense upon the air –

The inspiration of the dying day.
And Juan now, when Pablo's notes subside,
Soothes the regretful ear, and breaks the pause
With masculine voice in deep antiphony.

JUAN (*sings*).

> *Day is dying ! Float, O song,*
>   *Down the westward river*
> *Requiem chanting to the Day –*
>   *Day, the mighty Giver.*
>
> *Pierced by shafts of Time he bleeds,*
>   *Melted rubies sending*
> *Through the river and the sky,*
>   *Earth and heaven blending;*
>
> *All the long-drawn earthy banks*
>   *Up to cloud-land lifting:*
> *Slow between them drifts the swan,*
>   *'Twixt two heavens drifting.*
>
> *Wings half open, like a flow'r*
>   *Inly deeper flushing,*
> *Neck and breast as virgin's pure –*
>   *Virgin proudly blushing*
>
> *Day is aying ! Float, O swan,*
>   *Down the ruby river;*
> *Follow, song, in requiem*
>   *To the mighty Giver.*

The exquisite hour, the ardour of the crowd,
The strains more plenteous, and the gathering might
Of action passionate where no effort is,
But self's poor gates open to rushing power

That blends the inward ebb and outward vast –
All gathering influences culminate
And urge Fedalma. Earth and heaven seem one,
Life a glad trembling on the outer edge
Of unknown rapture. Swifter now she moves,
Filling the measure with a double beat
And widening circle; now she seems to glow
With more declaréd presence, glorified.
Circling, she lightly bends and lifts on high
The multitudinous-sounding tambourine,
And makes it ring and boom, then lifts it higher
Stretching her left arm beauteous; now the crowd
Exultant shouts, forgetting poverty
In the rich moment of possessing her.

But sudden, at one point, the exultant throng
Is pushed and hustled, and then thrust apart:
Something approaches – something cuts the ring
Of jubilant idlers – startling as a streak
From alien wounds across the blooming flesh
Of careless sporting childhood. 'Tis the band
Of Gypsy prisoners. Soldiers lead the van
And make sparse flanking guard, aloof surveyed
By gallant Lopez, stringent in command.
The Gypsies chained in couples, all save one,
Walk in dark file with grand bare legs and arms
And savage melancholy in their eyes
That star-like gleam from out black clouds of hair;
Now they are full in sight, and now they stretch
Right to the centre of the open space.
Fedalma now, with gentle wheeling sweep
Returning, like the loveliest of the Hours
Strayed from her sisters, truant lingering,
Faces again the centre, swings again
The uplifted tambourine. . . .

When lo ! with sound
Stupendous throbbing, solemn as a voice
Sent by the invisible choir of all the dead,
Tolls the great passing bell that calls to prayer
For souls departed: at the mighty beat
It seems the light sinks awe-struck − 'tis the note
Of the sun's burial; speech and action pause;
Religious silence and the holy sign
Of everlasting memories (the sign
Of death that turned to more diffusive life)
Pass o'er the Plaça. Little children gaze
With lips apart, and feel the unknown god;
And the most men and women pray. Not all.
The soldiers pray; the Gypsies stand unmoved
As pagan statues with proud level gaze.
But he who wears a solitary chain
Heading the file, has turned to face Feldama.
She motionless, with arm uplifted, guards
The tambourine aloft (lest, sudden-lowered,
Its trivial jingle mar the duteous pause),
Reveres the general prayer, but prays not, stands
With level glance meeting that Gypsy's eyes
That seem to her the sadness of the world
Rebuking her, the great bell's hidden thought
Now first unveiled − the sorrows unredeemed
Of races outcast, scorned, and wandering.
Why does he look at her ? why she at him ?
As if the meeting light between their eyes
Made permanent union ? His deep-knit brow,
Inflated nostril, scornful lip compressed,
Seem a dark hieroglyph of coming fate
Written before her. Father Isidor
Had terrible eyes and was her enemy;
She knew it and defied him; all her soul
Rounded and hardened in its separateness

When they encountered. But this prisoner –
This Gypsy, passing, gazing casually –
Was he her enemy too ? She stood all quelled,
The impetuous joy that hurried in her veins
Seemed backward rushing turned to chillest awe,
Uneasy wonder, and a vague self-doubt.
The minute brief stretched measureless, dream-filled
By a dilated new-fraught consciousness.

Now it was gone; the pious murmur ceased,
The Gypsies all moved onward at command
And careless noises blent confusedly.
But the ring closed again, and many ears
Waited for Pablo's music, many eyes
Turned towards the carpet: it lay bare and dim,
Twilight was there – the bright Fedalma gone.

A handsome room in the Castle.
On a table a rich jewel casket.

Silva had doffed his mail and with it all
The heavier harness of his warlike cares.
He had not seen Fedalma; miser-like
He hoarded through the hour a costlier joy
By longing oft-repressed. Now it was earned;
And with observance wonted he would send
To ask admission. Spanish gentlemen
Who wooed fair dames of noble ancestry
Did homage with rich tunics and slashed sleeves
And outward-surging linen's costly snow;
With broidered scarf transverse, and rosary
Handsomely wrought to fit high-blooded prayer;
So hinting in how deep respect they held
That self they threw before their lady's feet.

And Silva – that Fedalma's rate should stand
No jot below the highest, that her love
Might seem to all the royal gift it was –
Turned every trifle in his mien and garb
To scrupulous language, uttering to the world
That since she loved him he went carefully,
Bearing a thing so precious in his hand.
A man of high-wrought strain, fastidious
In his acceptance, dreading all delight
That speedy dies and turns to carrion:
His senses much exacting, deep instilled
With keen imagination's airy needs; –
Like strong-limbed monsters studded o'er with eyes,
Their hunger checked by overwhelming vision
Or that fierce lion in symbolic dream
Snatched from the ground by wings and new-endowed
With a man's thought-propelled relenting heart.
Silva was both the lion and the man;
First hesitating shrank, then fiercely sprang,
Or having sprung, turned pallid at his deed
And loosed the prize, paying his blood for nought.
A nature half-transformed, with qualities
That oft betrayed each other, elements
Not blent but struggling, breeding strange effects,
Passing the reckoning of his friends or foes.
Haughty and generous, grave and passionate;
With tidal moments of devoutest awe,
Sinking anon to farthest ebb of doubt;
Deliberating ever, till the sting
Of a recurrent ardour made him rush
Right against reasons that himself had drilled
And marshalled painfully. A spirit framed
Too proudly special for obedience,
Too subtly pondering for mastery:
Born of a goddess with a mortal sire,

Heir of flesh-fettered, weak divinity,
Doom-gifted with long resonant consciousness
And perilous heightening of the sentient soul.
But look less curiously: life itself
May not express us all, may leave the worst
And the best too, like tunes in mechanism
Never awaked. In various catalogues
Objects stand variously. Silva stands
As a young Spaniard, handsome, noble, brave,
With titles many, high in pedigree;
Or, as a nature quiveringly poised
In reach of storms, whose qualities may turn
To murdered virtues that still walk as ghosts
Within the shuddering soul and shriek remorse;
Or, as a lover . . . . In the screening time
Of purple blossoms, when the petals crowd
And softly crush like cherub cheeks in heaven,
Who thinks of greenly withered fruit and worms ?
O the warm southern spring is beauteous !
And in love's spring all good seems possible:
No threats, all promise, brooklets ripple full
And bathe the rushes, vicious crawling things
Are pretty eggs, the sun shines graciously
And parches not, the silent rain beats warm
As childhood's kisses, days are young and grow,
And earth seems in its sweet beginning time
Fresh made for two who live in Paradise.
Silva is in love's spring, its freshness breathed
Within his soul along the dusty ways
While marching homeward; 'tis around him now
As in a garden fenced in for delight, –
And he may seek delight. Smiling he lifts
A whistle from his belt, but lets it fall
Ere it has reached his lips, jarred by the sound

Of ushers' knocking, and a voice that craves
Admission for the Prior of San Domingo.

PRIOR (*entering*).
    You look perturbed, my son. I thrust myself
    Between you and some beckoning intent
    That wears a face more smiling than my own.

DON SILVA. Father, enough that you are here. I wait,
    As always, your commands – nay, should have sought
    An early audience.

PRIOR.   To give, I trust,
    God reasons for your change of policy ?

DON SILVA. Strong reasons, father.

PRIOR.   Ay, but are they good ?
    I have known reasons strong, but strongly evil.

DON SILVA. 'Tis possible. I but deliver mine
    To your strict judgment. Late despatches sent
    With urgence by the Count of Bavien,
    No hint on my part prompting, with besides
    The testified concurrence of the king
    And our Grand Master, have made peremptory
    The course which else had been but rational.
    Without the forces furnished by allies
    The siege of Guadix would be madness. More,
    El Zagal has his eyes upon Bedmár:
    Let him attempt it: in three weeks from hence
    The Master and the Lord of Aguilar
    Will bring their forces. We shall catch the Moors,
    The last gleaned clusters of their bravest men,
    As in a trap. You have my reasons, father.

PRIOR. And they sound well. But free-tongued rumour adds
A pregnant supplement – in substance this:
That inclination snatches arguments
To make indulgence seem judicious choice;
That you, commanding in God's Holy War,
Lift prayers to Satan to retard the fight
And give you time for feasting – wait a siege,
Call daring enterprise impossible,
Because you'd marry ! You, a Spanish duke,
Christ's general, would marry like a clown,
Who, selling fodder dearer for the war,
Is all the merrier; nay, like the brutes,
Who know no awe to check their appetite,
Coupling 'mid heaps of slain, while still in front
The battle rages.

DON SILVA.   Rumour on your lips
Is eloquent, father.

PRIOR.   Is she true ?

DON SILVA.   Perhaps.
I seek to justify my public acts
And not my private joy. Before the world
Enough if I am faithful in command,
Betray not by my deeds, swerve from no task
My knightly vows constrain me to: herein
I ask all men to test me.

PRIOR.   Knightly vows ?
Is it by their constraint that you must marry ?

DON SILVA. Marriage is not a breach of them. I use
A sanctioned liberty . . . . your pardon, father,
I need not teach you what the Church decrees.

But facts may weaken texts, and so dry up
The fount of eloquence. The Church relaxed
Our Order's rule before I took the vows.

PRIOR.   Ignoble liberty ! you snatch your rule
From what God tolerates, not what he loves ? –
Inquire what lowest offering may suffice,
Cheapen it meanly to an obolus,
Buy, and then count the coin left in your purs
For your debauch ? – Measure obedience
By scantest powers of brethren whose frail flesh
Our Holy Church indulges ? – Ask great Law,
The rightful Sovereign of the human soul,
For what it pardons, not what it commands ?
O fallen knighthood, penitent of high vows,
Asking a charter to degrade itself !
Such poor apology of rules relaxed
Blunts not suspicion of that doubleness
Your enemies tax you with.

DON SILVA.   Oh, for the rest
Conscience is harder than our enemies,
Knows more, accuses with more nicety,
Nor needs to question Rumour if we fall
Below the perfect model of our thought.
I fear no outward arbiter. – You smile ?

PRIOR.   Ay, at the contrast 'twixt your portraiture
And the true image of your conscience, shown
As now I see it in your acts. I see
A drunken sentinel who gives alarm
At his own shadow, but when scalers snatch
His weapon from his hand smiles idiotlike
At games he's dreaming of.

DON SILVA.   A parable !
   The husk is rough – holds something bitter, doubtless.

PRIOR. Oh, the husk gapes with meaning over-ripe.
   You boast a conscience that controls your deeds,
   Watches your knightly armour, guards your rank
   From stain of treachery – you, helpless slave,
   Whose will lies nerveless in the clutch of lust –
   Of blind mad passion – passion itself most helpless,
   Storm-driven, like the monsters of the sea.
   O famous conscience !

DON SILVA.   Pause there ! Leave unsaid
   Aught that will match that text. More were too much,
   Even from holy lips. I own no love
   But such as guards my honour, since it guards
   Hers whom I love ! I suffer no foul words
   To stain the gift I lay before her feet;
   And, being hers, my honour is more safe.

PRIOR. Versemakers' talk ! fit for as world of rhymes
   Where facts are feigned to tickle idle ears,
   Where good and evil play at tournament
   And end in amity – a world of lies –
   A carnival of words where every year
   Stale falsehoods serve fresh men. Your honour safe ?
   What honour has a man with double bonds ?
   Honour is shifting as the shadows are
   To souls that turn their passions into laws.
   A Christian knight who weds an infidel . . . .

DON SILVA (*fiercely*). An infidel !

PRIOR.   May one day spurn the Cross,
   And call that honour ! – one day find his sword

257

Stained with his brother's blood, and call that honour !
Apostates' honour ? – harlots' chastity !
Renegades' faithfulness ? – Iscariot's !

DON SILVA.

Strong words and burning; but they scorch not me.
Fedalma is a daughter of the Church –
Has been baptised and nurtured in the faith.

PRIOR.   Ay, as a thousand Jewesses, who yet
Are brides of Satan in a robe of flames.

DON SILVA.   Fedalma is no Jewess, bears no marks
That tell of Hebrew blood.

PRIOR   She bears the marks
Of races unbaptised, that never bowed
Before the holy signs, were never moved
By stirrings of the sacramental gifts.

DON SILVA   (*scornfully*).   Holy accusers practise palmistry,
And, other witness lacking, read the skin.

PRIOR.   I read a record deeper than the skin.
What! Shall the trick of nostrils and of lips
Descend through generations, and the soul
That moves within our frame like God in worlds –
Convulsing, urging, melting, withering –
Imprint no record, leave no documents,
Of her great history ?   Shall men bequeath
The fancies of their palate to their sons,
And shall the shudder of restraining awe,
The slow-wept tears of contrite memory,
Faith's prayerful labour, and the food divine
Of fasts ecstatic – shall these pass away

Like wind upon the waters, tracklessly ?
Shall the mere curl of eyelashes remain,
And god-enshrining symbols leave no trace
Of tremors reverent ? – That maiden's blood
Is as unchristian as the leopard's.

DON SILVA.   Say,
Unchristian as the Blessed Virgin's blood
Before the angel spoke the word, "All hail !"

PRIOR (*smiling bitterly*).
Said I not truly ? See, your passion weaves
Already blasphemies !

DON SILVA.   'Tis you provoke them.

PRIOR. I strive, as still the Holy Spirit strives,
To move the will perverse. But, failing this,
God commands other means to save our blood,
To save Castilian glory – nay, to save
The name of Christ from blot of traitorous deeds.

DON SILVA.
Of traitorous deeds ! Age, kindred, and your cowl,
Give an ignoble licence to your tongue.
As for your threats, fulfil them at your peril.
'Tis you, not I, will gibbet our great name
To rot in infamy. If I am strong
In patience now, trust me, I can be strong
Then in defiance.

PRIOR.   Miserable man !
Your strength will to to anguish, like the strength
Of fallen angels. Can you change your blood ?
You are a Christian, with the Christian awe

In every vein. A Spanish noble, born
To serve your people and your people's faith.
Strong, are you ? Turn your back upon the Cross –
Its shadow is before you. Leave your place:
Quit the great ranks of knighthood: you will walk
For ever with a tortured double self,
A self that will be hungry while you feast,
Will blush with shame while you are glorified,
Will feel the ache and chill of desolation,
Even in the very bosom of your love.
Mate yourself with this woman, fit for what ?
To make the sport of Moorish palaces,
A lewd Herodias . . . .

Don Silva.   Stop ! no other man,
Priest though he were, had had his throat left free
For passage of those words. I would have clutched
His serpent's neck, and flung him out to hell !
A monk must needs defile the name of love:
He knows it but as tempting devils paint it.
You think to scare my love from its resolve
With arbitrary consequences, strained
By rancorous effort from the thinnest motes
Of possibility ? – cite hideous lists
Of sins irrelevant, to frighten me
With bugbears' names, as women fright a child ?
Poor pallid wisdom, taught by inference
From blood-drained life, where phantom terrors rule,
And all achievement is to leave undone !
Paint the day dark, make sunshine cold to me,
Abolish the earth's fairness, prove it all
A fiction of my eyes – then, after that,
Profane Fedalma.

PRIOR.   O there is no need:
She has profaned herself. Go, raving man,
And see her dancing now. Go, see your bride
Flaunting her beauties grossly in the gaze
Of vulgar idlers – eking out the show
Made in the Plaça by a mountebank.
I hinder you no farther.

DON SILVA.   It is false !

PRIOR. Go, prove it false, then.

                         [Father Isidor
Drew on his cowl and turned away. The face
That flashed anathemas, in swift eclipse
Seemed Silva's vanished confidence. In haste
He rushed unsignalled through the corridor
To where the Duchess once, Fedalma now,
Had residence retired from din of arms –
Knocked, opened, found all empty – said
With muffled voice, "Fedalma !" – called more loud,
More oft on Iñez, the old trusted nurse –
Then searched the terrace-garden, calling still,
But heard no answering sound, and saw no face
Save painted faces staring all unmoved
By agitated tones. He hurried back,
Giving half-conscious orders as he went
To page and usher, that they straight should seek
Lady Fedalma; then with stinging shame
Wished himself silent; reached again the room
Where still the Father's menace seemed to hang
Thickening the air; snatched cloak and pluméd hat,
And grasped, not knowing why, his poniard's hilt;
Then checked himself and said: –]

                              If he spoke truth !
To know were wound enough – to see the truth
Were fire upon the wound. It must be false !
His hatred saw amiss, or snatched mistake
In other men's report. I am a fool !
But where can she be gone ? gone secretly ?
And in my absence ? Oh, she meant no wrong !
I am a fool ! – But where can she be gone ?
With only Iñez ? Oh, she meant no wrong !
I swear she never meant it. There's no wrong
But she would make it momentary right
By innocence in doing it. . . .

                         And yet,
What is our certainty ? Why, knowing all
That is not secret. Mighty confidence !
One pulse of Time makes the base hollow – sends
The towering certainty we built so high
Toppling in fragments meaningless. What is –
What will be – must be – pooh ! they wait the key
Of that which is not yet; all other keys
Are made of our conjectures, take their sense
From humours fooled by hope, or by despair.
Know what is good ? O God, we know not yet
If bliss itself is not young misery
With fangs swift growing. . . .

                              But some outward harm
May even now be hurting, grieving her.
Oh ! I must search – face shame – if shame be there.
Here, Perez ! hasten to Don Alvar – tell him
Lady Fedalma must be sought – is lost –
Has met, I fear, some mischance. He must send
Towards divers points. I go myself to seek
First in the town. . . .

                    [As Perez oped the door,

Then moved aside for passage of the Duke,
Fedalma entered, cast away the cloud
Of serge and linen, and outbeaming bright,
Advanced a pace towards Silva – but then paused,
For he had started and retreated; she,
Quick and responsive as the subtle air
To change in him, divined that she must wait
Until they were alone: they stood and looked.
Within the Duke was struggling confluence
Of feelings manifold – pride, anger, dread,
Meeting in stormy rush with sense secure
That she was present, with the new-stilled thirst
Of gazing love, with trust inevitable
As in beneficent virtues of the light
And all earth's sweetness, that Fedalma's soul
Was free from blemishing purpose. Yet proud wrath
Leaped in dark flood above the purer stream
That strove to drown it: Anger seeks its prey –
Something to tear with sharp-edged tooth and claw,
Likes not to go off hungry, leaving Love
To feast on milk and honeycomb at will.
Silva's heart said, he must be happy soon,
She being there; but to be happy – first
He must be angry, having cause. Yet love
Shot like a stifled cry of tenderness
All through the harshness he would fain have given
To the dear word,]

DON SILVA.   Fedalma !

FEDALMA.   O my lord !
    You are come back, and I was wandering !

DON SILVA (*coldly, but with suppressed agitation*).
    You meant I should be ignorant.

FEDALMA.   Oh no,
I should have told you after – not before,
Lest you should hinder me.

DON SILVA.   Then my known wish
Can make no hindrance ?

FEDALMA (*archly*).   That depends
On what the wish may be. You wished me once
Not to uncage the birds. I meant to obey:
But in a moment something – something stronger,
Forced me to let them out. It did no harm.
They all came back again – the silly birds !
I told you, after.

DON SILVA   (*with haughty coldness*). Will you tell me now
What was the prompting stronger than my wish
That made you wander ?

FEDALMA   (*advancing a step towards him, with a sudden
look of anxiety*).
                        Are you angry ?

DON SILVA (*smiling bitterly*).   Angry ?
A man deep-wounded may feel too much pain
To feel much anger.

FEDALMA   (*still more anxiously*).
                    You – deep-wounded ?

DON SILVA.   Yes !
Have I not made your place and dignity
The very heart of my ambition ? You –
No enemy could do it – you alone
Can strike it mortally.

FEDALMA.   Nay, Silva, nay.
  Has some one told you false ? I only went
  To see the world with Iñez – see the town,
  The people, everything. It was no harm.
  I did not mean to dance: it happened so
  At last . . .

DON SILVA.   O God, it's true then ! – true that you,
  A maiden nurtured as rare flowers are,
  The very air of heaven sifted fine
  Lest any mote should mar your purity,
  Have flung yourself out on the dusty way
  For common eyes to see your beauty soiled !
  You own it true – you danced upon the Plaça ?

FEDALMA (*proudly*).
  Yes, it is true. I was not wrong to dance.
  The air was filled with music, with a song
  That seemed the voice of the sweet eventide –
  The glowing light entering through eye and ear –
  That seemed our love – mine, yours – they are but one –
  Trembling through, all my limbs, as fervent words
  Tremble within my soul and must be spoken.
  And all the people felt a common joy
  And shouted for the dance. A brightness soft
  As of the angels moving down to see
  Illumined the broad space. The joy, the life
  Around, within me, were one heaven: I longed
  To blend them visibly: I longed to dance
  Before the people – be as mounting flame
  To all that burned within them ! Nay, I danced;
  There was no longing: I but did the deed
  Being moved to do it.

(*As* FEDALMA *speaks, she and* DON SILVA *are gradually drawn nearer to each other.*)

Oh ! I seemed new-waked
To life in unison with a multitude –
Feeling my soul upborne by all their souls
Floating within their gladness ! Soon I lost
All sense of separateness: Fedalma died
As a star dies, and melts into the light.
I was not, but joy was, and love and triumph.
Nay, my dear lord, I never could do aught
But I must feel you present. And once done,
Why, you must love it better than your wish.
I pray you, say so – say, it was not wrong !

(*While* FEDALMA *has been making this last appeal, they have gradually come close together, and at last embrace.*)

DON SILVA (*holding her hands*).
Dangerous rebel ! if the world without
Were pure as that within . . . but 'tis a book
Wherein you only read the poesy
And miss all wicked meanings. Hence the need
For trust – obedience – call it what you will –
Towards him whose life will be your guard – towards me
Who now am soon to be your husband.

FEDALMA.   Yes !
That very thing that when I am your wife
I shall be something different, – shall be
I know not what, a Duchess with new thoughts –
For nobles never think like common men,
Nor wives like maidens (Oh, you wot not yet
How much I note, with all my ignorance) –
That very thing has made me more resolve

To have my will before I am your wife.
How can the Duchess ever satisfy
Fedalma's unwed eyes ? and so to-day
I scolded Iñez till she cried and went.

DON SILVA. It was a guilty weakness: she knows well
  That since you pleaded to be left more free
  From tedious tendance and control of dames
  Whose rank matched better with your destiny,
  Her charge – my trust – was weightier.

FEDALMA.   Nay, my lord,
  You must not blame her, dear old nurse. She cried.
  Why, you would have consented too, at last.
  I said such things ! I was resolved to go,
  And see the streets, the shops, the men at work,
  The women, little children – everything,
  Just as it is when nobody looks on.
  And I have done it ! We were out four hours.
  I feel so wise.

DON SILVA   Had you but seen the town,
  You innocent naughtiness, not shown yourself –
  Shown yourself dancing – you bewilder me ! –
  Frustrate my judgment with strange negatives
  That seem like poverty, and yet are wealth
  In precious womanliness, beyond the dower
  Of other women: wealth in virgin gold,
  Outweighing all their petty currency.
  You daring modesty ! You shrink no more
  From gazing men than from the gazing flowers
  That, dreaming sunshine, open as you pass.

FEDALMA. No, I should like the world to look at me
  With eyes of love that make a second day.

267

I think your eyes would keep the life in me
Though I had nought to feed on else. Their blue
Is better than the heavens' — holds more love
For me, Fedalma — is a little heaven
For this one little world that looks up now.

DON SILVA.   O precious little world ! you make the heaven
As the earth makes the sky. But, dear, all eyes,
Though looking even on you, have not a glance
That cherishes . . . .

FEDALMA.   Ah no, I meant to tell you —
Tell how my dancing ended with a pang.
There came a man, one among many more,
But *he* came first, with iron on his limbs.
And when the bell tolled, and the people prayed,
And I stood pausing — then he looked at me.
O Silva, such a man ! I thought he rose
From the dark place of long-imprisoned souls,
To say that Christ had never come to them.
It was a look to shame a seraph's joy,
And make him sad in heaven. It found me there —
Seemed to have travelled far to find me there
And grasp me — claim this festal life of mine
As heritage of sorrow, chill my blood
With the cold iron of some unknown bonds.
The gladness hurrying full within my veins
Was sudden frozen, ana I danced no more.
But seeing you let loose the stream of joy,
Mingling the present with the sweetest past.
Yet, Silva, still I see him. Who is he ?
Who are those prisoners with him ? Are they Moors ?

DON SILVA.
No, they are Gypsies, strong and cunning knaves,

A double gain to us by the Moors' loss:
The man you mean – their chief – is an ally
The infidel will miss. His look might chase
A herd of monks, and make them fly more swift
Than from St Jerome's lion. Such vague fear,
Such bird-like tremors when that savage glance
Turned full upon you in your height of joy
Was natural, was not worth emphasis.
Forget it, dear. This hour is worth whole days
When we are sundered. Danger urges us
To quick resolve.

FEDALMA.   What danger ? what resolve ?
I never felt chill shadow in my heart
Until this sunset.

DON SILVA.   A dark enmity
Plots how to sever us. And our defence
Is speedy marriage, secretly achieved,
Then publicly declared. Beseech you, dear,
Grant me this confidence; do my will in this,
Trusting the reasons why I overset
All my own airy building raised so high
Of bridal honours, marking when you step
From off your maiden throne to come to me
And bear the yoke of love. There is great need.
I hastened home, carrying this prayer to you
Within my heart. The bishop is my friend,
Furthers our marriage, holds in enmity –
Some whom we love not and who love not us.
By this night's moon our priest will be despatched
From Jaën. I shall march an escort strong
To meet him. Ere a second sun from this
Has risen – you consenting – we may wed.

FEDALMA.   None knowing that we wed ?

DON SILVA.   Beforehand none
  Save Iñez and Don Alvar. But the vows
  Once safely binding us, my household all
  Shall know you as their Duchess. No man then
  Can aim a blow at you but through my breast,
  And what stains you must stain our ancient name;
  If any hate you I will take his hate,
  And wear it as a glove upon my helm;
  Nay, God himself will never have the power
  To strike you solely and leave me unhurt,
  He having made us one. Now put the seal
  Of your dear lips on that.

FEDALMA.   A solemn kiss ? –
  Such as I gave you when you came that day
  From Córdova, when first we said we loved ?
  When you had left the ladies of the Court
  For thirst to see me; and you told me so,
  And then I seemed to know why I had lived.
  I never knew before. A kiss like that ?

DON SILVA. Yes, yes, you face divine ! When was our kiss
  Like any other ?

FEDALMA.   Nay, I cannot tell
  What other kisses are. But that one kiss
  Remains upon my lips. The angels, spirits,
  Creatures with finer sense, may see it there.
  And now another kiss that will not die,
  Saying, To-morrow I shall be your wife !

    (*They kiss, and pause a moment, looking earnestly
    in each other's eyes. Then* FEDALMA, *breaking away*

Now I am glad I saw the town to-day
Before I am a Duchess – glad I gave
This poor Fedalma all her wish. For once,
Long years ago, I cried when Iñez said,
"You are no more a little girl;" I grieved
To part for ever from that little girl
And all her happy world so near the ground.
It must be sad to outlive aught we love.
So I shall grieve a little for these days
Of poor unwed Fedalma. Oh, they are sweet,
And none will come just like them. Perhaps the wind
Wails so in winter for the summers dead,
And all sad sounds are nature's funeral cries
For what has been and is not. Are they, Silva ?
    (*She comes nearer to him again, and lays her hand
    on his arm, looking up at him with melancholy.*)

DON SILVA. Why, dearest, you began in merriment,
    And end as sadly as a widowed bird.
    Some touch mysterious has new-tuned your soul
    To melancholy sequence. You soared high
    In that wild flight of rapture when you danced,
    And now you droop. 'Tis arbitrary grief,
    Surfeit of happiness, that mourns for loss
    Of unwed love, which does but die like seed
    For fuller harvest of our tenderness.
    We in our wedded life shall know no loss.
    We shall new-date our years. What went before
    Will be the time of promise, shadows, dreams;
    But this, all revelation of great love.
    For rivers blent take in a broader heaven,
    And we shall blend our souls.   Away with grief!

When this dear head shall wear the double crown
Of wife and Duchess — spiritually crowned
With sworn espousal before God and man —
Visibly crowned with jewels that bespeak
The chosen sharer of my heritage —
My love will gather perfectness, as thoughts
That nourish us to magnanimity
Grow perfect with more perfect utterance,
Gathering full-shapen strength. And then these gems,

(DON SILVA *draws* FEDALMA *towards the
jewel-casket on the table, and opens it.*)

Helping the utterance of my soul's full choice,
Will be the words made richer by just use,
And have new meaning in their lustrousness.
You know these jewels; they are precious signs
Of long-transmitted honour, heightened still
By worthy wearing; and I give them you —
Ask you to take them — place our house's trust
In her sure keeping whom my heart has found
Worthiest, most beauteous. These rubies — see —
Were falsely placed if not upon your brow.

(FEDALMA, *while* DON SILVA *holds open the casket,
bends over it, looking at the jewels with delight.*)

FEDALMA. Ah, I remember them. In childish days
I felt as if they were alive and breathed.
I used to sit with awe and look at them.
And now they will be mine ! I'll put them on.
Help me, my lord, and you shall see me now
Somewhat as I shall look at Court with you,
That we may know if I shall bear them well.
I have a fear sometimes: I think your love

Has never paused within your eyes to look,
And only passes through them into mine.
But when the Court is looking, and the queen,
Your eyes will follow theirs. Oh, if you saw
That I was other than you wished – 'twere death !

DON SILVA (*taking up a jewel and placing it against her ear*).
Nay, let us try. Take out your ear-ring, sweet.
This ruby glows with longing for your ear.

FEDALMA (*taking out her ear-rings, and then lifting up the other jewels, one by one*).
Pray, fasten in the rubies.
    (DON SILVA *begins to put in the ear-ring.*)
                    I was right !
These gems have life in them: their colours speak,
Say what words fail of. So do many things –
The scent of jasmine, and the fountain's plash,
The moving shadows on the far-off hills,
The slanting moonlight, and our clasping hands.
O Silva, there's an ocean round our words
That overflows and drowns them. Do you know
Sometimes when we sit silent, and the air
Breathes gently on us from the orange-trees,
It seems that with the whisper of a word
Our souls must shrink, get poorer, more apart.
Is it not true ?

DON SILVA.   Yes, dearest, it is true.
Speech is but broken light upon the depth
Of the unspoken: even your loved words
Float in the larger meaning of your voice
As something dimmer.

(He is still trying in vain to fasten the second ear-ring, while she has stooped again over the casket.)

FEDALMA *(raising her head).* Ah ! your lordly hands
Will never fix that jewel. Let me try.
Women's small finger-tips have eyes.

DON SILVA.   No, no !
I like the task, only you must be still.
(She stands perfectly still, clasping her hands together while he fastens the second ear-ring. Suddenly a clanking noise is heard without.)

FEDALMA *(starting with an expression of pain).*
What is that sound ? – that jarring cruel sound ?
'Tis there – outside.
(She tries to start away towards the window, but DON SILVA detains her.)

DON SILVA   O heed it not, it comes
From workmen in the outer gallery.

FEDALMA. It is the sound of fetters; sound of work
Is not so dismal. Hark, they pass along !
I know it is those Gypsy prisoners.
I saw them, heard their chains. O horrible,
To be in chains ! Why, I with all my bliss
Have longed sometimes to fly and be at large;
Have felt imprisoned in my luxury
With servants for my gaolers. O my lord,
Do you not wish the world were different ?

DON SILVA. It will be different when this war has ceased.
You, wedding me, will make it different,

Making one life more perfect.

FEDALMA.   That is true !
And I shall beg much kindness at your hands
For those who are less happy than ourselves. –
(*Brightening*) Oh I shall rule you ! ask for many things
Before the world, which you will not deny
For very pride, lest men should say, "The Duke
Holds lightly by his Duchess; he repents
His humble choice."

    (*She breaks away from him and returns to the
    jewels, taking up a necklace, and clasping it on her
    neck, while he takes a circlet of diamonds and
    rubies and raises it towards her head as he speaks.*)

DON SILVA.   Doubtless, I shall persist
In loving you, to disappoint the world;
Out of pure obstinacy feel myself
Happiest of men. Now, take the coronet.
    (*He places the circlet on her head.*)
The diamonds want more light. See, from this lamp
I can set tapers burning.

FEDALMA.   Tell me, now,
When all these cruel wars are at an end,
And when we go to Court at Córdova,
Or Seville, or Toledo – wait awhile,
I must be farther off for you to see –
    (*She retreats to a distance from him, and then
    advances slowly.*)
Now think (I would the tapers gave more light !)
If when you show me at the tournaments
Among the other ladies, they will say,
"Duke Silva is well matched. His bride was nought,

Was some poor foster-child, no man knows what;
Yet is her carriage noble, all her robes
Are worn with grace: she might have been well born."
Will they say so ? Think now we are at Court,
And all eyes bent on me.

Don Silva.   Fear not, my Duchess !
Some knight who loves may say his lady-love
Is fairer, being fairest. None can say
Don Silva's bride might better fit her rank.
You will make rank seem natural as kind,
As eagle's plumage or the lion's might.
A crown upon your brow would seem God-made.

Fedalma. Then I am glad ! I shall try on to-night
The other jewels – have the tapers lit,
And see the diamonds sparkle.
     (*She goes to the casket again.*)
                                        Here is gold –
A necklace of pure gold – most finely wrought.
     (*She takes out a large gold necklace and holds it
     up before her, then turns to* Don Silva.)
But this is one that you have worn, my lord ?

Don Silva. No, love, I never wore it. Lay it down.
     (*He puts the necklace gently out of her hand, then
     joins both her hands and holds them up between
     his own.*)
You must not look at jewels any more,
But look at me.

Fedalma (*looking up at him*). O you dear heaven !
I should see nought if you were gone. 'Tis true
My mind is too much given to gauds – to things
That fetter thought within this narrow space.

That comes of fear.

DON SILVA.   What fear ?

FEDALMA.   Fear of myself.
For when I walk upon the battlements
And see the river travelling toward the plain,
The mountains screening all the world beyond,
A longing comes that haunts me in my dreams –
Dreams where I seem to spring from off the walls,
And fly far, far away, until at last
I find myself alone among the rocks,
Remember then that I have left you – try
To fly back to you – and my wings are gone !

DON SILVA. A wicked dream ! If ever I left you,
Even in dreams, it was some demon dragged me,
And with fierce struggles I awaked myself.

FEDALMA. It is a hateful dream, and when it comes –
I mean, when in my waking hours there comes
That longing to be free, I am afraid:
I run down to my chamber, plait my hair,
Weave colours in it, lay out all my gauds,
And in my mind make new ones prettier.
You see I have two minds, and both are foolish.
Sometimes a torrent rushing through my soul
Escapes in wild strange wishes; presently,
It dwindles to a little babbling rill
And plays among the pebbles and the flowers.
Iñez will have it I lack broidery,
Says nought else gives content to noble maids.
But I have never broidered – never will.

No, when I am a Duchess and a wife
I shall ride forth – may I not ? – by your side.

DON SILVA. Yes, you shall ride upon a palfrey, black
To match Bavieca. Not Queen Isabel
Will be a sight more gladdening to men's eyes
Than my dark queen Fedalma.

FEDALMA.   Ah, but you,
You are my king, and I shall tremble still
With some great fear that throbs within my love.
Does your love fear ?

DON SILVA.   Ah, yes ! all preciousness
To mortal hearts is guarded by a fear.
All love fears loss, and most that loss supreme,
Its own perfection – seeing, feeling change
From high to lower, dearer to less dear.
Can love be careless ? If we lost our love
What should we find ? – with this sweet Past torn off,
Our lives deep scarred just where their beauty lay ?
The best we found thenceforth were still a worse:
The only better is a Past that lives
On through an added Present, stretching still
In hope unchecked by shaming memories
To life's last breath. And so I tremble too
Before my queen Fedalma.

FEDALMA.   That is just.
'Twere hard of Love to make us women fear
And leave you bold. Yet Love is not quite even.
For feeble creatures, little birds and fawns,
Are shaken more by fear, while large strong things
Can bear it stoutly. So we women still
Are not well dealt with. Yet I'd choose to be

Fedalma loving Silva. You, my lord,
Hold the worse share, since you must love poor me.
But is it what we love, or how we love,
That makes true good ?

DON SILVA.   O subtlety ! for me
'Tis what I love determines how I love.
The goddess with pure rites reveals herself
And makes pure worship.

FEDALMA.   Do you worship me ?

DON SILVA. Ay, with that best of worship which adores
Goodness adorable.

FEDALMA (*archly*).   Goodness obedient,
Doing your will, devoutest worshipper ?

DON SILVA. Yes – listening to this prayer. This very night
I shall go forth. And you will rise with day
And wait for me ?

FEDALMA   Yes.

DON SILVA   I shall surely come.
And then we shall be married. Now I go
To audience fixed in Abderahman's tower.
Farewell, love !
                    (*They embrace.*)

FEDALMA.   Some chill dread possesses me !

DON SILVA. Oh, confidence has oft been evil augury,
So dread may hold a promise. Sweet, farewell !
I shall send tendance as I pass, to bear

This casket to your chamber. – One more kiss.

(*Exit*)

FEDALMA (*when* DON SILVA *is gone, returning to the casket, and looking dreamily at the jewels*).
Yes, now that good seems less impossible !
Now it seems true that I shall be his wife,
Be ever by his side, and make a part
In all his purposes . . . .
These rubies greet me Duchess. How they glow !
Their prisoned souls are throbbing like my own.
Perchance they loved once, were ambitious, proud;
Or do they only dream of wider life,
Ache from intenseness, yearn to burst the wall
Compact of crystal splendour, and to flood
Some wider space with glory ? Poor, poor gems !
We must be patient in our prison-house,
And find our space in loving. Pray you, love me.
Let us be glad together. And you, gold –
    (*She takes up the gold necklace.*)
You wondrous necklace – will you love me too,
And be my amulet to keep me safe
From eyes that hurt ?
    (*She spreads out the necklace, meaning to clasp it on her neck. Then pauses, startled, holding it before her.*)
                              Why, it is magical !
He says he never wore it – yet these lines –
Nay, if he had, I should remember well
'Twas he, no other. And these twisted lines –
They seem to speak to me as writing would,
To bring a message from the dead, dead past
What is their secret? Are they characters ?
I never learned them; yet they stir some sense
That once I dreamed – I have forgotten what.

Or was it life ? Perhaps I lived before
In some strange world where first my soul was shaped,
And all this passionate love, and joy, and pain,
That come, I know not whence, and sway my deeds,
Are old imperious memories, blind yet strong,
That this world stirs within me; as this chain
Stirs some strange certainty of visions gone,
And all my mind is as an eye that stares
Into the darkness painfully.

> (*While* Fedalma *has been looking at the necklace,*
> Juan *has entered, and finding himself unobserved*
> *by her, says at last,*)

> Señora !

Fedalma (*starts, and gathering the necklace together, turns*
round).
Oh, Juan, it is you !

Juan.   I met the Duke –
Had waited long without, no matter why –
And when he ordered one to wait on you
And carry forth a burthen you would give,
I prayed for leave to be the servitor.
Don Silva owes me twenty granted wishes
That I have never tendered, lacking aught
That I could wish for and a Duke could grant;
But this one wish to serve you, weighs as much
As twenty other longings.

Fedalma (*smiling*).   That sounds well.
You turn your speeches prettily as songs.
But I will not forget the many days
You have neglected me. Your pupil learns
But little from you now. Her studies flag.

The Duke says, "That is idle Juan's way:
Poets must rove — are honey-sucking birds
And know not constancy."   Said he quite true ?

JUAN.   O lady, constancy has kind and rank.
One man's is lordly, plump, and bravely clad,
Holds its head high, and tells the world its name:
Another man's is beggared, must go bare,
And shiver through the world, the jest of all,
But that it puts the motley on, and plays
Itself the jester.   But I see you hold
The Gypsy's necklace: it is quaintly wrought.

FEDALMA.   The Gypsy's ?   Do you know its history ?

JUAN.   No farther back than when I saw it taken
From off its wearer's neck — the Gypsy chief's.

FEDALMA (*eagerly*).
What ! he who paused, at tolling of the bell,
Before me in the Plaça ?

JUAN.   Yes, I saw
His look fixed on you.

FEDALMA.   Know you aught of him ?

JUAN.   Something and nothing — as I know the sky,
Or some great story of the olden time
That hides a secret.   I have oft talked with him.
He seems to say much, yet is but a wizard
Who draws down rain by sprinkling; throws me out
Some pregnant text that urges comment; casts
A sharp-hooked question, baited with such skill
It needs must catch the answer.

FEDALMA.   It is hard
    That such a man should be a prisoner –
    Be chained to work.

JUAN.   Oh, he is dangerous !
    Granáda with this Zarca for a king
    Might still maim Christendom. He is of those
    Who steal the keys from snoring Destiny
    And make the prophets lie. A Gypsy, too,
    Suckled by hunted beasts, whose mother-milk
    Has filled his veins with hate.

FEDALMA.   I thought his eyes
    Spoke not of hatred – seemed to say he bore
    The pain of those who never could be saved.
    What if the Gypsies are but savage beasts
    And must be hunted ? – let them be set free,
    Have benefit of chase, or stand at bay
    And fight for life and offspring. Prisoners !
    Oh ! they have made their fires beside the streams,
    Their walls have been the rocks, the pillared pines,
    Their roof the living sky that breathes with light:
    They may well hate a cage, like strong-winged birds,
    Like me, who have no wings, but only wishes.
    I will beseech the Duke to set them free.

JUAN. Pardon me, lady, if I seem to warn,
    Or try to play the sage. What if the Duke
    Loved not to hear of Gypsies ? if their name
    Were poisoned for him once, being used amiss ?
    I speak not as of fact. Our nimble souls
    Can spin an insubstantial universe
    Suiting our mood, and call it possible,
    Sooner than see one grain with eye exact
    And give strict record of it. Yet by chance

Our fancies may be truth and make us seers.
'Tis a rare teeming world, so harvest-full,
Even guessing ignorance may pluck some fruit.
Note what I say no farther than will stead
The siege you lay. I would not seem to tell
Aught that the Duke may think and yet withhold:
It were a trespass in me.

FEDALMA.   Fear not, Juan.
Your words bring daylight with them when you speak
I understand your care. But I am brave –
Oh ! and so cunning ! – always I prevail.
Now, honoured Troubadour, if you will be
Your pupil's servant, bear this casket hence.
Nay, not the necklace: it is hard to place.
Pray go before me; Iñez will be there.

                    (*Exit* JUAN *with the casket*.)

FEDALMA (*looking again at the necklace*).
It is *his* past clings to you, not my own.
If we have each our angels, good and bad,
Fates, separate from ourselves, who act for us
When we are blind, or sleep, then this man's fate,
Hovering about the thing he used to wear,
Has laid its grasp on mine appealingly.
Dangerous, is he ? – well, a Spanish knight
Would have his enemy strong – defy, not bind him.
I can dare all things when my soul is moved
By something hidden that possesses me.
If Silva said this man must keep his chains
I should find ways to free him – disobey
And free him as I did the birds. But no !
As soon as we are wed, I'll put my prayer,
And he will not deny me: he is good.

284

Oh, I shall have much power as well as joy !
Duchess Fedalma may do what she will.

A Street by the Castle. Juan *leans against a parapet, in
moonlight, and touches his lute half unconsciously.*
Pepita *stands on tiptoe watching him, and then advances
till her shadow falls in front of him. He looks towards
her. A piece of white drapery thrown over her head
catches the moonlight.*

Juan. Ha ! my Pepíta ! see how thin and long
  Your shadow is. 'Tis so your ghost will be,
  When you are dead.

Pepita (*crossing herself*). Dead ! O the blessed saints !
  You would be glad, then, if Pepíta died ?

Juan. Glad ! why ? Dead maidens are not merry. Ghosts
  Are doleful company. I like you living.

Pepita. I think you like me not. I wish you did.
  Sometimes you sing to me and make me dance
  Another time you take no heed of me,
  Not though I kiss my hand to you and smile.
  But Andrès would be glad if I kissed *him*.

Juan. My poor Pepíta, I am old.

Pepita.   No, no.
  You have no wrinkles.

Juan.   Yes, I have – within;
  The wrinkles are within, my little bird.
  Why, I have lived through twice a thousand years,

285

And kept the company of men whose bones
Crumbled before the blessed Virgin lived.

PEPITA (*crossing herself*).
Nay, God defend us, that is wicked talk !
You say it but to scorn me. (*With a sob*) I will go.

JUAN. Stay, little pigeon. I am not unkind.
Come, sit upon the wall. Nay, never cry.
Give me your cheek to kiss. There, cry no more !

(PEPITA, *sitting on the low parapet, puts up her
cheek to* JUAN, *who kisses it, putting his hand under
her chin. She takes his hand and kisses it.*)

PEPITA. I like to kiss your hand. It is so good –
So smooth and soft.

JUAN.   Well, well, I'll sing to you.

PEPITA. A pretty song, loving and merry ?

JUAN.   Yes.

(JUAN *sings.*)
> *Memory,*
> *Tell to me*
> *What is fair,*
> *Past compare,*
> > *In the land of Tubal ?*
>
> *Is it Spring's*
> *Lovely things,*
> *Blossoms white,*
> *Rosy dight ?*
> > *Then it is Pepita.*

Summer's crest
Red-gold tressed,
  Cornflowers peeping under ? –
Idle noons,
Lingering moons,
Sudden cloud,
Lightning's shroud,
Sudden rain,
Quick again
  Smiles where late was thunder ? –
Are all these
Made to please ?
  So too is Pepíta.

Autumn's prime,
Apple-time,
Smooth cheek round,
Heart all sound ? –
Is it this
You would kiss ?
  Then it is Pepíta.
You can bring
No sweet thing,
But my mind
Still shall find
  It is my Pepíta.

Memory
Says to me
It is she –
She is fair
Past compare
  In the land of Tubal.

PEPITA (*seizing* JUAN's *hand again*)
Oh, then, you do love me ?

JUAN.   Yes, in the song.

PEPITA (*sadly*). Not out of it ? – not love me out of it ?

JUAN. Only a little out of it, my bird.
When I was singing I was Andrès, say,
Or one who loves you better still than he.

PEPITA. Not yourself ?

JUAN.   No !

PEPÍTA (*throwing his hand down pettishly*).
                                        Then take it back again !
I will not have it !

JUAN.   Listen, little one.
Juan is not a living man by himself:
His life is breathed in him by other men,
And they speak out of him. He is their voice.
Juan's own life he gave once quite away.
Pepíta's lover sang that song – not Juan.
We old, old poets, if we kept our hearts,
Should hardly know them from another man's.
They shrink to make room for the many more
We keep within us. There, now – one more kiss,
And then go home again.

PEPITA (*a little frightened, after letting* JUAN *kiss her*).
                                        You are not wicked ?

JUAN. Ask your confessor – tell him what I said.

(PEPITA *goes, while* JUAN *thrums his lute again, and sings.*)

> Came a pretty maid
>   By the moon's pure light,
> Loved me well, she said,
>   Eyes with tears all bright,
>   A pretty maid !
>
> But too late she strayed,
>   Moonlight pure was there;
> She was nought but shade
> Hiding the more fair,
>   The heavenly maid !

A vaulted room all stone. The light shed from a high lamp. Wooden chairs, a desk, book-shelves. The PRIOR, *in white frock, a black rosary with a crucifix of ebony and ivory at his side, is walking up and down, holding a written paper in his hands, which are clasped behind him.*

What if this witness lies ? he says he heard her
Counting her blasphemies on a rosary,
And in a bold discourse with Salomo,
Say that the Host was nought but ill-mixed flour,
That it was mean to pray — she never prayed.
I know the man who wrote this for a cur,
Who follows Don Diego, sees life's good
In scraps my nephew flings to him. What then ?
Particular lies may speak a general truth.
I guess him false, but know her heretic —
Know her for Satan's instrument, bedecked
With heathenish charms, luring the souls of men

To damning trust in good unsanctified.
Let her be prisoned – questioned – she will give
Witness against herself, that were this false . . .
> (*He looks at the paper again and reads, then again
> thrusts it behind him.*)

The matter and the colour are not false:
The form concerns the witness not the judge;
For proof is gathered by the sifting mind,
Not given in crude and formal circumstance.
Suspicion is a heaven-sent lamp, and I –
I, watchman of the Holy Office, bear
That lamp in trust. I will keep faithful watch.
The Holy Inquisition's discipline;
Is mercy, saving her, if penitent –
God grant it ! – else – root up the poison-plant,
Though 'twere a lily with a golden heart !
This spotless maiden with her pagan soul
Is the arch-enemy's trap: he turns his back
On all the prostitutes, and watches her
To see her poison men with false belief
In rebel virtues. She has poisoned Silva;
His shifting mind, dangerous in fitfulness,
Strong in the contradiction of itself,
Carries his young ambitions wearily,
As holy vows regretted. Once he seemed
The fresh-oped flower of Christian knighthood, born
For feats of holy daring; and I said:
"That half of life which I, as monk, renounce,
Shall be fulfilled in him: Silva will be
That saintly noble, that wise warrior,
That blameless excellence in worldly gifts
I would have been, had I not asked to live
The higher life of man impersonal
Who reigns o'er all things by refusing all."
What is his promise now ? Apostasy

From every high intent: − languid, nay, gone,
The prompt devoutness of a generous heart,
The strong obedience of a reverent will,
That breathes the Church's air and sees her light,
He peers and strains with feeble questioning,
Or else he jests. He thinks I know it not −
I who have read the history of his lapse,
As clear as it is writ in the angel's book.
He will defy me − flings great words at me −
Me who have governed all our house's acts,
Since I, a stripling, ruled his stripling father.
This maiden is the cause, and if they wed,
The Holy War may count a captain lost.
For better he were dead than keep his place,
And fill it infamously: in God's war
Slackness is infamy. Shall I stand by
And let the tempter win ? defraud Christ's cause,
And blot his banner ? − all for scruples weak
Of pity towards their young and frolicsome blood;
Or nice discrimination of the tool
By which my hand shall work a sacred rescue ?
The fence of rules is for the purblind crowd;
They walk by averaged precepts: sovereign men,
Seeing by God's light, see the general
By seeing all the special − own no rule
But their full vision of the moment's worth.
'Tis so God governs, using wicked men −
Nay, scheming fiends, to work his purposes.
Evil that good may come ? Measure the good
Before you say what's evil. Perjury ?
I scorn the perjurer, but I will use him
To serve the holy truth. There is no lie
Save in his soul, and let his soul be judged.
I know the truth, and act upon the truth.

O God, thou knowest that my will is pure.
Thy servant owns nought for himself, his wealth
Is but obedience. And I have sinned
In keeping small respects of human love –
Calling it mercy. Mercy ? Where evil is
True mercy holds a sword. Mercy would save.
Save whom ? Save serpents, locusts, wolves ?
Or out of pity let the idiots gorge
Within a famished town ? Or save the gains
Of men who trade in poison lest they starve ?
Save all things mean and foul that clog the earth
Stifling the better? Save the fools who cling
For refuge round their hideous idol's limbs,
So leave the idol grinning unconsumed,
And save the fools to breed idolaters ?
O mercy worthy of the licking hound
That knows no future but its feeding time !
Mercy has eyes that pierce the ages – sees
From heights divine of the eternal purpose
Far-scattered consequence in its vast sum;
Chooses to save, but with illumined vision
Sees that to save is greatly to destroy.
'Tis so the Holy Inquisition sees: its wrath
Is fed from the strong heart of wisest love.
For love must needs make hatred. He who loves
God and his law must hate the foes of God.
And I have sinned in being merciful:
Being slack in hate, I have been slack in love.
  (*He takes the crucfix and holds it up before him.*)
Thou shuddering, bleeding, thirsting, dying God,
Thou Man of Sorrows, scourged and bruised and torn,
Suffering to save – wilt thou not judge the world ?
This arm which held the children, this pale hand
That gently touched the eyelids of the blind,
And opened passive to the cruel nail,

Shall one day stretch to leftward of thy throne,
Charged with the power that makes the lightning strong,
And hurl thy foes to everlasting hell.
And thou, Immaculate Mother, Virgin mild,
Thou sevenfold-pierced, thou pitying, pleading Queen,
Shalt see and smile, while the black filthy souls
Sink with foul weight to their eternal place,
Purging the Holy Light. Yea, I have sinned
And called it mercy. But I shrink no more.
To-morrow morn this temptress shall be safe
Under the Holy Inquisition's key.
He thinks to wed her, and defy me then,
She being shielded by our house's name.
But he shall never wed her. I have said.
The time is come. *Exurge, Domine,*
Judica causam tuam. Let thy foes
Be driven as the smoke before the wind,
And melt like wax upon the furnace lip !

*A large chamber richly furnished opening on a
terrace-garden, the trees visible through the window in
faint moonlight. Flowers hanging about the window, lit
up by the tapers. The casket of jewels open on a table.
The gold necklace lying near.* FEDALMA, *splendidly dressed
and adorned with pearls and rubies, is walking up and
down.*

So soft a night was never made for sleep,
But for the waking of the finer sense
To every murmuring and gentle sound,
To subtlest odours, pulses, visitings
That touch our frames with wings too delicate
To be discerned amid the blare of day.

(She pauses near the window to gather some jasmine: then walks again.)

Surely these flowers keep happy watch – their breath
Is their fond memory of the loving light.
I often rue the hours I lose in sleep:
It is a bliss too brief, only to see
This glorious world, to hear the voice of love,
To feel the touch, the breath of tenderness,
And then to rest as from a spectacle.
I need the curtained stillness of the night
To live through all my happy hours again
With more selection – cull them quite away
From blemished moments. Then in loneliness
The face that bent before me in the day
Rises in its own light, more vivid seems
Painted upon the dark, and ceaseless glows
With sweet solemnity of gazing love,
Till like the heavenly blue it seems to grow
Nearer, more kindred, and more cherishing,
Mingling with all my being. Then the words,
The tender low-toned words come back again,
With repetition welcome as the chime
Of softly hurrying brooks – "My only love –
My love while life shall last – my own Fedalma !"
Oh it is mine – the joy that once has been !
Poor eager hope is but a stammerer,
Must listen dumbly to great memory,
Who makes our bliss the sweeter by her telling.

(She pauses a moment musingly.)

But that dumb hope is still a sleeping guard
Whose quiet rhythmic breath saves me from dread
In this fair paradise. For if the earth
Broke off with flower-fringed edge, visibly sheer
Leaving no footing for my forward step
But empty blackness . . .

Nay, there is no fear –
They will renew themselves, day and my joy,
And all that past which is securely mine,
Will be the hidden root that nourishes
Our still unfolding, ever-ripening love !
  (*While she is uttering the last words, a little bird*
  falls softly on the floor behind her; she hears the
  light sound of its fall, and turns round.)
Did something enter? . . . .

                    Yes, this little bird . . . .
        (*She lifts it.*)
Dead and yet warm; 'twas seeking sanctuary,
And died, perhaps of fright, at the altar foot.
Stay, there is something tied beneath the wing !
A strip of linen, streaked with blood – what blood ?
The streaks are written words – are sent to me –
O God, are sent to me ! *Dear child, Fedalma,*
Be brave, give no alarm – your Father comes !
    (*She lets the bird fall again.*)
My Father . . . comes . . . my Father . . .

  (*She turns in quivering expectation toward the*
  window. There is perfect stillness a few moments
  until Zarca *appears at the window. He enters*
  quickly and noiselessly; then stands still at his full
  height, and at a distance from Fedalma.)

Fedalma (*In a low distinct tone of terror*).

                              It is he !

I said his fate had laid its hold on mine.

Zarca (*advancing a step or two*).
  You know, then, who I am ?

295

FEDALMA   The prisoner –
  He whom I saw in fetters – and this necklace. . . .

ZARCA. Was played with by your fingers when it hung
  About my neck, full fifteen years ago.

FEDALMA (*looking at the necklace and handling it, then
  speaking, as if unconsciously*).
  Full fifteen years ago !

ZARCA.   The very day
  I lost you, when you wore a tiny gown
  Of scarlet cloth with golden broidery:
  'Twas clasped in front by coins – two golden coins.
  The one upon the left was split in two
  Across the king's head, right from brow to nape,
  A dent i' the middle nicking in the cheek.
  You see I know the little gown by heart.

FEDALMA (*growing paler and more tremulous*).
  Yes.   It is true – I have the gown – the clasps –
  The braid – sore tarnished: – it is long ago !

ZARCA. But yesterday to me; for till to-day
  I saw you always as that little child.
  And when they took my necklace from me, still
  Your fingers played about it on my neck,
  And still those buds of fingers on your feet
  Caught in its meshes as you seemed to climb
  Up to my shoulder.   You were not stolen all.
  You had a double life fed from my heart. . . .
      (FEDALMA, *letting fall the necklace, makes an
      impulsive movement towards him, with outstretched
      hands*.)
  The Gypsy father loves his children well.

FEDALMA (*shrinking, trembling, and letting fall her hands*).
How came it that you sought me – no – I mean
How came it that you knew me – that you lost me ?

ZARCA (*standing perfectly still*).
Poor child ! I see – your father and his rags
Are welcome as the piercing wintry wind
Within this silken chamber. It is well.
I would not have a child who stooped to feign,
And aped a sudden love. Better, true hate.

FEDALMA (*raising her eyes towards him, with a flash of
admiration, and looking at him fixedly*).
Father, how was it that we lost each other ?

ZARCA. I lost you as a man may lose a gem
Wherein he has compressed his total wealth,
Or the right hand whose cunning makes him great:
I lost you by a trivial accident.
Marauding Spaniards sweeping like a storm
Over a spot within the Moorish bounds,
Near where our camp lay, doubtless snatched you up,
When Zind, your nurse, as she confessed, was urged
By burning thirst to wander toward the stream
And leave you on the sand some paces off
Playing with pebbles, while she dog-like lapped.
'Twas so I lost you – never saw you more
Until to-day I saw you dancing ! Saw
The daughter of the Zíncalo make sport
For those who spit upon her people's name.

FEDALMA (*vehemently*).
It was not sport. What if the world looked on ?
I danced for joy – for love of all the world
But when you looked at me my joy was stabbed –

Stabbed with your pain. I wondered . . . now I know . .
It was my father's pain.

> (*She pauses a moment with eyes bent downward,
> during which* ZARCA *examines her face. Then she
> says quickly,*)

                              How were you sure
At once I was your child ?

ZARCA.   I had witness strong
  As any Cadi needs, before I saw you !
  I fitted all my memories with the chat
  Of one named Juan – one whose rapid talk
  Showers like the blossoms from a light-twigged shrub,
  If you but cough beside it. I learned all
  The story of your Spanish nurture – all
  The promise of your fortune. When at last
  I fronted you, my little maid full-grown,
  Belief was turned to vision: then I saw
  That she whom Spaniards called the bright Fedalma –
  The little red-frocked foundling three years old –
  Grown to such perfectness the Spanish Duke
  Had wooed her for his Duchess – was the child,
  Sole offspring of my flesh, that Lambra bore
  One hour before, the Christian, hunting us,
  Hurried her on to death. Therefore I sought –
  Therefore I come to claim you – claim my child,
  Not from the Spaniard, not from him who robbed,
  But from herself.

> (FEDALMA *has gradually approached close to* ZARCA,
> *and with a low sob sinks on her knees before him.
> He stoops to kiss her brow and lays his hands on
> her head.*)

ZARCA (*with solemn tenderness*).
Then my child owns her father ?

FEDALMA.   Father ! yes.
I will eat dust before I will deny
The flesh I spring from.

ZARCA.   There my daughter spoke.
Away then with these rubies !
       (*He seizes the circlet of rubies and flings it on the
       ground.*   FEDALMA, *starting from the ground with
       strong emotion, shrinks backward.*)
                              Such a crown
Is infamy around a Zíncala's brow.
It is her people's blood, decking her shame.

FEDALMA   (*after a moment, slowly and distinctly, as if
   accepting a doom*).
Then . . . I was born . . . a Zíncala ?

ZARCA.   Of a blood
Unmixed as virgin wine juice.

FEDALMA.   Of a race
More outcast and despised than Moor or Jew ?

ZARCA. Yes: wanderers whom no God took knowledge of
To give them laws, to fight for them, or blight
Another race to make them ampler room;
Who have no Whence or Whither in their souls,
No dimmest lore of glorious ancestors
To make a common hearth for piety.

FEDALMA. A race that lives on prey as foxes do
With stealthy, petty rapine: so despised,

299

It is not persecuted, only spurned,
Crushed underfoot, warred on by chance like rats,
Or swarming flies, or reptiles of the sea
Dragged in the net unsought, and flung far off
To perish as they may ?

ZARCA   You paint us well.
So abject are the men whose blood we share:
Untutored, unbefriended, unendowed;
No favourites of heaven or of men.
Therefore I cling to them ! Therefore no lure
Shall draw me to disown them, or forsake
The meagre wandering herd that lows for help
And needs me for its guide, to seek my pasture
Among the well-fed beeves that graze at will.
Because our race has no great memories,
I will so live, it shall remember me
For deeds of such divine beneficence
As rivers have, that teach men what is good
By blessing them. I have been schooled – have caught
Lore from the Hebrew, deftness from the Moor –
Know the rich heritage, the milder life,
Of nations fathered by a mighty Past;
But were our race accursed (as they who make
Good luck a god count all unlucky men)
I would espouse their curse sooner than take
My gifts from brethren naked of all good,
And lend them to the rich for usury.

(FEDALMA *again advances, and putting forth her right
hand grasps* ZARCA'S *left. He places his other hand
on her shoulder. They stand so, looking at each
other.*)

300

ZARCA. And you, my child ? are you of other mind,
Choosing forgetfulness, hating the truth
That says you are akin to needy men ? –
Wishing your father were some Christian Duke,
Who could hang Gypsies when their task was done
While you, his daughter, were not bound to care ?

FEDALMA (*in a troubled eager voice*).
No, I should always care – I cared for you –
For all, before I dreamed . . . .

ZARCA.   Before you dreamed
That you were born a Zíncala – your flesh
Stamped with your people's faith.

FEDALMA (*bitterly*).   The Gypsies' faith ?
Men say they have none.

ZARCA.   Oh, it is a faith
Taught by no priest, but by their beating hearts:
Faith to each other: the fidelity
Of fellow-wanderers in a desert place
Who share the same dire thirst, and therefore share
The scanty water: the fidelity
Of men whose pulses leap with kindred fire,
Who in the flash of eyes, the clasp of hands,
The speech that even in lying tells the truth
Of heritage inevitable as birth,
Nay, in the silent bodily presence feel
The mystic stirring of a common life
Which makes the many one: fidelity
To the consecrating oath our sponsor Fate
Made through our infant breath when we were born
The fellow-heirs of that small island, Life,
Where we must dig and sow and reap with brothers.

Fear thou that oath, my daughter – nay, not fear,
But love it; for the sanctity of oaths
Lies not in lightning that avenges them,
But in the injury wrought by broken bonds
And in the garnered good of human trust.
And you have sworn – even with your infant breath
You too were pledged . . . .

FEDALMA (*letting go* ZARCA's *hand, and sinking backward on her knees, with bent head, as if before some impending crushing weight*).

To what ? what have I sworn ?

ZARCA. To take the heirship of the Gypsy's child:
The child of him who, being chief, will be
The saviour of his tribe, or if he fail
Will choose to fail rather than basely win
The prize of renegades. Nay, will not choose –
Is there a choice for strong souls to be weak ?
For men erect to crawl like hissing snakes ?
I choose not – I *am* Zarca. Let him choose
Who halts and wavers, having appetite
To feed on garbage. You, my child – are you
Halting and wavering ?

FEDALMA (*raising her head*). Say what is my task.

ZARCA. To be the angel of a homeless tribe:
To help me bless a race taught by no prophet
And make their name, now but a badge of scorn,
A glorious banner floating in their midst,
Stirring the air they breathe with impulses
Of generous pride, exalting fellowship
Until it soars to magnanimity.
I'll guide my brethren forth to their new land,

Where they shall plant and sow and reap their own,
Serving each other's needs, and so be spurred
To skill in all the arts that succour life;
Where we may kindle our first altar-fire
From settled hearths, and call our Holy Place
The hearth that binds us in one family.
That land awaits them: they await their chief –
Me who am prisoned. All depends on you.

FEDALMA (*rising to her full height, and looking solemnly at* ZARCA).
Father, your child is ready ! She will not
Forsake her kindred: she will brave all scorn
Sooner than scorn herself. Let Spaniards all,
Christians, Jews, Moors, shoot out the lip and say,
"Lo, the first hero in a tribe of thieves."
Is it not written so of them? They, too,
Were slaves, lost, wandering, sunk beneath a curse,
Till Moses, Christ, and Mahomet were born,
Till beings lonely in their greatness lived,
And lived to save their people. Father, listen.
The Duke to-morrow weds me secretly:
But straight he will present me as his wife
To all his household, cavaliers and dames
And noble pages. Then I will declare
Before them all, "I am his daughter, his,
The Gypsy's, owner of this golden badge."
Then I shall win your freedom; then the Duke –
Why, he will be your son ! – will send you forth
With aid and honours. Then, before all eyes
I'll clasp this badge on you, and lift my brow
For you to kiss it, saying by that sign,
"I glory in my father." This, to-morrow.

ZARCA. A woman's dream – who thinks by smiling well
To ripen figs in frost. What ! marry first,
And then proclaim your birth ? Enslave yourself
To use your freedom ? Share another's name,
Then treat it as you will ? How will that tune
Ring in your bridegroom's ears – that sudden song
Of triumph in your Gypsy father ?

FEDALMA (*discouraged*).   Nay,
I meant not so. We marry hastily –
Yet there is time – there will be: – in less space
Than he can take to look at me, I'll speak
And tell him all. Oh, I am not afraid !
His love for me is stronger than all hate;
Nay, stronger than my love, which cannot sway
Demons that haunt me – tempt me to rebel.
Were he Fedalma and I Silva, he
Could love confession, prayers, and tonsured monks
If my soul craved them. He will never hate
The race that bore him what he loves the most.
I shall but do more strongly what I will,
Having his will to help me. And to-morrow,
Father, as surely as this heart shall beat,
You – every Gypsy chained, shall be set free.

ZARCA (*coming nearer to her, and laying his hand on her
shoulder*).
Too late, too poor a service that, my child !
Not so the woman who would save her tribe
Must help its heroes – not by wordy breath,
By easy prayers strong in a lover's ear,
By showering wreaths and sweets and wafted kisses,
And then, when all the smiling work is done,
Turning to rest upon her down again,
And whisper languid pity for her race

304

Upon the bosom of her alien spouse.
Not to such petty mercies as can fall
'Twixt stitch and stitch of silken broidery,
Such miracles of mitred saints who pause
Beneath their gilded canopy to heal
A man sun-stricken: not to such trim merit
As soils its dainty shoes for charity
And simpers meekly at the pious stain,
But never trod with naked bleeding feet
Where no man praised it, and where no Church blessed:
Not to such almsdeeds fit for holidays
Were you, my daughter, consecrated – bound
By laws that, breaking, you will dip your bread
In murdered brother's blood and call it sweet –
When you were born beneath the dark man's tent,
And lifted up in sight of all your tribe,
Who greeted you with shouts of loyal joy,
Sole offspring of the chief in whom they trust
As in the oft-tried never-failing flint
They strike their fire from. Other work is yours.

FEDALMA. What work ? – what is it that you ask of me ?

ZARCA. A work as pregnant as the act of men
Who set their ships aflame and spring to land,
A fatal deed . . . .

FEDALMA.   Stay ! never utter it !
If it can part my lot from his whose love
Has chosen me. Talk not of oaths, of birth,
Of men as numerous as the dim white stars –
As cold and distant, too, for my heart's pulse.
No ills on earth, though you should count them up
With grains to make a mountain, can outweigh
For me, his ill who is my supreme love.

All sorrows else are but imagined flames,
Making me shudder at an unfelt smart;
But his imagined sorrow is a fire
That scorches me.

ZARCA.   I know, I know it well –
The first young passionate wail of spirits called
To some great destiny. In vain, my daughter !
Lay the young eagle in what nest you will,
The cry and swoop of eagles overhead
Vibrate prophetic in its kindred frame,
And make it spread its wings and poise itself
For the eagle's flight. Hear what you have to do.
    (FEDALMA *stands half averted, as if she dreaded the
    effect of his looks and words*.)
My comrades even now file off their chains
In a low turret by the battlements,
Where we were locked with slight and sleepy guard –
We who had files hid in our shaggy hair,
And possible ropes that waited but our will
In half our garments. Oh, the Moorish blood
Runs thick and warm to us, though thinned by chrism.
I found a friend among our gaolers – one
Who loves the Gypsy as the Moor's ally.
I know the secrets of this fortress. Listen.
Hard by yon terrace is a narrow stair,
Cut in the living rock, and at one point
In its slow straggling course it branches off
Towards a low wooden door, that art has bossed
To such unevenness, it seems one piece
With the rough-hewn rock. Open that door, it leads
Through a broad passage burrowed under-ground
A good half-mile out to the open plain:
Made for escape, in dire extremity
From siege or burning, of the house's wealth

306

In women or in gold. To find that door
Needs one who knows the number of the steps
Just to the turning-point; to open it,
Needs one who knows the secret of the bolt.
You have that secret: you will ope that door,
And fly with us.

FEDALMA (*receding a little, and gathering herself up in an*
attitude of resolve opposite to ZARCA
              No, I will never fly !
Never forsake that chief half of my soul
Where lies my love. I swear to set you free.
Ask for no more; it is not possible.
Father, my soul is not too base to ring
At touch of your great thoughts; nay, in my blood
There streams the sense unspeakable of kind,
As leopard feels at ease with leopard. But –
Look at these hands ! You say when they were little
They played about the gold upon your neck.
I do believe it, for their tiny pulse
Made record of it in the inmost coil
Of growing memory. But see them now !
Oh, they have made fresh record; twined themselves
With other throbbing hands whose pulses feed
Not memories only but a blended life –
Life that will bleed to death if it be severed.
Have pity on me, father ! Wait the morning;
Say you will wait the morning. I will win
Your freedom openly: you shall go forth
With aid and honours, Silva will deny
Nought to my asking . . . .

ZARCA (*with contemptuous decision*).
              Till you ask him aught
Wherein he is powerless. Soldiers even now

Murmur against him that he risks the town,
And forfeits all the prizes of a foray
To get his bridal pleasure with a bride
Too low for him. They'll murmur more and louder
If captives of our pith and sinew, fit
For all the work the Spaniard hates, are freed –
Now, too, when Spanish hands are scanty. What,
Turn Gypsies loose instead of hanging them !
'Tis flat against the edict. Nay, perchance
Murmurs aloud may turn to silent threats
Of some well-sharpened dagger; for your Duke
Has to his heir a pious cousin, who deems
The Cross were better served if he were Duke.
Such good you'll work your lover by your prayers.

FEDALMA. Then, I will free you now ! You shall be safe,
Nor he be blamed, save for his love to me.
I will declare what I have done: the deed
May put our marriage off . . . .

ZARCA.   Ay, till the time
When you shall be a queen in Africa,
And he be prince enough to sue for you.
You cannot free us and come back to him.

FEDALMA. And why ?

ZARCA.   I would compel you to go forth.

FEDALMA. You tell me that ?

ZARCA.   Yes, for I'd have you choose;
Though, being of the blood you are – my blood –
You have no right to choose.

FEDALMA.   I only owe
    A daughter's debt; I was not born a slave.

ZARCA. No, not a slave; but you were born to reign.
    'Tis a compulsion of a higher sort,
    Whose fetters are the net invisible
    That hold all life together. Royal deeds
    May make long destinies for multitudes,
    And you are called to do them. You belong
    Not to the petty round of circumstance
    That makes a woman's lot, but to your tribe,
    Who trust in me and in my blood with trust
    That men call blind; but it is only blind
    As unyeaned reason is, that grows and stirs
    Within the womb of superstition.

FEDALMA.   No !
    I belong to him who loves me – whom I love –
    Who chose me – whom I chose – to whom I pledged
    A woman's truth. And that is nature too,
    Issuing a fresher law than laws of birth.

ZARCA. Unmake yourself, then, from a Zíncala –
    Unmake yourself from being child of mine !
    Take holy water, cross your dark skin white;
    Round your proud eyes to foolish kitten looks;
    Walk mincingly, and smirk, and twitch your robe:
    Unmake yourself – doff all the eagle plumes
    And be a parrot, chained to a ring that slips
    Upon a Spaniard's thumb, at will of his
    That you should prattle o'er his words again !
    Get a small heart that flutters at the smiles
    Of that plump penitent, that greedy saint –
    Who breaks all treaties in the name of God,
    Saves souls by confiscation, sends to heaven

The altar-fumes of burning heretics,
And chaffers with the Levite for the gold;
Holds Gypsies beasts unfit for sacrifice,
So sweeps them out like worms alive or dead.
Go, trail your gold and velvet in her court ! –
A conscious Zíncala, smile at your rare luck,
While half your brethren . . . .

FEDALMA.   I am not so vile !
It is not to such mockeries that I cling,
Not to the flaring tow of gala-lights;
It is to him – my love – the face of day.

ZARCA. What, will you part him from the air he breathes,
Never inhale with him although you kiss him ?
Will you adopt a soul without its thoughts,
Or grasp a life apart from flesh and blood ?
Till then you cannot wed a Spanish Duke
And not wed shame at mention of your race,
And not wed hardness to their miseries –
Nay, not wed murder. Would you save my life
Yet stab my purpose ? maim my every limb,
Put out my eyes, and turn me loose to feed ?
Is that salvation ? rather drink my blood.
That child of mine who weds my enemy –
Adores a God who took no heed of Gypsies –
Forsakes her people, leaves their poverty
To join the luckier crowd that mocks their woes –
That child of mine is doubly murderess,
Murdering her father's hope, her people's trust.
Such draughts are mingled in your cup of love !
And when you have become a thing so poor,
Your life is all a fashion without law
Save frail conjecture of a changing wish,
Your worshipped sun, your smiling face of day,

Will turn to cloudiness, and you will shiver
In your thin finery of vain desire.
Men call his passion madness; and he, too,
May learn to think it madness: 'tis a thought
Of ducal sanity.

FEDALMA.   No, he is true !
And if I part from him I part from joy.
Oh, it was morning with us – I seemed young.
But now I know I am an aged sorrow –
My people's sorrow. Father, since I am yours –
Since I must walk an unslain sacrifice,
Carrying the knife within me, quivering –
Put cords upon me, drag me to the doom
My birth has laid upon me. See, I kneel:
I cannot will to go.

ZARCA.   Will then to stay !
Say you will take your better, painted such
By blind desire, and choose the hideous worse
For thousands who were happier but for you.
My thirty followers are assembled now
Without this terrace: I your father wait
That you may lead us forth to liberty –
Restore me to my tribe – five hundred men
Whom I alone can save, alone can rule,
And plant them as a mighty nation's seed.
Why, vagabonds who clustered round one man,
Their voice of God, their prophet and their king,
Twice grew to empire on the teeming shores
Of Africa, and sent new royalties
To feed afresh the Arab sway in Spain.
My vagabonds are a seed more generous,
Quick as the serpent, loving as the hound,
And beautiful as disinherited gods.

They have a promised land beyond the sea
There I may lead them, raise my standard call
The wandering Zíncali to that new home
And make a nation – bring light, order, law,
Instead of chaos. You, my only heir,
Are called to reign for me when I am gone.
Now choose your deed: to save or to destroy.
You, a born Zíncala, you, fortunate
Above your fellows – you who hold a curse
Or blessing in the hollow of your hand –
Say you will loose that hand from fellowship,
Let go the rescuing rope, hurl all the tribes,
Children and countless beings yet to come,
Down from the upward path of light and joy,
Back to the dark and marshy wilderness
Where life is nought but blind tenacity
Of that which is. Say you will curse your race !

FEDALMA (*rising and stretching out her arms in
    deprecation*).
No, no – I will not say it – I will go !
Father, I choose ! I will not take a heaven
Haunted by shrieks of far-off misery.
This deed and I have ripened with the hours
It is a part of me – a wakened thought
That, rising like a giant, masters me,
And grows into a doom. O mother life,
That seemed to nourish me so tenderly,
Even in the womb you vowed me to the fire,
Hung on my soul the burden of men's hopes,
And pledged me to redeem ! – I'll pay the debt.
You gave me strength that I should pour it all
Into this anguish. I can never shrink
Back into bliss – my heart has grown too big
With things that might be. Father, I will go.

I will strip off these gems. Some happier bride
Shall wear them, since Fedalma would be dowered
With nought but curses, dowered with misery
Of men — of women, who have hearts to bleed
As hers is bleeding.

   (*She sinks on a seat, and begins to take off her
   jewels.*)

                      Now, good gems, we part.
Speak of me always tenderly to Silva.

   (*She pauses, turning to* Zarca.)
O father, will the women of our tribe
Suffer as I do, in the years to come
When you have made them great in Africa ?
Redeemed from ignorant ills only to feel
A conscious woe ? Then — is it worth the pains ?
Were it not better when we reach that shore
To raise a funeral-pile and perish all,
So closing up a myriad avenues
To misery yet unwrought ? My soul is faint —
Will these sharp pangs buy any certain good ?

Zarca. Nay, never falter: no great deed is done
By falterers who ask for certainty.
No good is certain, but the steadfast mind,
The undivided will to seek the good:
'Tis that compels the elements, and wrings
A human music from the indifferent air.
The greatest gift the hero leaves his race
Is to have been a hero. Say we fail ! —
We feed the high tradition of the world,
And leave our spirit in our children's breasts.

Fedalma   (*unclasping her jewelled belt, and throwing it
   down*).
Yes, say that we shall fail ! I will not count

On aught but being faithful. I will take
This yearning self of mine and strangle it.
I will not be half-hearted: never yet
Fedalma did aught with a wavering soul.
Die, my young joy — die, all my hungry hopes —
The milk you cry for from the breast of life
Is thick with curses. Oh, all fatness here
Snatches its meat from leanness — feeds on graves.
I will seek nothing but to shun base joy.
The saints were cowards who stood by to see
Christ crucified: they should have flung themselves
Upon the Roman spears, and died in vain —
The grandest death, to die in vain — for love
Greater than sways the forces of the world !
That death shall be my bridegroom. I will wed
The curse that blights my people. Father, come !

ZARCA. No curse has fallen on us till we cease
To help each other. You, if you are false
To that first fellowship, lay on the curse:
But write now to the Spaniard: briefly say
That I, your father, came; that you obeyed
The fate which made you Zíncala, as his fate
Made him a Spanish duke and Christian knight.
He must not think . . .

FEDALMA   Yes, I will write, but he —
Oh, he would know it — he would never think
The chain that dragged me from him could be aught
But scorching iron entering in my soul.
                (She writes.)
Silva, sole love — he came — my father came.
I am the daughter of the Gypsy chief
Who means to be the Saviour of our tribe.
He calls on me to live for his great end.

314

To live ? nay, die for it. Fedalma dies
In leaving Silva: all that lives henceforth
Is the poor Zíncala.

(*She rises.*)

Father, now I go
To wed my people's lot.

ZARCA.   To wed a crown.
Our people's lowly lot we will make royal –
Give it a country, homes, and monuments
Held sacred through the lofty memories
That we shall leave behind us. Come, my Queen !

FEDALMA. Stay, my betrothal ring ! – one kiss – farewell !
O love, you were my crown. No other crown
Is aught but thorns on my poor woman's brow.

BOOK II

SILVA was marching homeward while the moon
Still shed mild brightness like the far-off hope
Of those pale virgin lives that wait and pray.
The stars thin-scattered made the heavens large,
Bending in slow procession; in the east
Emergent from the dark waves of the hills,
Seeming a little sister of the moon,
Glowed Venus all unquenched. Silva, in haste,
Exultant and yet anxious, urged his troop
To quick and quicker march: he had delight
In forward stretching shadows, in the gleams
That travelled on the armour of the van,
And in the many-hoofed sound: in all that told
Of hurrying movement to o'ertake his thought
Already in Bedmár, close to Fedalma,
Leading her forth a wedded bride, fast vowed,
Defying Father Isidor. His glance
Took in with much content the priest who rode
Firm in his saddle, stalwart and broad-backed,
Crisp-curled, and comfortably secular,
Right in the front of him. But by degrees
Stealthily faint, disturbing with slow loss
That showed not yet full promise of a gain,
The light was changing, and the watch intense
Of moon and stars seemed weary, shivering:
The sharp white brightness passed from off the rocks
Carrying the shadows: beauteous Night lay dead
Under the pall of twilight, and the love-star
Sickened and shrank. The troop was winding now
Upward to where a pass between the peaks
Seemed like an opened gate – to Silva seemed
An outer-gate of heaven, for through that pass

They entered his own valley, near Bedmár.
Sudden within the pass a horseman rose,
One instant dark upon the banner pale
Of rock-cut sky, the next in motion swift
With hat and plume high shaken – ominous.
Silva had dreamed his future, and the dream
Held not this messenger. A minute more –
It was his friend Don Alvar whom he saw
Reining his horse up, face to face with him,
Sad as the twilight, all his clothes ill girt-
As if he had been roused to see one die,
And brought the news to him whom death had robbed.
Silva believed he saw the worst – the town
Stormed by the infidel – or, could it be
Fedalma dragged – no, there was not yet time.
But with a marble face, he only said,
"What evil, Alvar ?"

                     "What this paper speaks."
It was Fedalma's letter folded close
And mute as yet for Silva. But his friend
Keeping it still sharp-pinched against his breast,
"It will smite hard, my lord: a private grief.
I would not have you pause to read it here.
Let us ride on – we use the moments best,
Reaching the town with speed. The smaller ill
Is that our Gypsy prisoners have escaped."
"No more. Give me the paper – nay, I know –
'Twill make no difference. Bid them march on faster."
Silva pushed forward – held the paper crushed
Close in his right. "They have imprisoned her,"
He said to Alvar in low, hard-cut tones,
Like a dream-speech of slumbering revenge.
"No – when they came to fetch her she was gone."
Swift as the right touch on a spring, that word
Made Silva read the letter. She was gone !

But not into locked darkness – only gone
Into free air – where he might find her yet.
The bitter loss had triumph in it – what !
They would have seized her with their holy claws
The Prior's sweet morsel of despotic hate
Was snatched from off his lips. This misery
Had yet a taste of joy.

                       But she was gone !
The sun had risen, and in the castle walls
The light grew strong and stronger. Silva walked
Through the long corridor where dimness yet
Cherished a lingering, flickering, dying hope:
Fedalma still was there – he could not see
The vacant place that once her presence filled.
Can we believe that the dear dead are gone ?
Love in sad weeds forgets the funeral day,
Opens the chamber door and almost smiles –
Then sees the sunbeams pierce athwart the bed
Where the pale face is not. So Silva's joy,
Like the sweet habit of caressing hands
That seek the memory of another hand,
Still lived on fitfully in spite of words,
And, numbing thought with vague illusion, dulled
The slow and steadfast beat of certainty.
But in the rooms inexorable light
Streamed through the open window where she fled,
Streamed on the belt and coronet thrown down –
Mute witnesses – sought out the typic ring
That sparkled on the crimson, solitary,
Wounding him like a word. O hateful light !
It filled the chambers with her absence, glared
On all the motionless things her hand had touched,
Motionless all – save where old Iñez lay
Sunk on the floor holding her rosary,
Making its shadow tremble with her fear.

And Silva passed her by because she grieved:
It was the lute, the gems, the pictured heads,
He longed to crush, because they made no sign
But of insistance that she was not there,
She who had filled his sight and hidden them.
He went forth on the terrace tow'rd the stairs,
Saw the rained petals of the cistus flowers
Crushed by large feet; but on one shady spot
Far down the steps, where dampness made a home,
He saw a footprint delicate-slippered, small,
So dear to him, he searched for sister-prints,
Searched in the rock-hewn passage with a lamp
For other trace of her, and found a glove;
But not Fedalma's. It was Juan's glove,
Tasselled, perfumed, embroidered with his name,
A gift of dames. Then Juan, too, was gone ?
Full-mouthed conjecture, hurrying through the town,
Had spread the tale already: it was he
That helped the Gypsies' flight. He talked and sang
Of nothing but the Gypsies and Fedalma.
He drew the threads together, wove the plan;
Had lingered out by moonlight, had been seen
Strolling, as was his wont, within the walls,
Humming his ditties. So Don Alvar told,
Conveying outside rumour. But the Duke,
Making of haughtiness a visor closed,
Would show no agitated front in quest
Of small disclosures. What her writing bore
Had been enough. He knew that she was gone,
Knew why.

   "The Duke," some said, "will send a force,
Retake the prisoners, and bring back his bride."
But others, winking, "Nay, her wedding dress
Would be the *san-benito*. 'Tis a fight
Between the Duke and Prior. Wise bets will choose

The churchman: he's the iron, and the Duke . . . ."
"Is a fine piece of pottery," said mine host,
Softening the sarcasm with a bland regret.

There was the thread that in the new-made knot
Of obstinate circumstance seemed hardest drawn,
Vexed most the sense of Silva, in these hours
Of fresh and angry pain – there, in that fight
Against a foe whose sword was magical,
His shield invisible terrors – against a foe
Who stood as if upon the smoking mount
Ordaining plagues. All else, Fedalma's flight,
The father's claim, her Gypsy birth disclosed,
Were momentary crosses, hindrances
A Spanish noble might despise. This Chief
Might still be treated with, would not refuse
A proffered ransom, which would better serve
Gypsy prosperity, give him more power
Over his tribe, than any fatherhood:
Nay, all the father in him must plead loud
For marriage of his daughter where she loved –
Her love being placed so high and lustrously.
The Gypsy chieftain had foreseen a price
That would be paid him for his daughter's dower –
Might soon give signs. Oh, all his purpose lay
Face upward. Silva here felt strong, and smiled.
What could a Spanish noble not command ?
He only helped the Queen, because he chose;
Could war on Spaniards, and could spare the Moor;
Buy justice, or defeat it – if he would:
Was loyal, not from weakness but from strength
Of high resolve to use his birthright well.
For nobles too are gods, like Emperors,
Accept perforce their own divinity,
And wonder at the virtue of their touch,

Till obstinate resistance shakes their creed,
Shattering that self whose wholeness is not rounded
Save in the plastic souls of other men.
Don Silva had been suckled in that creed
(A high-taught speculative noble else),
Held it absurd as foolish argument
If any failed in deference, was too proud
Not to be courteous to so poor a knave
As one who knew not necessary truths
Of birth and dues of rank; but cross his will,
The miracle-working will, his rage leaped out
As by a right divine to rage more fatal
Than a mere mortal man's. And now that will
Had met a stronger adversary – strong
As awful ghosts are whom we cannot touch,
While they clutch *us*, subtly as poisoned air,
In deep-laid fibres of inherited fear
That lie below all courage.

                    Silva said,
"She is not lost to me, might still be mine
But for the Inquisition – the dire hand
That waits to clutch her with a hideous grasp
Not passionate, human, living, but a grasp
As in the death-throe when the human soul
Departs and leaves force unrelenting, locked,
Not to be loosened save by slow decay
That frets the universe. Father Isidor
Has willed it so: his phial dropped the oil
To catch the air-borne motes of idle slander;
He fed the fascinated gaze that clung
Round all her movements, frank as growths of spring,
With the new hateful interest of suspicion.
What barrier is this Gypsy? a mere gate
I'll find the key for. The one barrier,
The tightening cord that winds about my limbs,

Is this kind uncle, this imperious saint,
He who will save me, guard me from myself.
And he can work his will: I have no help
Save reptile secrecy, and no revenge
Save that I *will* do what he schemes to hinder.
Ay, secrecy, and disobedience – these
No tyranny can master. Disobey !
You may divide the universe with God,
Keeping your will unbent, and hold a world
Where He is not supreme. The Prior shall know it !
His will shall breed resistance: he shall do
The thing he would not, further what he hates
By hardening my resolve."

                     But 'neath this speech –
Defiant, hectoring, the more passionate voice
Of many-blended consciousness – there breathed
Murmurs of doubt, the weakness of a self
That is not one; denies and yet believes:
Protests with passion, "This is natural" –
Yet owns the other still were truer, better,
Could nature follow it: a self disturbed
By budding growths of reason premature
That breed disease. With all his outflung rage
Silva half shrank before the steadfast man
Whose life was one compacted whole, a realm
Where the rule changed not, and the law was strong.
Then that reluctant homage stirred new hate,
And gave rebellion an intenser will.

But soon this inward strife the slow-paced hours
Slackened; and the soul sank with hunger-pangs,
Hunger of love. Debate was swept right down
By certainty of loss intolerable.
A little loss ! only a dark-tressed maid
Who had no heritage save her beauteous being !

But in the candour of her virgin eyes
Saying, I love; and in the mystic charm
Of her dear presence, Silva found a heaven
Where faith and hope were drowned as stars in day.
Fedalma there, each momentary Now
Seemed a whole blest existence, a full cup
That, flowing over, asked no pouring hand
From past to future. All the world was hers.
Splendour was but the herald trumpet-note
Of her imperial coming: penury
Vanished before her as before a gem,
The pledge of treasuries. Fedalma there,
He thought all loveliness was lovelier,
She crowning it: all goodness credible,
Because of that great trust her goodness bred.
For the strong current of the passionate love
Which urged his life tow'rd hers, like urgent floods
That hurry through the various-mingled earth,
Carried within its stream all qualities
Of what it penetrated, and made love
Only another name, as Silva was,
For the whole man that breathed within his frame
And she was gone. Well, goddesses will go;
But for a noble there were mortals left
Shaped just like goddesses – O hateful sweet !
O impudent pleasures that should dare to front
With vulgar visage memories divine !
The noble's birthright of miraculous will
Turning *I would* to *must be*, spurning all
Offered as substitute for what it chose,
Tightened and fixed in strain irrevocable
The passionate selection of that love
Which came not first but as all-conquering last.
Great Love has many attributes, and shrines
For varied worship, but his force divine

Shows most its many-named fulness in the man
Whose nature multitudinously mixed –
Each ardent impulse grappling with a thought –
Resists all easy gladness, all content
Save mystic rapture, where the questioning soul
Flooded with consciousness of good that is
Finds life one bounteous answer. So it was
In Silva's nature, Love had mastery there,
Not as a holiday ruler, but as one
Who quells a tumult in a day of dread,
A welcomed despot.

                O all comforters,
All soothing things that bring mild ecstasy
Came with her coming, in her presence lived.
Spring afternoons, when delicate shadows fall
Pencilled upon the grass; high summer morns
When white light rains upon the quiet sea
And corn-fields flush with ripeness; odours soft –
Dumb vagrant bliss that seems to seek a home
And find it deep within, 'mid stirrings vague
Of far-off moments when our life was fresh;
All sweetly-tempered music, gentle change
Of sound, form, colour, as on wide lagoons
At sunset when from black far-floating prows
Comes a clear wafted song; all exquisite joy
Of a subdued desire, like some strong stream
Made placid in the fulness of a lake –
All came with her sweet presence, for she brought
The love supreme which gathers to its realm
All powers of loving. Subtle nature's hand
Waked with a touch the far-linked harmonies
In her own manifold work. Fedalma there,
Fastidiousness became the prelude fine
For full contentment; and young melancholy,
Lost for its origin, seemed but the pain

324

Of waiting for that perfect happiness.
The happiness was gone !
                              He sate alone,
Hating companionship that was not hers;
Felt bruised with hopeless longing; drank, as wine,
Illusions of what had been, would have been;
Weary with anger and a strained resolve,
Sought passive happiness in waking dreams.
It has been so with rulers, emperors,
Nay, sages who held secrets of great Time,
Sharing his hoary and beneficent life –
Men who sate throned among the multitudes –
They have sore sickened at the loss of one.
Silva sat lonely in her chamber, leaned
Where she had leaned, to feel the evening breath
Shed from the orange trees; when suddenly
His grief was echoed in a sad young voice
Far and yet near, brought by aërial wings.

The world is great: the birds all fly from me,
The stars are golden fruit upon a tree
All out of reach: my little sister went,
        And I am lonely.

The world is great: I tried to mount the hill
Above the pines, where the light lies so still,
But it rose higher: little Lisa went,
        And I am lonely.

The world is great: the wind comes rushing by,
I wonder where it comes from; sea-birds cry
And hurt my heart: my little sister went,
        And I am lonely.

The world is great: the people laugh and talk,
And make loud holiday: how fast they walk !
I'm lame, they push me: little Lisa went,
And I am lonely.

'Twas Pablo, like the wounded spirit of song
Pouring melodious pain to cheat the hour
For idle soldiers in the castle court.
Dreamily Silva heard and hardly felt
The song was outward, rather felt it part
Of his own aching, like the lingering day,
Or slow and mournful cadence of the bell.
But when the voice had ceased he longed for it,
And fretted at the pause, as memory frets
When words that made its body fall away
And leave it yearning dumbly. Silva then
Bethought him whence the voice came, framed perforce
Some outward image of a life not his
That made a sorrowful centre to the world:
A boy lame, melancholy-eyed, who bore
A viol – yes, that very child he saw
This morning eating roots by the gateway – saw
As one fresh-ruined sees and spells a name
And knows not what he does, yet finds it writ
Full in the inner record. Hark, again !
The voice and viol. Silva called his thought
To guide his ear and track the travelling sound

O bird that used to press
  Thy head against my cheek
  With touch that seemed to speak
And ask a tender "yes" –
    Ay de mi, my bird !

> O tender downy breast
> And warmly beating heart,
> That beating seemed a part
> Of me who gave it rest –
> Ay de mi, my bird !

The western court ! The singer might be seen
From the upper gallery: quick the Duke was there
Looking upon the court as on a stage.
Men eased of armour, stretched upon the ground
Gambling by snatches; shepherds from the hills
Who brought their bleating friends for slaughter; grooms
Shouldering loose harness; leather-aproned smiths,
Traders with wares, green-suited serving-men,
Made a round audience; and in their midst
Stood little Pablo, pouring forth his song,
Just as the Duke had pictured. But the song
Was strangely companied by Roldan's play
With the swift gleaming balls, and now was crushed
By peals of laughter at grave Annibal,
Who carrying stick and purse o'erturned the pence,
Making mistake by rule. Silva had thought
To melt hard bitter grief by fellowship
With the world-sorrow trembling in his ear
In Pablo's voice; had meant to give command
For the boy's presence; but this company,
This mountebank and monkey, must be – stay !
Not be excepted – must be ordered too
Into his private presence; they had brought
Suggestion of a ready shapen tool
To cut a path between his helpless wish
And what it imaged. A ready shapen tool !
A spy, an envoy whom he might despatch.
In unsuspected secrecy, to find

The Gypsies' refuge so that none beside
Might learn it. And this juggler could be bribed,
Would have no fear of Moors – for who would kill
Dancers and monkeys ? – could pretend a journey
Back to his home, leaving his boy the while
To please the Duke with song. Without such chance –
An envoy cheap and secret as a mole
Who could go scatheless, come back for his pay
And vanish straight, tied by no neighbourhood –
Without such chance as this poor juggler brought,
Finding Fedalma was betraying her.

Short interval betwixt the thought and deed.
Roldan was called to private audience
With Annibal and Pablo. All the world
(By which I mean the score or two who heard)
Shrugged high their shoulders, and supposed the Duke
Would fain beguile the evening and replace
His lacking happiness, as was the right
Of nobles, who could pay for any cure,
And wore nought broken, save a broken limb.
In truth, at first, the Duke bade Pablo sing,
But, while he sang, called Roldan wide apart,
And told him of a mission secret, brief –
A quest which well performed might earn much gold,
But, if betrayed, another sort of pay.
Roldan was ready; "wished above all for gold
And never wished to speak; had worked enough
At wagging his old tongue and chiming jokes;
Thought it was others' turn to play the fool.
Give him but pence enough, no rabbit, sirs,
Would eat and stare and be more dumb than he.
Give him his orders."

                They were given straight;
Gold for the journey, and to buy a mule

Outside the gates through which he was to pass
Afoot and carelessly. The boy would stay
Within the castle, at the Duke's command,
And must have nought but ignorance to betray
For threats or coaxing. Once the quest performed,
The news delivered with some pledge of truth
Safe to the Duke, the juggler should go forth,
A fortune in his girdle, take his boy
And settle firm as any planted tree
In fair Valencia, never more to roam.
"Good ! good ! most worthy of a great hidalgo !
And Roldan was the man ! But Annibal –
A monkey like no other, though morose
In private character, yet full of tricks –
'Twere hard to carry him, yet harder still
To leave the boy and him in company
And free to slip away. The boy was wild
And shy as mountain kid; once hid himself
And tried to run away; and Annibal,
Who always took the lad's side (he was small,
And they were nearer of a size, and, sirs,
Your monkey has a spite against us men
For being bigger) – Annibal went too.
Would hardly know himself, were he to lose
Both boy and monkey – and 'twas property,
The trouble he had put in Annibal.
He didn't choose another man should beat
His boy and monkey. If they ran away
Some man would snap them up, and square himself
And say they were his goods – he'd taught them – no !
He Roldan had no mind another man
Should fatten by his monkey, and the boy
Should not be kicked by any pair of sticks
Calling himself a juggler." . . .

329

                    But the Duke,
Tired of that hammering, signed that it should cease;
Bade Roldan quit all fears – the boy and ape
Should be safe lodged in Abderahman's tower,
In keeping of the great physician there,
The Duke's most special confidant and friend,
One skilled in taming brutes, and always kind.
The Duke himself this eve would see them lodged.
Roldan must go – spend no more words – but go.

The Astrologer's Study

A room high up in Abderahman's tower,
A window open to the still warm eve,
And the bright disc of royal Jupiter.
Lamps burning low make little atmospheres
Of light amid the dimness; here and there
Show books and phials, stones and instruments.
In carved dark-oaken chair, unpillowed, sleeps
Right in the rays of Jupiter a small man,
In skull-cap bordered close with crisp grey curls,
And loose black gown showing a neck and breast
Protected by a dim-green amulet;
Pale-faced, with finest nostril wont to breathe
Ethereal passion in a world of thought;
Eyebrows jet-black and firm, yet delicate;
Beard scant and grizzled; mouth shut firm, with curves
So subtly turned to meanings exquisite,
You seem to read them as you read a word
Full-vowelled, long-descended, pregnant – rich
With legacies from long, laborious lives.
Close by him, like a genius of sleep,
Purrs the grey cat, bridling, with snowy breast.
A loud knock. "Forward !" in clear vocal ring.

                    330

Enter the Duke, Pablo, and Annibal.
Exit the cat, retreating toward the dark.

DON SILVA.   You slept, Sephardo. I am come too soon.

SEPHARDO.   Nay, my lord, it was I who slept too long.
I go to court among the stars to-night,
So bathed my soul beforehand in deep sleep,
But who are these ?

DON SILVA.   Small guests, for whom I ask
Your hospitality. Their owner comes
Some short time hence to claim them. I am pledged
To keep them safely; so I bring them you,
Trusting your friendship for small animals.

SEPHARDO.   Yea, am not I too a small animal ?

DON SILVA.   I shall be much beholden to your love
If you will be their guardian. I can trust
No other man so well as you. The boy
Will please you with his singing, touches too
The viol wondrously.

SEPHARDO.   They are welcome both.
Their names are – ?

DON SILVA.   Pablo, this – this Annibal,
And yet, I hope, no warrior.

SEPHARDO.   We'll make peace.
Come, Pablo, let us loosen our friend's chain.
Deign you, my lord, to sit. Here Pablo, thou –
Close to my chair. Now Annibal shall choose.

[The cautious monkey, in a Moorish dress,
A tunic white, turban and scimitar,
Wears these stage garments, nay, his very flesh
With silent protest; keeps a neutral air
As aiming at a metaphysic state
'Twixt "is" and "is not;" lets his chain be loosed
By sage Sephardo's hands, sits still at first,
Then trembles out of his neutrality,
Looks up and leaps into Sephardo's lap,
And chatters forth his agitated soul,
Turning to peep at Pablo on the floor.]

SEPHARDO. See, he declares we are at amity !

DON SILVA. No brother sage had read your nature faster.

SEPHARDO. Why, so he is a brother sage. Man thinks
Brutes have no wisdom, since they know not his:
Can we divine their world? – the hidden life
That mirrors us as hideous shapeless power,
Cruel supremacy of sharp-edged death,
Or fate that leaves a bleeding mother robbed ?
Oh, they have long tradition and swift speech,
Can tell with touches and sharp darting cries
Whole histories of timid races taught
To breathe in terror by red-handed man.

DON SILVA.
Ah, you denounce my sport with hawk and hound.
I would not have the angel Gabriel
As hard as you in noting down my sins.

SEPHARDO. Nay, they are virtues for you warriors –
Hawking and hunting ! You are merciful
When you leave killing men to kill the brutes.

332

But, for the point of wisdom, I would choose
To know the mind that stirs between the wings
Of bees and building wasps, or fills the woods
With myriad murmurs of responsive sense
And true-aimed impulse, rather than to know
The thoughts of warriors.

DON SILVA.   Yet they are warriors too –
   Your animals. Your judgment limps, Sephardo:
   Death is the king of this world; 'tis his park
   Where he breeds life to feed him. Cries of pain
   Are music for his banquet; and the masque –
   The last grand masque for his diversion, is
   The Holy Inquisition.

SEPHARDO.   Ay, anon
   I may chime in with you. But not the less
   My judgment has firm feet. Though death were king,
   And cruelty his right-hand minister,
   Pity insurgent in some human breasts
   Makes spiritual empire, reigns supreme
   As persecuted faith in faithful hearts.
   Your small physician, weighing ninety pounds,
   A petty morsel for a healthy shark,
   Will worship mercy throned within his soul
   Though all the luminous angels of the stars
   Burst into cruel chorus on his ear,
   Singing, "We know no mercy." He would cry
   "I know it" still, and soothe the frightened bird
   And feed the child a-hungered, walk abreast
   Of persecuted men, and keep most hate
   For rational torturers. There I stand firm.
   But you are bitter, and my speech rolls on
   Out of your note.

DON SILVA.   No, no, I follow you.
I too have that within which I will worship
In spite of . . . Yes, Sephardo, I am bitter.
I need your counsel, foresight, all your aid.
Lay these small guests to bed, then we will talk.

SEPHARDO.   See, they are sleeping now. The boy has made
My leg his pillow. For my brother sage,
He'll never heed us; he knit long ago
A sound ape-system, wherein men are brutes
Emitting doubtful noises. Pray, my lord,
Unlade what burthens you: my ear and hand
Are servants of a heart much bound to you.

DON SILVA.   Yes, yours is love that roots in gifts bestowed
By you on others, and will thrive the more
The more it gives. I have a double want:
First a confessor – not a Catholic;
A heart without a livery – naked manhood.

SEPHARDO.   My lord, I will be frank; there's no such thing
As naked manhood. If the stars look down
On any mortal of our shape, whose strength
Is to judge all things without preference,
He is a monster, not a faithful man.
While my heart beats, it shall wear livery –
My people's livery, whose yellow badge
Marks them for Christian scorn. I will not say
Man is first man to me, then Jew or Gentile:
That suits the rich *marranos*; but to me
My father is first father and then man.
So much for frankness' sake. But let that pass,
'Tis true at least, I am no Catholic
But Salomo Sephardo, a born Jew,
Willing to serve Don Silva.

334

DON SILVA. Oft you sing
Another strain, and melt distinctions down
As no more real than the wall of dark
Seen by small fishes' eyes, that pierce a span
In the wide ocean. Now you league yourself
To hem me, hold me prisoner in bonds
Made, say you – how ? – by God or Demiurge,
By spirit or flesh – I care not ! Love was made
Stronger than bonds, and where they press must break
    them.
I came to you that I might breathe at large,
And now you stifle me with talk of birth,
Of race and livery. Yet you knew Fedalma.
She was your friend, Sephardo. And you know
She is gone from me – know the hounds are loosed
To dog me if I seek her.

SEPHARDO. Yes, I know.
Forgive me that I used untimely speech,
Pressing a bruise. I loved her well, my lord:
A woman mixed of such fine elements
That were all virtue and religion dead
She'd make them newly, being what she was.

DON SILVA. *Was ?* say not *was*, Sephardo ! She still lives –
Is, and is mine; and I will not renounce
What heaven, nay, what she gave me. I will sin,
If sin I must, to win my life again.
The fault lie with those powers who have embroiled
The world in hopeless conflict, where all truth
Fights manacled with falsehood, and all good
Makes but one palpitating life with ill.
    (DON SILVA *pauses*. SEPHARDO *is silent.*)
Sephardo, speak ! am I not justified ?

You taught my mind to use the wing that soars
Above the petty fences of the herd:
Now, when I need your doctrine, you are dumb.

SEPHARDO. Patience ! Hidalgos want interpreters
Of untold dreams and riddles; they insist
On dateless horoscopes, on formulas
To raise a possible spirit, nowhere named.
Science must be their wishing-cap; the stars
Speak plainer for high largesse. No, my lord !
I cannot counsel you to unknown deeds.
This much I can divine: you wish to find
Her whom you love – to make a secret search.

DON SILVA. That is begun already: a messenger
Unknown to all has been despatched this night.
But forecast must be used, a plan devised,
Ready for service when my scout returns,
Bringing the invisible thread to guide my steps
Toward that lost self my life is aching with.
Sephardo, I will go: and I must go
Unseen by all save you; though at our need
We may trust Alvar.

SEPHARDO.   A grave task, my lord.
Have you a shapen purpose, or mere will
That sees the end alone and not the means?
Resolve will melt no rocks.

DON SILVA.   But it can scale them.
This fortress has two private issues: one,
Which served the Gypsies' flight, to me is closed:
Our bands must watch the outlet, now betrayed
To cunning enemies. Remains one other,
Known to no man save me: a secret left

As heirloom in our house: a secret safe
Even from him – from Father Isidor.
'Tis he who forces me to use it – he:
All's virtue that cheats bloodhounds.   Hear, Sephardo.
Given, my scout returns and brings me news
I can straight act on, I shall want your aid.
The issue lies below this tower, your fastness,
Where, by my charter, you rule absolute.
I shall feign illness; you with mystic air
Must speak of treatment asking vigilance
(Nay I *am* ill – my life has half ebbed out).
I shall be whimsical, devolve command
On Don Diego, speak of poisoning,
Insist on being lodged within this tower,
And rid myself of tendance save from you
And perhaps from Alvar.   So I shall escape
Unseen by spies, shall win the days I need
To ransom her and have her safe enshrined.
No matter, were my flight disclosed at last:
I shall come back as from a duel fought
Which no man can undo.   Now you know all.
Say, can I count on you ?

SEPHARDO.   For faithfulness
In aught that I may promise, yes, my lord.
But – for a pledge of faithfulness – this warning.
I will betray nought for your personal harm:
I love you.   But note this – I am a Jew;
And while the Christian persecutes my race,
I'll turn at need even the Christian's trust
Into a weapon and a shield for Jews.
Shall Cruelty crowned – wielding the savage force
Of multitudes, and calling savageness God
Who gives it victory – upbraid deceit
And ask for faithfulness ?   I love you well.

You are my friend. But yet you are a Christian,
Whose birth has bound you to the Catholic kings.
There may come moments when to share my joy
Would make you traitor, when to share your grief
Would make me other than a Jew . . . .

DON SILVA.   What need
To urge that now, Sephardo ? I am one
Of many Spanish nobles who detest
The roaring bigotry of the herd, would fain
Dash from the lips of king and queen the cup
Filled with besotting venom, half infused
By avarice and half by priests. And now –
Now when the cruelty you flout me with
Pierces me too in the apple of my eye,
Now when my kinship scorches me like hate
Flashed from a mother's eye, you choose this time
To talk of birth as of inherited rage
Deep-down, volcanic, fatal, bursting forth
From under hard-taught reason ? Wondrous friend !
My uncle Isidor's echo, mocking me,
From the opposing quarter of the heavens,
With iteration of the thing I know,
That I'm a Christian knight and Spanish duke !
The consequence ? Why, that I know. It lies
In my own hands and not on raven tongues.
The knight and noble shall not wear the chain
Of false-linked thoughts in brains of other men.
What question was there 'twixt us two, of aught
That makes division? When I come to you
I come for other doctrine than the Prior's.

SEPHARDO.
My lord, you are o'erwrought by pain. My words,
That carried innocent meaning, do but float

Like little emptied cups upon the flood
Your mind brings with it. I but answered you
With regular proviso, such as stands
In testaments and charters, to forefend
A possible case which none deem likelihood;
Just turned my sleeve, and pointed to the brand
Of brotherhood that limits every pledge.
Superfluous nicety – the student's trick,
Who will not drink until he can define
What water is and is not. But enough.
My will to serve you now knows no division
Save the alternate beat of love and fear.
There's danger in this quest – name, honour, life –
My lord, the stake is great, and are you sure . . . .

DON SILVA. No, I am sure of nought but this, Sephardo,
That I will go. Prudence is but conceit
Hoodwinked by ignorance. There's nought exists
That is not dangerous and holds not death
For souls or bodies. Prudence turns its helm
To flee the storm and lands 'mid pestilence.
Wisdom would end by throwing dice with folly
But for dire passion which alone makes choice.
And I have chosen as the lion robbed
Chooses to turn upon the ravisher.
If love were slack, the Prior's imperious will
Would move it to outmatch him. But, Sephardo,
Were all else mute, all passive as sea-calms,
My soul is one great hunger – I must see her.
Now you are smiling. Oh, you merciful men
Pick up coarse griefs and fling them in the face
Of us whom life with long descent has trained
To subtler pains, mocking your ready balms.
You smile at my soul's hunger.

SEPHARDO.   Science smiles
  And sways our lips in spite of us, my lord,
  When thought weds fact – when maiden prophecy
  Waiting, believing, sees the bridal torch.
  I use not vulgar measures for your grief,
  My pity keeps no cruel feasts; but thought
  Has joys apart, even in blackest woe,
  And seizing some fine thread of verity
  Knows momentary godhead.

DON SILVA.   And your thought ?

SEPHARDO. Seized on the close agreement of your words
  With what is written in your horoscope.

DON SILVA. Reach it me now.

SEPHARDO.   By your leave, Annibal.
  (*He places* ANNIBAL *on* PABLO'*s lap and rises. The boy*
  moves without waking, and his head falls on the
  opposite side. SEPHARDO *fetches a cushion and lays*
  PABLO'*s head gently down upon it, then goes to reach*
  the parchment from a cabinet. ANNIBAL, *having waked*
  up in alarm, shuts his eyes quickly again and pretends
  to sleep.)

DON SILVA. I wish, by new appliance of your skill,
  Reading afresh the records of the sky,
  You could detect more special augury.
  Such chance oft happens, for all characters
  Must shrink or widen, as our wine-skins do,
  For more or less that we can pour in them;
  And added years give ever a new key
  To fixed prediction.

SEPHARDO   *(returning with the parchment and reseating himself).*

                                True; our growing thought
Makes growing revelation. But demand not
Specific augury, as of sure success
In meditated projects, or of ends
To be foreknown by peeping in God's scroll.
I say – nay, Ptolemy said it, but wise books
For half the truths they hold are honoured tombs –
Prediction is contingent, of effects
Where causes and concomitants are mixed
To seeming wealth of possibilities
Beyond our reckoning. Who will pretend
To tell the adventures of each single fish
Within the Syrian Sea ? Show me a fish,
I'll weigh him, tell his kind, what he devoured,
What would have devoured *him* – but for one Blas
Who netted him instead; nay, could I tell
That had Blas missed him, he would not have died
Of poisonous mud, and so made carrion,
Swept off at last by some sea-scavenger ?

DON SILVA. Ay, now you talk of fishes, you get hard.
I note you merciful men: you can endure
Torture of fishes and hidalgos. Follows ?

SEPHARDO. By how much, then, the fortunes of a man
Are made of elements refined and mixed
Beyond a tunny's, what our science tells
Of the star's influence hath contingency
In special issues. Thus, the loadstone draws,
Acts like a will to make the iron submiss;
But garlick rubbing it, that chief effect
Lies in suspense; the iron keeps at large
And garlick is controller of the stone.

And so, my lord, your horoscope declares
Not absolutely of your sequent lot,
But, by our lore's authentic rules, sets forth
What gifts, what dispositions, likelihoods
The aspects of the heavens conspired to fuse
With your incorporate soul. Aught more than this
Is vulgar doctrine. For the ambient,
Though a cause regnant, is not absolute,
But suffers a determining restraint
From action of the subject qualities
In proximate motion.

DON SILVA.   Yet you smiled just now
At some close fitting of my horoscope
With present fact – with this resolve of mine
To quit the fortress ?

SEPHARDO.   Nay, not so; I smiled,
Observing how the temper of your soul
Sealed long tradition of the influence shed
By the heavenly spheres. Here is your horoscope:
The aspects of the Moon with Mars conjunct,
Of Venus and the Sun with Saturn, lord
Of the ascendant, make symbolic speech
Whereto your words gave running paraphrase.

DON SILVA *(impatiently)*.
What did I say ?

SEPHARDO.   You spoke as oft you did
When I was schooling you at Córdova,
And lessons on the noun and verb were drowned
With sudden stream of general debate
On things and actions. Always in that stream
I saw the play of babbling currents, saw

A nature o'er-endowed with opposites
Making a self alternate, where each hour
Was critic of the last, each mood too strong
For tolerance of its fellow in close yoke.
The ardent planets stationed as supreme,
Potent in action, suffer light malign
From luminaries large and coldly bright
Inspiring meditative doubt, which straight
Doubts of itself, by interposing act
Of Jupiter in the fourth house fortified
With power ancestral. So, my lord, I read
The changeless in the changing; so I read
The constant action of celestial powers
Mixed into waywardness of mortal men,
Whereof no sage's eye can trace the course
And see the close.

DON SILVA.   Fruitful result, O sage !
    Certain uncertainty.

SEPHARDO.   Yea, a result
    Fruitful as seeded earth, where certainty
    Would be as barren as a globe of gold.
    I love you, and would serve you well, my lord.
    Your rashness vindicates itself too much,
    Puts harness on of cobweb theory
    While rushing like a cataract. Be warned.
    Resolve with you is a fire-breathing steed,
    But it sees visions, and may feel the air
    Impassable with thoughts that come too late,
    Rising from out the grave of murdered honour.
    Look at your image in your horoscope:
        (Laying the horoscope before DON SILVA.)
    You are so mixed, my lord, that each to-day
    May seem a maniac to its morrow.

DON SILVA (*pushing away the horoscope, rising and turning to look out at the open window*).

No !

No morrow e'er will say that I am mad
Not to renounce her. Risks ! I know them all.
I've dogged each lurking, ambushed consequence.
I've handled every chance to know its shape
As blind men handle bolts. Oh, I'm too sane !
I see the Prior's nets. He does my deed;
For he has narrowed all my life to this –
That I must find her by some hidden means.
  (*He turns and stands close in front of* SEPHARDO.)
One word, Sephardo – leave that horoscope,
Which is but iteration of myself,
And give me promise. Shall I count on you
To act upon my signal ? Kings of Spain
Like me have found their refuge in a Jew,
And trusted in his counsel. You will help me ?

SEPHARDO. Yes, my lord, I will help you. Israel
Is to the nations as the body's heart:
Thus writes our poet Jehuda. I will act
So that no man may ever say through me
"Your Israel is nought," and make my deeds
The mud they fling upon my brethren.
I will not fail you, save – you know the terms:
I am a Jew, and not that infamous life
That takes on bastardy, will know no father,
So shrouds itself in the pale abstract, Man.
You should be sacrificed to Israel
If Israel needed it.

DON SILVA.   I fear not that.
I am no friend of fines and banishment,
Or flames that, fed on heretics, still gape,

344

And must have heretics made to feed them still.
I take your terms, and for the rest, your love
Will not forsake me.

SEPHARDO.   'Tis hard Roman love,
That looks away and stretches forth the sword
Bared for its master's breast to run upon.
But you will have it so. Love shall obey.

(DON SILVA *turns to the window again, and is silent
for a few moments, looking at the sky.*)

DON SILVA. See now, Sephardo, you would keep no faith
To smooth the path of cruelty. Confess,
The deed I would not do, save for the strait
Another brings me to (quit my command,
Resign it for brief space, I mean no more) –
Were that deed branded, then the brand should fix
On him who urged me.

SEPHARDO.   Will it, though, my lord ?

DON SILVA. I speak not of the fact but of the right.

SEPHARDO. My lord, you said but now you were resolved.
Question not if the world will be unjust
Branding your deed. If conscience has two courts
With differing verdicts, where shall lie the appeal ?
Our law must be without us or within.
The Highest speaks through all our people's voice,
Custom, tradition, and old sanctities;
Or he reveals himself by new decrees
Of inward certitude.

Don Silva.   My love for her
  Makes highest law, must be the voice of God.

Sephardo.   I thought, but now, you seemed to make excuse,
  And plead as in some court where Spanish knights
  Are tried by other laws than those of love.

Don Silva.   'Twas momentary. I shall dare it all.
  How the great planet glows, and looks at me,
  And seems to pierce me with his effluence !
  Were he a living God, these rays that stir
  In me the pulse of wonder were in him
  Fulness of knowledge. Are you certified,
  Sephardo, that the astral science shrinks
  To such pale ashes, dead symbolic forms
  For that congenital mixture of effects
  Which life declares without the aid of lore ?
  If there are times propitious or malign
  To our first framing, then must all events
  Have favouring periods: you cull your plants
  By signal of the heavens, then why not trace
  As others would by astrologic rule
  Times of good augury for momentous acts, –
  As secret journeys ?

Sephardo.   Oh, my lord, the stars
  Act not as witchcraft or as muttered spells.
  I said before they are not absolute,
  And tell no fortunes. I adhere alone
  To such tradition of their agencies
  As reason fortifies.

Don Silva.   A barren science !
  Some argue now 'tis folly. 'Twere as well
  Be of their mind. If those bright stars had will –

But they are fatal fires, and know no love.
Of old, I think, the world was happier
With many gods, who held a struggling life
As mortals do, and helped men in the straits
Of forced misdoing. I doubt that horoscope.
> (Don Silva *turns from the window and reseats
> himself opposite* Sephardo.)
I am most self-contained, and strong to bear.
No man save you has seen my trembling lip
Utter her name, since she was lost to me.
I'll face the progeny of all my deeds.

Sephardo. May they be fair ! No horoscope makes slaves.
'Tis but a mirror, shows one image forth,
And leaves the future dark with endless "ifs."

Don Silva. I marvel, my Sephardo, you can pinch
With confident selection these few grains,
And call them verity, from out the dust
Of crumbling error. Surely such thought creeps,
With insect exploration of the world.
Were I a Hebrew, now, I would be bold.
Why should you fear, not being Catholic ?

Sephardo. Lo ! you yourself, my lord, mix subtleties
With gross belief; by momentary lapse
Conceive, with all the vulgar, that we Jews
Must hold ourselves God's outlaws, and defy
All good with blasphemy, because we hold
Your good is evil; think we must turn pale
To see our portraits painted in your hell,
And sin the more for knowing we are lost.

Don Silva Read not my words with malice. I but meant,
My temper hates an over-cautious march.

SEPHARDO The Unnameable made not the search for truth
To suit hidalgos' temper. I abide
By that wise spirit of listening reverence
Which marks the boldest doctors of our race.
For Truth, to us, is like a living child
Born of two parents: if the parents part
And will divide the child, how shall it live ?
Or, I will rather say: Two angels guide
The path of man, both aged and yet young,
As angels are, ripening through endless years.
On one he leans: some call her Memory,
And some, Tradition; and her voice is sweet,
With deep mysterious accords: the other,
Floating above, holds down a lamp which streams
A light divine and searching on the earth,
Compelling eyes and footsteps. Memory yields,
Yet clings with loving check, and shines anew
Reflecting all the rays of that bright lamp
Our angel Reason holds. We had not walked
But for Tradition; we walk evermore
To higher paths, by brightening Reason's lamp.
Still we are purblind, tottering. I hold less
Than Aben-Ezra, of that aged lore
Brought by long centuries from Chaldaean plains;
The Jew-taught Florentine rejects it all.
For still the light is measured by the eye,
And the weak organ fails. I may see ill;
But over all belief is faithfulness,
Which fulfils vision with obedience.
So, I must grasp my morsels: truth is oft
Scattered in fragments round a stately pile
Built half of error; and the eye's defect
May breed too much denial. But, my lord,
I weary your sick soul. Go now with me
Into the turret. We will watch the spheres,

And see the constellations bend and plunge
Into a depth of being where our eyes
Hold them no more. We'll quit ourselves and be
The red Aldebaran or bright Sirius,
And sail as in a solemn voyage, bound
On some great quest we know not.

Don Silva.   Let us go.
She may be watching too, and thought of her
Sways me, as if she knew, to every act
Of pure allegiance.

Sephardo.   That is love's perfection –
Tuning the soul to all her harmonies
So that no chord can jar. Now we will mount.

*A large hall in the Castle, of Moorish architecture. On
the side where the windows are, an outer gallery. Pages
and other young gentlemen attached to* Don Silva's
*household, gathered chiefly at one end of the hall. Some
are moving about; others are lounging on the carved
benches; others, half stretched on pieces of matting and
carpet, are gambling.* Arias, *a stripling of fifteen, sings by
snatches in a boyish treble, as he walks up and down,
and tosses back the nuts which another youth flings
towards him. In the middle* Don Amador, *a gaunt, grey-
haired soldier, in a handsome uniform, sits in a marble
red-cushioned chair, with a large book spread out on his
knees, from which he is reading aloud, while his voice is
half drowned by the talk that is going on around him,
first one voice and then another surging above the hum.*

ARIAS *(singing).*

> *There was a holy hermit*
> > *Who counted all things loss*
> *For Christ his Master's glory:*
> > *He made an ivory cross,*
> *And as he knelt before it*
> > *And wept his murdered Lord,*
> *The ivory turned to iron,*
> > *The cross became a sword.*

JOSÉ *(from the floor).* I say, twenty cruzados !
thy Galician wit can never count.

HERNANDO *(also from the floor).*
And thy Sevillian wit always counts double.

ARIAS *(singing).*

> *The tears that fell upon it,*
> > *They turned to red, red rust,*
> *The tears that fell from off it*
> > *Made writing in the dust.*
> *The holy hermit, gazing,*
> > *Saw words upon the ground:*
> *"The sword be red for ever*
> > *With the blood of false Mahound."*

DON AMADOR *(looking up from his book, and raising his voice).*
What, gentlemen ! Our Glorious Lady defend us !

ENRIQUEZ *(from the benches).*

Serves the infidels right! They have sold Christians enough to people half the towns in Paradise. If the Queen, now, had divided the pretty damsels of Malaga among the Castilians who have been helping in the holy war, and not sent half of them to Naples . . .

ARIAS *(singing again).*

> *At the battle of Clavijo*
> *In the days of King Ramiro,*
> *Help us, Allah ! cried the Moslem,*
> *Cried the Spaniard, Heaven's chosen,*
> > *God and Santiago !*

FABIAN. Oh, the very tail of our chance has vanished. The royal army is breaking up – going home for the winter. The Grand Master sticks to his own border.

ARIAS *(singing).*

> *Straight out-flushing like the rainbow,*
> *See him come, celestial Baron,*
> *Mounted knight, with red-crossed banner,*
> *Plunging earthward to the battle,*
> > *Glorious Santiago !*

HURTADO. Yes, yes, through the pass of By-and-by, you go to the valley of Never. We might have done a great feat, if the Marquis of Cadiz . . .

ARIAS *(sings).*

> *As the flame before the swift wind,*
> *See, he fires us, we burn with him !*
> *Flash our swords, dash Pagans backward –*
> *Victory he ! pale fear is Allah !*
> > *God with Santiago !*

DON AMADOR *(raising his voice to a cry).*
Sangre de Dios, gentlemen !
  (He shuts the book, and lets it fall with a bang on the
  floor. There is instant silence.)
To what good end is it that I, who studied at Salamanca,
and can write verses agreeable to the Glorious Lady with
the point of a sword which hath done harder service, am
reading aloud in a clerkly manner from a book which
hath been culled from the flowers of all books, to instruct
you in the knowledge befitting those who would be
knights and worthy hidalgos ? I had as lief be reading
in a belfry. And gambling too ! As if it were a time
when we needed not the help of God and the saints !
Surely for the space of one hour ye might subdue your
tongues to your ears, that so your tongues might learn
somewhat of civility and modesty. Wherefore am I master
of the Duke's retinue, if my voice is to run along like a
gutter in a storm ?

HURTADO *(lifting up the book, and respectfully presenting it*
to DON AMADOR).
Pardon, Don Amador! The air is so commoved by your
voice, that it stirs our tongues in spite of us.

DON AMADOR *(reopening the book).*
Confess, now, it is a goose-headed trick, that when
rational sounds are made for your edification, you find

nought in it but an occasion for purposeless gabble. I will report it to the Duke, and the reading-time shall be doubled, and my office of reader shall be handed over to Fray Domingo.

(While Don Amador *has been speaking,* Don Silva, *with* Don Alvar, *has appeared walking in the outer gallery on which the windows are opened.)*

All *(in concert).* No, no, no.

Don Amador. Are ye ready, then, to listen, if I finish the wholesome extract from the Seven Parts, wherein the wise King Alfonso hath set down the reason why knights should be of gentle birth ? Will ye now be silent ?

All. Yes, silent.

Don Amador. But when I pause, and look up, I give any leave to speak, if he hath aught pertinent to say.
(Reads.)
"And this nobility cometh in three ways: *first,* by lineage, *secondly,* by science, and *thirdly,* by valour and worthy behaviour. Now, although they who gain nobility through science or good deeds are rightfully called noble and gentle; nevertheless, they are with the highest fitness so called who are noble by ancient lineage, and lead a worthy life as by inheritance from afar; and hence are more bound and constrained to act well, and guard themselves from error and wrong-doing; for in their case it is more true that by evil-doing they bring injury and shame not only on themselves, but also on those from whom they are derived."

Don Amador *(placing his forefinger for a mark on the page, and looking up, while he keeps his voice raised, as wishing* Don Silva *to overhear him in the judicious discharge of his function*).

Hear ye that, young gentlemen ? See ye not that if ye have but bad manners even, they disgrace you more than gross misdoings disgrace the low-born ? Think you, Arias, it becomes the son of your house irreverently to sing and fling nuts, to the interrup tion of your elders ?

Arias *(sitting on the floor, and leaning backward on his elbows).*

Nay, Don Amador; King Alfonso, they say, was a heretic, and I think that is not true writing. For noble birth gives us more leave to do ill if we like.

Don Amador *(lifting his brows).*

What bold and blasphemous talk is this?

Arias. Why, nobles are only punished now and then, in a grand way, and have their heads cut off, like the Grand Constable. I shouldn't mind that.

José. Nonsense, Arias ! nobles have their heads cut off because their crimes are noble. If they did what was unknightly, they would come to shame. Is not that true, Don Amador?

Don Amador. Arias is a contumacious puppy, who will bring dishonour on his parentage. Pray, sirrah, whom did you ever hear speak as you have spoken?

Arias. Nay, I speak out of my own head. I shall go and ask the Duke.

Hurtado. Now, now ! you are too bold, Arias.

354

ARIAS. Oh, he is never angry with me, – *(Dropping his* voice) because the Lady Fedalma liked me. She said I was a good boy, and pretty, and that is what you are not, Hurtado.

HURTADO. Girl-face ! See, now, if you dare ask the Duke.

(DON SILVA *is just entering the hall from the gallery, with* DON ALVAR *behind him, intending to pass out at the other end. All rise with homage.* DON SILVA *bows coldly and abstractedly.* ARIAS *advances from the group, and goes up to* DON SILVA.)

ARIAS. My lord, is it true that a noble is more dishonoured than other men if he does aught dishonourable ?

DON SILVA *(first blushing deeply, and grasping his sword, then raising his hand and giving* ARIAS *a blow on the ear).*
Varlet !

ARIAS. My lord, I am a gentleman.

(DON SILVA *pushes him away, and passes on hurriedly.*)

DON ALVAR *(following and turning to speak).*
Go, go ! you should not speak to the Duke when you are not called upon. He is ill and much distempered.
(ARIAS *retires, flushed, with tears in his eyes. His companions look too much surprised to triumph.* DON AMADOR *remains silent and confused.*)

The Plaça Santiago during busy market-time. Mules and asses laden with fruits and vegetables. Stalls and booths filled with wares of all sorts. A crowd of buyers and sellers. A stalwart woman, with keen eyes, leaning over the panniers of a mule laden with apples, watches LORENZO, *who is lounging through the market. As he approaches her, he is met by* BLASCO.

LORENZO. Well met, friend.

BLASCO.   Ay, for we are soon to part,
And I would see you at the hostelry,
To take my reckoning. I go forth to-day.

LORENZO. 'Tis grievous parting with good company.
I would I had the gold to pay such guests
For all my pleasure in their talk.

BLASCO.   Why, yes;
A solid-headed man of Aragon
Has matter in him that you Southerners lack.
You like my company – 'tis natural.
But, look you, I have done my business well,
Have sold and ta'en commissions. I come straight
From – you know who – I like not naming him.
I'm a thick man: you reach not my backbone
With any tooth-pick; but I tell you this:
He reached it with his eye, right to the marrow.
It gave me heart that I had plate to sell,
For, saint or no saint, a good silversmith
Is wanted for God's service; and my plate –
He judged it well – bought nobly.

LORENZO.   A great man,
And holy !

BLASCO.   Yes, I'm glad I leave to-day.
For there are stories give a sort of smell –
One's nose has fancies. A good trader, sir,
Likes not this plague of lapsing in the air,
Most caught by men with funds. And they *do* say
There's a great terror here in Moors and Jews,
I would say, Christians of unhappy blood.
'Tis monstrous, sure, that men of substance lapse,
And risk their property. I know I'm sound.
No heresy was ever bait to me. Whate'er
Is the right faith, that I believe – nought else.

LORENZO. Ay, truly, for the flavour of true faith
Once known must sure be sweetest to the taste,
But an uneasy mood is now abroad
Within the town; partly, for that the Duke
Being sorely sick, has yielded the command
To Don Diego, a most valiant man,
More Catholic than the Holy Father's self,
Half chiding God that He will tolerate
A Jew or Arab; though 'tis plain they're made
For profit of good Christians. And weak heads –
Panic will knit all disconnected facts –
Draw hence belief in evil auguries,
Rumours of accusation and arrest,
All air-begotten. Sir, you need not go.
But if it must be so, I'll follow you
In fifteen minutes – finish marketing,
Then be at home to speed you on your way.

BLASCO. Do so. I'll back to Saragossa straight.
The court and nobles are retiring now
And wending northward. There'll be fresh demand
For bells and images against the Spring,

357

When doubtless our great Catholic sovereigns
Will move to conquest of these eastern parts,
And cleanse Granada from the infidel.
Stay, sir, with God, until we meet again !

LORENZO. Go, sir, with God, until I follow you !
(*Exit* BLASCO. LORENZO *passes on towards the market-
woman, who, as he approaches, raises herself from her
leaning attitude.*)

LORENZO.

Good day, my mistress. How's your merchandise.?
Fit for a host to buy ? Your apples now,
They have fair cheeks; how are they at the core ?

MARKET-WOMAN.

Good, good, sir ! Taste and try. See, here is one
Weighs a man's head. The best are bound with tow:
They're worth the pains, to keep the peel from splits.
(*She takes out an apple bound with tow, and, as she
puts it into* LORENZO'*s hand, speaks in a lower tone.*)
'Tis called the Miracle. You open it,
And find it full of speech.

LORENZO.   Ay, give it me,
I'll take it to the Doctor in the tower.
He feeds on fruit, and if he likes the sort
I'll buy them for him. Meanwhile, drive your ass
Round to my hostelry. I'll straight be there.
You'll not refuse some barter ?

MARKET-WOMAN.   No, not I.
Feathers and skins.

LORENZO.   Good, till we meet again.

(LORENZO, *after smelling at the apple, puts it into a pouch-like basket which hangs before him, and walks away. The woman drives off the mule.*)

A LETTER

"Zarca, the chieftain of the Gypsies, greets
"The King El Zagal. Let the force be sent
"With utmost swiftness to the Pass of Luz.
"A good five hundred added to my bands
"Will master all the garrison: the town
"Is half with us, and will not lift an arm
"Save on our side. My scouts have found a way
"Where once we thought the fortress most secure:
"Spying a man upon the height, they traced,
"By keen conjecture piecing broken sight,
"His downward path, and found its issue. There
"A file of us can mount, surprise the fort
"And give the signal to our friends within
"To ope the gates for our confederate bands,
"Who will lie eastward ambushed by the rocks,
"Waiting the night. Enough; give me command,
"Bedmár is yours. Chief Zarca will redeem
"His pledge of highest service to the Moor:
"Let the Moor too be faithful and repay
"The Gypsy with the furtherance he needs
"To lead his people over Bahr el Scham
"And plant them on the shore of Africa.
"So may the King El Zagal live as one
"Who, trusting Allah will be true to him,
"Maketh himself as Allah true to friends."

BOOK III

Quit now the town, and with a journeying dream
Swift as the wings of sound yet seeming slow
Through multitudinous pulsing of stored sense
And spiritual space, see walls and towers
Lie in the silent whiteness of a trance,
Giving no sign of that warm life within
That moves and murmurs through their hidden heart.
Pass o'er the mountain, wind in sombre shade,
Then wind into the light and see the town
Shrunk to white crust upon the darker rock.
Turn east and south, descend, then rise anew
'Mid smaller mountains ebbing towards the plain:
Scent the fresh breath of the height-loving herbs
That, trodden by the pretty parted hoofs
Of nimble goats, sigh at the innocent bruise,
And with a mingled difference exquisite
Pour a sweet burthen on the buoyant air.
Pause now and be all ear. Far from the south,
Seeking the listening silence of the heights,
Comes a slow-dying sound – the Moslems' call
To prayer in afternoon. Bright in the sun
Like tall white sails on a green shadowy sea
Stand Moorish watch-towers: 'neath that eastern sky
Couches unseen the strength of Moorish Baza;
Where the meridian bends lies Guadix, hold
Of brave El Zagal. This is Moorish land,
Where Allah lives unconquered in dark breasts
And blesses still the many-nourishing earth
With dark-armed industry. See from the steep
The scattered olives hurry in grey throngs
Down towards the valley, where the little stream
Parts a green hollow 'twixt the gentler slopes;
And in that hollow, dwellings: not white homes

Of building Moors, but little swarthy tents
Such as of old perhaps on Asian plains,
Or wending westward past the Caucasus,
Our fathers raised to rest in. Close they swarm
About two taller tents, and viewed afar
Might seem a dark-robed crowd in penitence
That silent kneel; but come now in their midst
And watch a busy, bright-eyed, sportive life !
Tall maidens bend to feed the tethered goat,
The ragged kirtle fringing at the knee
Above the living curves, the shoulder's smoothness
Parting the torrent strong of ebon hair.
Women with babes, the wild and neutral glance
Swayed now to sweet desire of mothers' eyes,
Rock their strong cradling arms and chant low strains
Taught by monotonous and soothing winds
That fall at night-time on the dozing ear.
The crones plait reeds, or shred the vivid herbs
Into the caldron: tiny urchins crawl
Or sit and gurgle forth their infant joy.
Lads lying sphinx-like with uplifted breast
Propped on their elbows, their black manes tossed back,
Fling up the coin and watch its fatal fall,
Dispute and scramble, run and wrestle fierce,
Then fall to play and fellowship again;
Or in a thieving swarm they run to plague
The grandsires, who return with rabbits slung,
And with the mules fruit-laden from the fields.
Some striplings choose the smooth stones from the brook
To serve the slingers, cut the twigs for snares,
Or trim the hazel-wands, or at the bark
Of some exploring dog they dart away
With swift precision towards a moving speck.
These are the brood of Zarca's Gypsy tribe;
Most like an earth-born race bred by the Sun

361

On some rich tropic soil, the father's light
Flashing in coal-black eyes, the mother's blood
With bounteous elements feeding their young limbs.
The stalwart men and youths are at the wars
Following their chief, all save a trusty band
Who keep strict watch along the northern heights.

But see, upon a pleasant spot removed
From the camp's hubbub, where the thicket strong
Of huge-eared cactus makes a bordering curve
And casts a shadow, lies a sleeping man
With Spanish hat screening his upturned face,
His doublet loose, his right arm backward flung,
His left caressing close the long-necked lute
That seems to sleep too, leaning tow'rds its lord.
He draws deep breath secure but not unwatched.
Moving a-tiptoe, silent as the elves,
As mischievous too, trip three bare-footed girls
Not opened yet to womanhood – dark flowers
In slim long buds: some paces further off
Gathers a little white-teethed shaggy group
A grinning chorus to the merry play.
The tripping girls have robbed the sleeping man
Of all his ornaments. Hita is decked
With an embroidered scarf across her rags;
Tralla, with thorns for pins, sticks two rosettes
Upon her threadbare woollen; Hinda now,
Prettiest and boldest, tucks her kirtle up
As wallet for the stolen buttons – then
Bends with her knife to cut from off the hat
The aigrette and long feather; deftly cuts,
Yet wakes the sleeper, who with sudden start
Shakes off the masking hat and shows the face
Of Juan: Hinda swift as thought leaps back,
But carries off the spoil triumphantly,

And leads the chorus of a happy laugh,
Running with all the naked-footed imps,
Till with safe survey all can face about
And watch for signs of stimulating chase,
While Hinda ties long grass around her brow
To stick the feather in with majesty.
Juan still sits contemplative, with looks
Alternate at the spoilers and their work.

JUAN. Ah, you marauding kite – my feather gone !
My belt, my scarf, my buttons and rosettes !
This is to be a brother of your tribe !
The fiery-blooded children of the Sun –
So says chief Zarca – children of the Sun !
Ay, ay, the black and stinging flies he breeds
To plague the decent body of mankind.
"Orpheus, professor of the *gai saber,*
Made all the brutes polite by dint of song."
Pregnant – but as a guide in daily life
Delusive. For if song and music cure
The barbarous trick of thieving, 'tis a cure
That works as slowly as old Doctor Time
In curing folly. Why, the minxes there
Have rhythm in their toes, and music rings
As readily from them as from little bells
Swung by the breeze. Well, I will try the physic.
                    (*He touches his lute.*)
Hem ! taken rightly, any single thing,
The Rabbis say, implies all other things.
A knotty task, though, the unravelling
Meum and *Tuum* from a saraband:
It needs a subtle logic, nay, perhaps
A good large property, to see the thread.
                    (*He touches the lute again.*)
There's more of odd than even in this world.

Else pretty sinners would not be let off
Sooner than ugly; for if honeycombs
Are to be got by stealing, they should go
Where life is bitterest on the tongue. And yet –
Because this minx has pretty ways I wink
At all her tricks, though if a flat-faced lass,
With eyes askew, were half as bold as she,
I should chastise her with a hazel switch.
I'm a plucked peacock – even my voice and wit
Without a tail ! – why, any fool detects
The absence of your tail, but twenty fools
May not detect the presence of your wit.

(*He touches his lute again.*)

Well, I must coax my tail back cunningly,
For to run after these brown lizards – ah!
I think the lizards lift their ears at this.

(*As he thrums his lute the lads and girls gradually
approach: he touches it more briskly, and* HINDA,
*advancing, begins to move arms and legs with an
initiatory dancing movement, smiling coaxingly at*
JUAN. *He suddenly stops, lays down his lute and
folds his arms.*)

JUAN. What, you expect a tune to dance to, eh ?

HINDA, HITA, TRALIA, AND THE REST (*clapping their hands*).
Yes, yes, a tune, a tune !

JUAN. But that is what you cannot have, my sweet brothers
and sisters. The tunes are all dead – dead as the tunes
of the lark when you have plucked his wings off; dead as
the song of the grasshopper when the ass has swallowed
him. I can play and sing no more. Hinda has killed my
tunes.

(All cry out in consternation. HINDA *gives a wail and tries to examine the lute.)*

JUAN *(waving her off).*
Understand, Señora Hinda, that the tunes are in me; they are not in the lute till I put them there. And if you cross my humour, I shall be as tuneless as a bag of wool. If the tunes are to be brought to life again, I must have my feather back.

*(*HINDA *kisses his hand and feet coaxingly.)*
No, no ! not a note will come for coaxing. The feather, I say, the feather !

*(*HINDA *sorrowfully takes off the feather, and gives it to* JUAN.)*
Ah, now let us see. Perhaps a tune will come.

(He plays a measure, and the three girls begin to dance; then he suddenly stops.)

JUAN. No, the tune will not come: it wants the aigrette.
(pointing to it on HINDA'S *neck.* HINDA, *with rather less hesitation, but again sorrowfully, takes off the aigrette, and gives it to him.)*

JUAN. Ha ! *(He plays again, but, after rather a longer time, again stops.)* No, no; 'tis the buttons are wanting, Hinda, the buttons. This tune feeds chiefly on buttons — a greedy tune. It wants one, two, three, four, five, six. Good !

(After HINDA *has given up the buttons, and* JUAN *has laid them down one by one, he begins to play again, going on longer than before, so that the dancers become excited by the movement. Then he stops.)*

JUAN. Ah, Hita, it is the belt, and, Tralla, the rosettes – both
are wanting. I see the tune will not go on without them.
    (HITA *and* TRALLA *take off the belt and rosettes, and
    lay them down quickly, being fired by the dancing,
    and eager for the music. All the articles lie by*
    JUAN's *side on the ground*.)

JUAN. Good, good, my docile wild-cats ! Now I think the
tunes are all alive again. Now you may dance and sing
too. Hinda, my little screamer, lead off with the song I
taught you, and let us see if the tune will go right on
from beginning to end.
    (*He plays. The dance begins again,* HINDA *singing.
    All the other boys and girls join in the chorus, and
    all at last dance wildly.*)

SONG

> *All things journey: sun and moon,*
> *Morning, noon, and afternoon,*
>   *Night and all her stars:*
> *'Twixt the east and western bars*
>   *Round they journey,*
>   *Come and go !*
>   *We go with them !*
> *For to roam and ever roam*
> *Is the Zíncali's loved home.*
>
> *Earth is good, the hillside breaks*
> *By the ashen roots and makes*
>   *Hungry nostrils glad:*
> *Then we run till we are mad,*
>   *Like the horses,*
>   *And we cry,*
>   *None shall catch us !*

Swift winds wing us – we are free –
Drink the air – we Zíncali !

Falls the snow: the pine-branch split,
Call the fire out, see it flit,
    Through the dry leaves run
Spread and glow, and make a sun
    In the dark tent:
        O warm dark !
    Warm as conies !
Strong fire loves us, we are warm !
Who the Zíncali shall harm ?

Onward journey: fires are spent;
Sunward, sunward ! lift the tent,
    Run before the rain,
Through the pass, along the plain.
    Hurry, hurry,
        Lift us, wind !
    Like the horses.
For to roam and ever roam
Is the Zíncali's loved home.

(When the dance is at its height, HINDA *breaks away*
from the rest, and dances round JUAN, *who is now*
standing. As he turns a little to watch her movement,
some of the boys skip towards the feather, aigrette,
&c., snatch them up, and run away, swiftly followed
by HITA, TRALIA, *and the rest.* HINDA, *as she turns*
again, sees them, screams, and falls in her whirling;
but immediately gets up, and rushes after them, still
screaming with rage.)

367

JUAN. Santiago ! these imps get bolder. Haha ! Señora
Hinda, this finishes your lesson in ethics. You have seen
the advantage of giving up stolen goods. Now you see
the ugliness of thieving when practised by others. That
fable of mine about the tunes was excellently devised. I
feel like an ancient sage instructing our lisping ancestors.
My memory will descend as the Orpheus of Gypsies. But
I must prepare a rod for those rascals. I'll bastinado
them with prickly pears. It seems to me these needles
will have a sound moral teaching in them.

   (*While* JUAN *takes a knife from his belt, and surveys
   a bush of the prickly pear*, HINDA *returns.*)

JUAN. Pray, Señora, why do you fume ? Did you want to
steal my ornaments again yourself ?

HINDA (*sobbing*). No; I thought you would give them me
back again.

JUAN. What, did you want the tunes to die again ? Do you
like finery better than dancing ?

HINDA. Oh, that was a tale ! I shall tell tales too, when I
want to get anything I can't steal. And I know what I
will do. I shall tell the boys I've found some little foxes,
and I will never say where they are till they give me back
the feather !

   (*She runs off again.*)

JUAN. Hem ! the disciple seems to seize the mode sooner
than the matter. Teaching virtue with this prickly pear
may only teach the youngsters to use a new weapon; as
your teaching orthodoxy with faggots may only bring up
a fashion of roasting. Dios ! my remarks grow too

368

pregnant – my wits get a plethora by solitary feeding on
the produce of my own
wisdom.

> *(As he puts up his knife again,* HINDA *comes running
> back, and crying, "Our Queen ! our Queen !"* JUAN
> *adjusts his garments and his lute, while* HINDA *turns
> to meet* FEDALMA, *who wears a Moorish dress, her
> black hair hanging round her in plaits, a white
> turban on her head, a dagger by her side. She
> carries a scarf on her left arm, which she holds up
> as a shade.)*

FEDALMA *(patting* HINDA's *head).*
How now, wild one ? You are hot and panting. Go up
to my tent, and help Nouna to plait reeds.

> (HINDA *kisses* FEDALMA's *hand, and runs off.* FEDALMA
> *advances towards* JUAN, *who kneels to take up the
> edge of her cymar, and kisses it.*)

JUAN. How is it with you, lady? You look sad.

FEDALMA. Oh, I am sick at heart. The eye of day,
The insistent summer sun, seems pitiless,
Shining in all the barren crevices
Of weary life, leaving no shade, no dark,
Where I may dream that hidden waters lie;
As pitiless as to some shipwrecked man,
Who gazing from his narrow shoal of sand
On the wide unspecked round of blue and blue
Sees that full light is errorless despair.
The insects' hum that slurs the silent dark
Startles and seems to cheat me, as the tread
Of coming footsteps cheats the midnight watcher
Who holds her heart and waits to hear them pause,

And hears them never pause, but pass and die.
Music sweeps by me as a messenger
Carrying a message that is not for me.
The very sameness of the hills and sky
Is obduracy, and the lingering hours
Wait round me dumbly, like superfluous slaves,
Of whom I want nought but the secret news
They are forbid to tell. And, Juan, you –
You, too, are cruel – would be over-wise
In judging your friend's needs, and choose to hide
Something I crave to know.

JUAN.   I, lady ?

FEDALMA.   You.

JUAN. I never had the virtue to hide aught,
    Save what a man is whipped for publishing.
    I'm no more reticent than the voluble air –
    Dote on disclosure – never could contain
    The latter half of all my sentences,
    But for the need to utter the beginning.
    My lust to tell is so importunate
    That it abridges every other vice,
    And makes me temperate for want of time.
    I dull sensation in the haste to say
    'Tis this or that, and choke report with surmise.
    Judge, then, dear lady, if I could be mute
    When but a glance of yours had bid me speak.

FEDALMA. Nay, sing such falsities ! – you mock me worse
    By speech that gravely seems to ask belief
    You are but babbling in a part you play
    To please my father. Oh, 'tis well meant, say you –
    Pity for woman's weakness. Take my thanks.

JUAN. Thanks angrily bestowed are red-hot coin
Burning your servant's palm.

FEDALMA.   Deny it not,
You know how many leagues this camp of ours
Lies from Bedmár – what moutains lie between –
Could tell me if you would about the Duke –
That he is comforted, sees how he gains
Losing the Zíncala, finds now how slight
The thread Fedalma made in that rich web,
A Spanish noble's life. No, that is false !
He never would think lightly of our love.
Some evil has befallen him – he's slain –
Has sought for danger and has beckoned death
Because I made all life seem treachery.
Tell me the worst – be merciful – no worst,
Against the hideous painting of my fear,
Would not show like a better.

JUAN.   If I speak,
Will you believe your slave? For truth is scant;
And where the appetite is still to hear
And not believe, falsehood would stint it less.
How say you? Does your hunger's fancy choose
The meagre fact?

FEDALMA *(seating herself on the ground)*.
                    Yes, yes, the truth, dear Juan.
Sit now, and tell me all.

JUAN.   That all is nought.
I can unleash my fancy if you wish
And hunt for phantoms: shoot an airy guess
And bring down airy likelihood – some lie
Masked cunningly to look like royal truth

And cheat the shooter, while King Fact goes free;
Or else some image of reality
That doubt will handle and reject as false.
As for conjecture – I can thread the sky
Like any swallow, but, if you insist
On knowledge that would guide a pair of feet
Right to Bedmár, across the Moorish bounds,
A mule that dreams of stumbling over stones
Is better stored.

FEDALMA.   And you have gathered nought
About the border wars ? No news, no hint
Of any rumours that concern the Duke –
Rumours kept from me by my father?

JUAN.   None.
Your father trusts no secret to the echoes.
Of late his movements have been hid from all
Save those few hundred chosen Gypsy breasts
He carries with him. Think you he's a man
To let his projects slip from out his belt,
Then whisper him who haps to find them strayed
To be so kind as keep his counsel well?
Why, if he found me knowing aught too much,
He would straight gag or strangle me, and say,
"Poor hound ! it was a pity that his bark
Could chance to mar my plans: he loved my daughter –
The idle hound had nought to do but love,
So followed to the battle and got crushed."

FEDALMA *(holding out her hand, which* JUAN *kisses.)*
Good Juan, I could have no nobler friend.
You'd ope your veins and let your life-blood out
To save another's pain, yet hide the deed
With jesting – say, 'twas merest accident,

A sportive scratch that went by chance too deep –
And die content with men's slight thoughts of you,
Finding your glory in another's joy.

JUAN. Dub not my likings virtues, lest they get
A drug-like taste, and breed a nausea.
Honey's not sweet, commended as cathartic.
Such names are parchment labels upon gems
Hiding their colour. What is lovely seen
Priced in a tarif ? – lapis lazuli,
Such bulk, so many drachmas: amethysts
Quoted at so much; sapphires higher still.
The stone like solid heaven in its blueness
Is what I care for, not its name or price.
So, if I live or die to serve my friend
'Tis for my love – 'tis for my friend alone,
And not for any rate that friendship bears
In heaven or on earth. Nay, I romance –
I talk of Roland and the ancient peers.
In me 'tis hardly friendship, only lack
Of a substantial self that holds a weight;
So I kiss larger things and roll with them.

FEDALMA. Oh, you will never hide your soul from me;
I've seen the jewel's flash, and know 'tis there,
Muffle it as you will. That foam-like talk
Will not wash out a fear which blots the good
Your presence brings me. Oft I'm pierced afresh
Through all the pressure of my selfish griefs
By thought of you. It was a rash resolve
Made you disclose yourself when you kept watch
About the terrace wall: – your pity leaped,
Seeing alone my ills and not your loss,
Self-doomed to exile. Juan, you must repent.
'Tis not in nature that resolve, which feeds

373

On strenuous actions, should not pine and die
In these long days of empty listlessness.

JUAN. Repent? Not I. Repentance is the weight
Of indigested meals ta'en yesterday.
'Tis for large animals that gorge on prey,
Not for a honey-sipping butterfly.
I am a thing of rhythm and redondillas –
The momentary rainbow on the spray
Made by the thundering torrent of men's lives:
No matter whether I am here or there;
I still catch sunbeams. And in Africa,
Where melons and all fruits, they say, grow large
Fables are real, and the apes polite,
A poet, too, may prosper past belief:
I shall grow epic, like the Florentine,
And sing the founding of our infant state,
Sing the new Gypsy Carthage.

FEDALMA.   Africa
Would we were there ! Under another heaven,
In lands where neither love nor memory
Can plant a selfish hope – in lands so far
I should not seem to see the outstretched arms
That seek me, or to hear the voice that calls.
I should feel distance only and despair;
So rest for ever from the thought of bliss,
And wear my weight of life's great chain unstruggling.
Juan, if I could know he would forget –
Nay, not forget, forgive me – be content
That I forsook him for no joy, but sorrow,
For sorrow chosen rather than a joy
That destiny made base ! Then he would taste
No bitterness in sweet, sad memory,
And I should live unblemished in his thought,

374

Hallowed like her who dies an unwed bride.
Our words have wings, but fly not where we would.
Could mine but reach him, Juan !

JUAN.   Speak the wish –
My feet have wings – I'll be your Mercury.
I fear no shadowed perils by the way.
No man will wear the sharpness of his sword
On me. Nay, I'm a herald of the Muse,
Sacred for Moors and Spaniards. I will go –
Will fetch you tidings for an amulet.
But stretch not hope too strongly towards that mark
As issue of my wandering. Given, I cross
Safely the Moorish border, reach Bedmár:
Fresh counsels may prevail there, and the Duke
Being absent in the field, I may be trapped.
Men who are sour at missing larger game
May wing a chattering sparrow for revenge,
It is a chance no further worth the note
Than as a warning, lest you feared worse ill
If my return were stayed. I might be caged;
They would not harm me else. Untimely death,
The red auxiliary of the skeleton,
Has too much work on hand to think of me;
Or, if he cares to slay me, I shall fall
Choked with a grape-stone for economy.
The likelier chance is that I go and come,
Bringing you comfort back.

FEDALMA *(starts from her seat and walks to a little distance,*
standing a few moments with her back towards JUAN,
then she turns round quickly, and goes towards him).
                              No, Juan, no !
Those yearning words came from a soul infirm,
Crying and struggling at the pain of bonds

375

Which yet it would not loosen. He knows all –
All that he needs to know: I said farewell:
I stepped across the cracking earth and knew
'Twould yawn behind me. I must walk right on
No, I will not win aught by risking you:
That risk would poison my poor hope. Besides,
'Twere treachery in me: my father wills
That we – all here – should rest within this camp.
If I can never live, like him, on faith
In glorious morrows, I am resolute.
While he treads painfully with stillest step
And beady brow, pressed 'neath the weight of arms,
Shall I, to ease my fevered restlessness,
Raise peevish moans, shattering that fragile silence ?
No ! On the close-thronged spaces of the earth
A battle rages: Fate has carried me
'Mid the thick arrows: I will keep my stand –
Not shrink and let the shaft pass by my breast
To pierce another. Oh, 'tis written large
The thing I have to do. But you, dear Juan,
Renounce, endure, are brave, unurged by aught
Save the sweet overflow of your good will.
    (She seats herself again.)

JUAN. Nay, I endure nought worse than napping sheep
When nimble birds uproot a fleecy lock
To line their nest with. See ! your bondsman, Queen,
The minstrel of your court, is featherless;
Deforms your presence by a moulting garb;
Shows like a roadside bush culled of its buds.
Yet, if your graciousness will not disdain
A poor plucked songster – shall he sing to you?
Some lay of afternoons – some ballad strain

376

Of those who ached once but are sleeping now
Under the sun-warmed flowers ?   'Twill cheat the time.

FEDALMA. Thanks, Juan – later, when this hour is passed.
My soul is clogged with self; it could not float
On with the pleasing sadness of your song.
Leave me in this green spot, but come again, –
Come with the lengthening shadows.

JUAN.   Then your slave
Will go to chase the robbers.   Queen, farewell !

FEDALMA. Best friend, my well-spring in the wilderness !

[While Juan sped along the stream, there came
From the dark tents a ringing joyous shout
That thrilled Fedalma with a summons grave
Yet welcome, too.   Straightway she rose and stood,
All languor banished, with a soul suspense,
Like one who waits high presence, listening.
Was it a message, or her father's self
That made the camp so glad ?
                                        It was himself !
She saw him now advancing, girt with arms
That seemed like idle trophies hung for show
Beside the weight and fire of living strength
That made his frame.   He glanced with absent triumph,
As one who conquers in some field afar
And bears off unseen spoil.   But nearing her,
His terrible eyes intense sent forth new rays –
A sudden sunshine where the lightning was
'Twixt meeting dark.   All tenderly he laid
His hand upon her shoulder; tenderly,
His kiss upon her brow.]

377

ZARCA.   My royal daughter !

FEDALMA.   Father, I joy to see your safe return.

ZARCA.   Nay, I but stole the time, as hungry men
Steal from the morrow's meal, made a forced march,
Left Hassan as my watchdog, all to see
My daughter, and to feed her famished hope
With news of promise.

FEDALMA.   Is the task achieved
That was to be the herald of our flight ?

ZARCA.   Not outwardly, but to my inward vision
Things are achieved when they are well begun.
The perfect archer calls the deer his own
While yet the shaft is whistling. His keen eye
Never sees failure, sees the mark alone.
You have heard nought, then – had no messenger ?

FEDALMA.   I, Father? no: each quiet day has fled
Like the same moth, returning with slow wing,
And pausing in the sunshine.

ZARCA.   It is well.
You shall not long count days in weariness.
Ere the full moon has waned again to new,
We shall reach Almería: Berber ships
Will take us for their freight, and we shall go
With plenteous spoil, not stolen, bravely won
By service done on Spaniards. Do you shrink ?
Are you aught less than a true Zíncala?

FEDALMA.   No; but I am more. The Spaniards fostered me.

Seen them so levelled to a handsome steed
That yesterday was Moorish property,
To-day is Christian – wears new-fashioned gear,
Neighs to new feeders, and will prance alike
Under all banners, so the banner be
A master's who caresses. Such light change
You call conversion; but we Zíncali call
Conversion infamy. Our people's faith
Is faithfulness; not the rote-learned belief
That we are heaven's highest favourites,
But the resolve that being most forsaken
Among the sons of men, we will be true
Each to the other, and our common lot.
You Christians burn men for their heresy:
Our vilest heretic is that Zíncala
Who, choosing ease, forsakes her people's woes.
The dowry of my daughter is to be
Chief woman of her tribe, and rescue it.
A bride with such a dowry has no match
Among the subjects of that Catholic Queen
Who would have Gypsies swept into the sea
Or else would have them gibbeted.

Don Silva.   And you,
    Fedalma's father – you who claim the dues
Of fatherhood – will offer up her youth
To mere grim idols of your phantasy !
Worse than all Pagans with no oracle
To bid you murder, no sure good to win,
Will sacrifice your daughter – to no god,
But to a ravenous fire within your soul,
Mad hopes, blind hate, that like possessing fiends
Shriek at a name ! This sweetest virgin, reared
As garden flowers, to give the sordid world
Glimpses of perfectness, you snatch and thrust

On dreary wilds; in visions mad, proclaim
Semiramis of Gypsy wanderers;
Doom, with a broken arrow in her heart,
To wait for death 'mid squalid savages:
For what? You would be saviour of your tribe;
So said Fedalma's letter; rather say,
You have the will to save by ruling men
But first to rule; and with that flinty will
You cut your way, though the first cut you give
Gash your child's bosom.

(*While* Don Silva *has been speaking with growing passion,* Fedalma *has placed herself between him and her father.*)

Zarca (*with calm irony*).   You are loud, my lord !
You only are the reasonable man;
You have a heart, I none. Fedalma's good
Is what you see, you care for; while I seek
No good, not even my own, urged on by nought
But hellish hunger, which must still be fed
Though in the feeding it I suffer throes.
Fume at your own opinion as you will:
I speak not now to you, but to my daughter.
If she still calls it good to mate with you,
To be a Spanish duchess, kneel at court,
And hope her beauty is excuse to men
When women whisper, "A mere Zíncala !"
If she still calls it good to take a lot
That measures joy for her as she forgets
Her kindred and her kindred's misery,
Nor feels the softness of her downy couch
Marred by remembrance that she once forsook
The place that she was born to – let her go !
If life for her still lies in alien love,

That forces her to shut her soul from truth
As men in shameful pleasures shut out day;
And death, for her, is to do rarest deeds,
Which, even failing, leave new faith to men,
The faith in human hearts – then, let her go !
She is my only offspring; in her veins
She bears the blood her tribe has trusted in;
Her heritage is their obedience,
And if I died, she might still lead them forth
To plant the race her lover now reviles
Where they may make a nation, and may rise
To grander manhood than his race can show;
Then live a goddess, sanctifying oaths,
Enforcing right, and ruling consciences,
By law deep-graven in exalting deeds,
Through the long ages of her people's life.
If she can leave that lot for silken shame,
For kisses honeyed by oblivion –
The bliss of drunkards or the blank of fools –
Then let her go ! You Spanish Catholics,
When you are cruel, base, and treacherous,
For ends not pious, tender gifts to God,
And for men's wounds offer much oil to churches:
We have no altars for such healing gifts
As soothe the heavens for outrage done on earth.
We have no priesthood and no creed to teach
That she – the Zíncala – who might save her race
And yet abandons it, may cleanse that blot,
And mend the curse her life has been to men,
By saving her own soul. Her one base choice
Is wrong unchangeable, is poison shed
Where men must drink, shed by her poisoning will-
Now choose, Fedalma !

[But her choice was made.
Slowly, while yet her father spoke, she moved
From where oblique with deprecating arms
She stood between the two who swayed her heart:
Slowly she moved to choose sublimer pain;
Yearning, yet shrinking; wrought upon by awe,
Her own brief life seeming a little isle
Remote through visions of a wider world
With fates close-crowded; firm to slay her joy
That cut her heart with smiles beneath the knife,
Like a sweet babe foredoomed by prophecy.
She stood apart, yet near her father: stood
Hand clutching hand, her limbs all tense with will
That strove 'gainst anguish, eyes that seemed a soul
Yearning in death towards him she loved and left.
He faced her, pale with passion and a will
Fierce to resist whatever might seem strong
And ask him to submit: he saw one end –
He must be conqueror; monarch of his lot
And not its tributary. But she spoke
Tenderly, pleadingly.]

FEDALMA.   My lord, farewell !
   'Twas well we met once more; now we must part.
   I think we had the chief of all love's joys
   Only in knowing that we loved each other.

DON SILVA. I thought we loved with love that clings till death,

   Clings as brute mothers bleeding to their young,
   Still sheltering, clutching it, though it were dead;
   Taking the death-wound sooner than divide.
   I thought we loved so.

FEDALMA.   Silva, it is fate.

Great Fate has made me heiress of this woe.
You must forgive Fedalma all her debt:
She is quite beggared: if she gave herself,
'Twould be a self corrupt with stifled thoughts
Of a forsaken better. It is truth
My father speaks: the Spanish noble's wife
Were a false Zíncala. No ! I will bear
The heavy trust of my inheritance.
See, 'twas my people's life that throbbed in me:
An unknown need stirred darkly in my soul,
And made me restless even in my bliss.
Oh, all my bliss was in our love; but now
I may not taste it: some deep energy
Compels me to choose hunger. Dear, farewell !
I must go with my people.

                        [She stretched forth
Her tender hands, that oft had lain in his,
The hands he knew so well, that sight of them
Seemed like their touch. But he stood still as death;
Locked motionless by forces opposite:
His frustrate hopes still battled with despair;
His will was prisoner to the double grasp
Of rage and hesitancy. All the way
Behind him he had trodden confident,
Ruling munificently in his thought
This Gypsy father. Now the father stood
Present and silent and unchangeable
As a celestial portent. Backward lay
The traversed road, the town's forsaken wall,
The risk, the daring; all around him now
Was obstacle, save where the rising flood
Of love close pressed by anguish of denial
Was sweeping him resistless; save where she

Gazing stretched forth her tender hands, that hurt
Like parting kisses. Then at last he spoke.]

DON SILVA. No, I can never take those hands in mine
Then let them go for ever !

FEDALMA.   It must be.
We may not make this world a paradise
By walking it together hand in hand,
With eyes that meeting feed a double strength.
We must be only joined by pains divine
Of spirits blent in mutual memories.
Silva, our joy is dead.

DON SILVA.   But love still lives,
And has a safer guard in wretchedness.
Fedalma, women know no perfect love:
Loving the strong, they can forsake the strong;
Man clings because the being whom he loves
Is weak and needs him. I can never turn
And leave you to your difficult wandering;
Know that you tread the desert, bear the storm,
Shed tears, see terrors, faint with weariness,
Yet live away from you. I should feel nought
But your imagined pains: in my own steps
See your feet bleeding, taste your silent tears,
And feel no presence but your loneliness.
No, I will never leave you !

ZARCA.   My lord Duke,
I have been patient, given room for speech,
Bent not to move my daughter by command,
Save that of her own faithfulness. But now,
All further words are idle elegies
Unfitting times of action. You are here

With the safe-conduct of that trust you showed
Coming unguarded to the Gypsy's camp.
I would fain meet all trust with courtesy
As well as honour; but my utmost power
Is to afford you Gypsy guard to-night
Within the tents that keep the northward lines,
And for the morrow, escort on your way
Back to the Moorish bounds.

DON SILVA.   What if my words
Were meant for deeds, decisive as a leap
Into the current? It is not my wont
To utter hollow words, and speak resolves
Like verses bandied in a madrigal.
I spoke in action first: I faced all risks
To find Fedalma. Action speaks again
When I, a Spanish noble, here declare
That I abide with her, adopt her lot,
Claiming alone fulfilment of her vows
As my betrothéd wife.

FEDALMA (*wresting herself from him, and standing opposite
with a look of terror*).   Nay, Silva, nay !
You could not live so − spring from your high place . . .

DON SILVA. Yes, I have said it. And you, chief, are bound
By her strict vows, no stronger fealty
Being left to cancel them.

ZARCA.   Strong words, my lord !
Sounds fatal as the hammer-strokes that shape
The glowing metal: they must shape your life.
That you will claim my daughter is to say
That you will leave your Spanish dignities,
Your home, your wealth, your people, to become

Wholly a Zíncalo: share our wanderings,
And be a match meet for my daughter's dower
By living for her tribe; take the deep oath
That binds you to us; rest within our camp,
Nevermore hold command of Spanish men,
And keep my orders. See, my lord, you lock
A many-winding chain – a heavy chain.

DON SILVA. I have but one resolve: let the rest follow.
What is my rank? To-morrow it will be filled
By one who eyes it like a carrion bird,
Waiting for death. I shall be no more missed
Than waves are missed that leaping on the rock
Find there a bed and rest. Life's a vast sea
That does its mighty errand without fail,
Panting in unchanged strength though waves are changing.
And I have said it: she shall be my people,
And where she gives her life I will give mine.
She shall not live alone, nor die alone.
I will elect my deeds, and be the liege
Not of my birth, but of that good alone
I have discerned and chosen.

ZARCA.   Our poor faith
Allows not rightful choice, save of the right
Our birth has made for us. And you, my lord,
Can still defer your choice, for some days' space.
I march perforce to-night; you, if you will,
Under a Gypsy guard, can keep the heights
With silent Time that slowly opes the scroll
Of change inevitable – take no oath
Till my accomplished task leave me at large
To see you keep your purpose or renounce it.

DON SILVA. Chief, do I hear amiss, or does your speech
    Ring with a doubleness which I had held
    Most alien to you? You would put me off,
    And cloak evasion with allowance ? No !
    We will complete our pledges. I will take
    That oath which binds not me alone, but you,
    To join my life for ever with Fedalma's.

ZARCA. I wrangle not – time presses. But the oath
    Will leave you that same post upon the heights;
    Pledged to remain there while my absence lasts.
    You are agreed, my lord?

DON SILVA.   Agreed to all.

ZARCA. Then I will give the summons to our camp.
    We will adopt you as a brother now,
    After our wonted fashion.
                    (*Exit* ZARCA.)
                    (SILVA *takes* FEDALMA's *hand*.)

FEDALMA.   O my lord !
    I think the earth is trembling: nought is firm.
    Some terror chills me with a shadowy grasp.
    Am I about to wake, or do you breathe
    Here in this valley? Did the outer air
    Vibrate to fatal words, or did they shake
    Only my dreaming soul? You join – our tribe?

DON SILVA. Is then your love too faint to raise belief
    Up to that height?

FEDALMA.   Silva, had you but said
    That you would die – that were an easy task
    For you who oft have fronted death in war.

But so to live for me – you, used to rule –
You could not breathe the air my father breathes:
His presence is subjection. Go, my lord !
Fly, while there yet is time. Wait not to speak.
I will declare that I refused your love
Would keep no vows to you . . .

DON SILVA.   It is too late.
You shall not thrust me back to seek a good
Apart from you. And what good? Why, to face
Your absence – all the want that drove me forth –
To work the will of a more tyrannous friend
Than any uncowled father. Life at least
Gives choice of ills; forces me to defy,
But shall not force me to a weak defiance.
The power that threatened you, to master me,
That scorches like a cave-hid dragon's breath,
Sure of its victory in spite of hate,
Is what I last will bend to – most defy.
Your father has a chieftain's ends, befitting
A soldier's eye and arm: were he as strong
As the Moors' prophet, yet the prophet too
Had younger captains of illustrious fame
Among the infidels. Let him command,
For when your father speaks, I shall hear you.
Life were no gain if you were lost to me:
I would straight go and seek the Moorish walls,
Challenge their bravest, and embrace swift death.
The Glorious Mother and her pitying Son
Are not Inquisitors, else their heaven were hell.
Perhaps they hate their cruel worshippers,
And let them feed on lies. I'll rather trust
They love you and have sent me to defend you.

FEDALMA. I made my creed so, just to suit my mood
   And smooth all hardship, till my father came
   And taught my soul by ruling it. Since then
   I cannot weave a dreaming happy creed
   Where our love's happiness is not accursed.
   My father shook my soul awake. And you –
   The bonds Fedalma may not break for you,
   I cannot joy that you should break for her.

DON SILVA. Oh, Spanish men are not a petty band
   Where one deserter makes a fatal breach.
   Men, even nobles, are more plenteous
   Than steeds and armour; and my weapons left
   Will find new hands to wield them. Arrogance
   Makes itself champion of mankind, and holds
   God's purpose maimed for one hidalgo lost.

   See where your father comes and brings a crowd
   Of witnesses to hear my oath of love;
   The low red sun glows on them like a fire.
   This seems a valley in some strange new world,
   Where we have found each other, my Fedalma.

BOOK IV

Now twice the day had sunk from off the hills
While Silva kept his watch there, with the band
Of stalwart Gypsies. When the sun was high
He slept; then, waking, strained impatient eyes
To catch the promise of some moving form
That might be Juan − Juan who went and came
To soothe two hearts, and claimed nought for his own:
Friend more divine than all divinities,
Quenching his human thirst in others' joy.
All through the lingering nights and pale chill dawns
Juan had hovered near; with delicate sense,
As of some breath from every changing mood,
Had spoken or kept silence; touched his lute
To hint of melody, or poured brief strains
That seemed to make all sorrows natural,
Hardly worth weeping for, since life was short,
And shared by loving souls. Such pity welled
Within the minstrel's heart of light-tongued Juan
For this doomed man, who with dream-shrouded eyes
Had stepped into a torrent as a brook,
Thinking to ford it and return at will,
And now waked helpless in the eddying flood,
Hemmed by its raging hurry. Once that thought,
How easy wandering is, how hard and strict
The homeward way, had slipped from reverie
Into low-murmured song; − (brief Spanish song
'Scaped him as sighs escape from other men).

> *Push off the boat,*
>> *Quit, quit the shore,*
>>> *The stars will guide us back:*
> *O gathering cloud,*
>> *O wide, wide sea,*
>>> *O waves that keep no track !*

> *On through the pines !*
>> *The pillared woods,*
>>> *Where silence breathes sweet breath: –*
> *O labyrinth,*
>> *O sunless gloom,*
>>> *The other side of death !*

Such plaintive song had seemed to please the Duke –
Had seemed to melt all voices of reproach
To sympathetic sadness; but his moods
Had grown more fitful with the growing hours,
And this soft murmur had the iterant voice
Of heartless Echo, whom no pain can move
To say aught else than we have said to her.
He spoke, impatient: "Juan, cease thy song.
Our whimpering poesy and small-paced tunes
Have no more utterance than the cricket's chirp
For souls that carry heaven and hell within."
Then Juan, lightly: "True, my lord, I chirp
For lack of soul; some hungry poets chirp
For lack of bread. 'Twere wiser to sit down
And count the star-seed, till I fell asleep –
With the cheap wine of pure stupidity."
And Silva, checked by courtesy: "Nay, Juan,
Were speech once good, thy song were best of speech.
I meant, all life is but poor mockery:
Action, place, power, the visible wide world
Are tattered masquerading of this self,

This pulse of conscious mystery: all change,
Whether to high or low, is change of rags.
But for her love, I would not take a good
Save to burn out in battle, in a flame
Of madness that would feel no mangled limbs,
And die not knowing death, but passing straight
Well, well, to other flames – in purgatory."
Keen Juan's ear caught the self-discontent
That vibrated beneath the changing tones
Of life-contemning scorn. Gently he said:
"But *with* her love, my lord, the world deserves
A higher rate; were it but masquerade,
The rags were surely worth the wearing ?" "Yes.
No misery shall force me to repent
That I have loved her."

                       So with wilful talk,
Fencing the wounded soul from beating winds
Of truth that came unasked, companionship
Made the hours lighter. And the Gypsy guard,
Trusting familiar Juan, were content,
At friendly hint from him, to still their songs
And busy jargon round the nightly fires.
Such sounds, the quick-conceiving poet knew
Would strike on Silva's agitated soul
Like mocking repetition of the oath
That bound him in strange clanship with the tribe
Of human panthers, flame-eyed, lithe-limbed, fierce,
Unrecking of time-woven subtleties
And high tribunals of a phantom-world.

But the third day, though Silva southward gazed
Till all the shadows slanted towards him, gazed
Till all the shadows died, no Juan came,
Now in his stead came loneliness, and Thought
Inexorable, fastening with firm chain

What is to what hath been. Now awful Night,
The prime ancestral mystery, came down
Past all the generations of the stars,
And visited his soul with touch more close
Than when he kept that younger, briefer watch
Under the church's roof beside his arms,
And won his knighthood.

                   Well, this solitude,
This company with the enduring universe,
Whose mighty silence carrying all the past
Absorbs our history as with a breath,
Should give him more assurance, make him strong
In all contempt of that poor circumstance
Called human life – customs and bonds and laws
Wherewith men make a better or a worse,
Like children playing on a barren mound
Feigning a thing to strive for or avoid.
Thus Silva argued with his many-voiced self,
Whose thwarted needs, like angry multitudes,
Lured from the home that nurtured them to strength,
Made loud insurgence. Thus he called on Thought,
On dexterous Thought, with its swift alchemy
To change all forms, dissolve all prejudice
Of man's long heritage, and yield him up
A crude fused world to fashion as he would.
Thought played him double; seemed to wear the yoke
Of sovereign passion in the noon-day height
Of passion's prevalence; but served anon
As tribune to the larger soul which brought
Loud-mingled cries from every human need
That ages had instructed into life.
He could not grasp Night's black blank mystery
And wear it for a spiritual garb
Creed-proof: he shuddered at its passionless touch.
On solitary souls, the universe

Looks down inhospitable; the human heart
Finds nowhere shelter but in human kind.
He yearned towards images that had breath in them,
That sprang warm palpitant with memories
From streets and altars, from ancestral homes
Banners and trophies and the cherishing rays
Of shame and honour in the eyes of man.
These made the speech articulate of his soul,
That could not move to utterance of scorn
Save in words bred by fellowship; could not feel
Resolve of hardest constancy to love
The firmer for the sorrows of the loved,
Save by concurrent energies high-wrought
To sensibilities transcending sense
Through close community, and long-shared pains
Of far-off generations. All in vain
He sought the outlaw's strength, and made a right
Contemning that hereditary right
Which held dim habitations in his frame,
Mysterious haunts of echoes old and far,
The voice divine of human loyalty.
At home, among his people, he had played
In sceptic ease with saints and litanies,
And thunders of the Church that deadened fell
Through screens of priests plethoric. Awe, unscathed
By deeper trespass, slept without a dream.
But for such trespass as made outcasts, still
The ancient Furies lived with faces new
And lurked with lighter slumber than of old
O'er Catholic Spain, the land of sacred oaths
That might be broken.
                                    Now the former life
Of close-linked fellowship, the life that made
His full-formed self, as the impregnate sap
Of years successive frames the full-branched tree –

Was present in one whole; and that great trust
His deed had broken turned reproach on him
From faces of all witnesses who heard
His uttered pledges; saw him hold high place
Centring reliance; use rich privilege
That bound him like a victim-nourished god
By tacit covenant to shield and bless;
Assume the Cross and take his knightly oath
Mature, deliberate: faces human all,
And some divine as well as human: His
Who hung supreme, the suffering Man divine
Above the altar; Hers, the Mother pure
Whose glance informed his masculine tenderness
With deepest reverence; the Archangel armed,
Trampling man's enemy: all heroic forms
That fill the world of faith with voices, hearts,
And high companionship, to Silva now
Made but one inward and insistent world
With faces of his peers, with court and hall
And deference, and reverent vassalage,
And filial pieties – one current strong,
The warmly mingled life-blood of his mind,
Sustaining him even when he idly played
With rules, beliefs, charges, and ceremonies
As arbitrary fooling. Such revenge
Is wrought by the long travail of mankind
On him who scorns it, and would shape his life
Without obedience.

                But his warrior's pride
Would take no wounds save on the breast. He faced
The fatal crowd: "I never shall repent !
If I have sinned, my sin was made for me
By men's perverseness. There's no blameless life
Save for the passionless, no sanctities
But have the self-same roof and props with crime,

Or have their roots close interlaced with wrong.
If I had loved her less, been more a craven,
I had kept my place and won the easy praise
Of a true Spanish noble. But I loved,
And, loving, dared – not Death the warrior
But Infamy that binds and strips, and holds
The brand and lash. I have dared all for her.
She was my good – what other men call heaven,
And for the sake of it bear penances;
Nay, some of old were baited, tortured, flayed
To win their heaven. Heaven was their good,
She, mine. And I have braved for her all fires
Certain or threatened; for I go away
Beyond the reach of expiation – far away
From sacramental blessing. Does God bless
No outlaw ? Shut his absolution fast
In human breath ? Is there no God for me
Save him whose cross I have forsaken ? – Well,
I am for ever exiled – but with her !
She is dragged out into the wilderness;
I, with my love, will be her providence.
I have a right top choose my good or ill,
A right to damn myself ! The ill is mine.
I never will repent ! " . . .
Thus Silva, inwardly debating, all his ear
Turned into audience of a twofold mind;
For even in tumult full-fraught consciousness
Had plenteous being for a self aloof
That gazed and listened, like a soul in dreams
Weaving the wondrous tale it marvels at.
But oft the conflict slackened, oft strong Love
With tidal energy returning laid
All other restlessness: Fedalma came,
And with her visionary presence brought
What seemed a waking in the warm spring morn.

He still was pacing on the stony earth
Under the deepening night; the fresh-lit fires
Were flickering on dark forms and eyes that met
His forward and his backward tread; but she,
She was within him, making his whole self
Mere correspondence with her image: sense,
In all its deep recesses where it keeps
The mystic stores of ecstasy, was turned
To memory that killed the hour, like wine.
Then Silva said, "She, by herself, is life.
What was my joy before I loved her – what
Shall heaven lure us with, love being lost ?" –
For he was young.

                But now around the fires
The Gypsy band felt freer; Juan's song
Was no more there, nor Juan's friendly ways
For links of amity 'twixt their wild mood
And this strange brother, this pale Spanish duke,
Who with their Gypsy badge upon his breast
Took readier place within their alien hearts
As a marked captive, who would fain escape.
And Nadar, who commanded them, had known
The prison in Bedmár. So now, in talk
Foreign to Spanish ears, they said their minds,
Discussed their chief's intent, the lot marked out
For this new brother. Would he wed their queen ?
And some denied, saying their queen would wed
Only a Gypsy duke – one who would join
Their bands in Telemsán. But others thought
Young Hassan was to wed her; said their chief
Would never trust this noble of Castile,
Who in his very swearing was forsworn.
And then one fell to chanting, in wild notes
Recurrent like the moan of outshut winds,
The adjuration they were wont to use

To any Spaniard who would join their tribe:
Words of plain Spanish, lately stirred anew
And ready at new impulse. Soon the rest,
Drawn to the stream of sound, made unison
Higher and lower, till the tidal sweep
Seemed to assail the Duke and close him round
With force daemonic. All debate till now
Had wrestled with the urgence of that oath
Already broken; now the newer oath
Thrust its loud presence on him. He stood still,
Close baited by loud-barking thoughts − fierce hounds
Of that Supreme, the irreversible Past.

The Zincali *sing.*

Brother, hear and take the curse,
Curse of soul's and body's throes,
If you hate not all our foes,
Cling not fast to all our woes,
  Turn false Zíncalo !

May you be accurst
By hunger and by thirst
 By spikéd pangs,
  Starvation's fangs
 Clutching you alone
When none but peering vultures hear your moan.
 Curst by burning hands,
  Curst by aching brow,
 When on sea-wide sands
  Fever lays you low;
 By the maddened brain
 When the running water glistens,
 And the deaf ear listens, listens,
  Prisoned fire within the vein,

On the tongue and on the lip
Not a sip
From the earth or skies;
Hot the desert lies
Pressed into your anguish,
Narrowing earth and narrowing sky
Into lonely misery.
Lonely may you languish
Through the day and through the night,
Hate the darkness, hate the light,
Pray and find no ear,
Feel no brother near,
Till on death you cry,
Death who passes by,
And anew you groan,
Scaring the vultures all to leave you living lone:
Curst by souls and body's throes
If you love the dark men's foes,
Cling not fast to all the dark men's woes,
Turn false Zíncalo !

Swear to hate the cruel cross,
The silver cross !
Glittering, laughing at the blood
Shed below it in a flood
When it glitters over Moorish porches;
Laughing at the scent of flesh
When it glitters where the faggot scorches,
Burning life's mysterious mesh:
Blood of wandering Israël,
Blood of wandering Ismaël,
Blood, the drink of Christian scorn,
Blood of wanderers, sons of morn
Where the life of men began:
Swear to hate the cross ! –

Sign of all the wanderers' foes,
Sign of all the wanderers' woes –
    Else its curse light on you !
Else the curse upon you light
Of its sharp red-sworded might.
May it lie a blood-red blight
On all things within your sight:
On the white haze of the morn,
On the meadows and the corn,
On the sun and on the moon,
On the clearness of the noon,
On the darkness of the night.
May it fill your aching sight –
Red-cross sword and sword blood-red –
Till it press upon your head,
Till it lie within your brain,
Piercing sharp, a cross of pain,
Till it lie upon your heart,
    Burning hot, a cross of fire,
Till from sense in every part
Pains have clustered like a stinging swarm
    In the cross's form,
And you see nought but the cross of blood,
And you feel nought but the cross of fire:
    Curst by all the cross's throes
    If you hate not all our foes,
    Fling not fast to all our woes,
      Turn false Zíncalo !

A fierce delight was in the Gypsies' chant:
They thought no more of Silva, only felt
Like those broad-chested rovers of the night
Who pour exuberant strength upon the air.
To him it seemed as if the hellish rhythm,
Revolving in long curves that slackened now,

416

Now hurried, sweeping round again to slackness,
Would cease no more. What use to raise his voice,
Or grasp his weapon ? He was powerless now,
With these new comrades of his future – he
Who had been wont to have his wishes feared
And guessed at as a hidden law for men.
Even the passive silence of the night
That left these howlers mastery, even the moon,
Rising and staring with a helpless face,
Angered him. He was ready now to fly
At some loud throat, and give the signal so
For butchery of himself.

> But suddenly
The sounds that travelled towards no foreseen close
Were torn right off and fringed into the night;
Sharp Gypsy ears had caught the onward strain
Of kindred voices joining in the chant.
All started to their feet and mustered close,
Auguring long-waited summons. It was come:
The summons to set forth and join their chief.
Fedalma had been called, and she was gone
Under safe escort, Juan following her:
The camp – the women, children, and old men –
Were moving slowly southward on the way
To Almería. Silva learned no more.
He marched perforce; what other goal was his
Than where Fedalma was ? And so he marched
Through the dim passes and o'er rising hills,
Not knowing whither, till the morning came.

*The Moorish hall in the castle at Bedmár.   The
morning twilight dimly shows stains of blood on
the white marble floor; yet there has been a careful
restoration of order among the sparse objects of*

*furniture. Stretched on mats lie three corpses, the
faces bare, the bodies covered with mantles. A little
way off, with rolled matting for a pillow, lies* ZARCA,
*sleeping. His chest and arms are bare; his
weapons, turban, mail-shirt, and other upper
garments lie on the floor beside him. In the outer
gallery Zíncali are pacing, at intervals, past the
arched openings.*

ZARCA (*half rising and resting his elbow on the pillow while
he looks round*).
The morning ! I have slept for full three hours;
Slept without dreams, save of my daughter's face.
Its sadness waked me. Soon she will be here,
Soon must outlive the worst of all the pains
Bred by false nurture in an alien home –
As if a lion in fangless infancy
Learned love of creatures that with fatal growth
It scents as natural prey, and grasps and tears
Yet with heart-hunger yearns for, missing them.
She is a lioness. And they – the race
That robbed me of her – reared her to this pain.
He will be crushed and torn. There was no help.
But she, my child, will bear it. For strong souls
Live like fire-hearted suns to spend their strength
In farthest striving action; breathe more free
In mighty anguish than in trivial ease.
Her sad face waked me. I shall meet it soon
Waking . . .
    (*He rises and stands looking at the corpses.*)
                As now I look on these pale dead,
These blossoming branches crushed beneath the fall
Of that broad trunk to which I laid my axe
With fullest foresight. So will I ever face
In thought beforehand to its utmost reach

418

The consequences of my conscious deeds;
So face them after, bring them to my bed,
And never drug my soul to sleep with lies.
If they are cruel, they shall be arraigned
By that true name; they shall be justified
By my high purpose, by the clear-seen good
That grew into my vision as I grew,
And makes my nature's function, the full pulse
Of inbred kingship. Catholics,
Arabs, and Hebrews, have their god apiece
To fight and conquer for them, or be bruised,
Like Allah now, yet keep avenging stores
Of patient wrath. The Zíncali have no god
Who speaks to them and calls them his, unless
I, Zarca, carry living in my frame
The power divine that chooses them and saves.
"Life and more life unto the chosen, death
To all things living that would stifle them !"
So speaks each god that makes a nation strong;
Burns trees and brutes and slays all hindering men.
The Spaniards boast their god the strongest now;
They win most towns by treachery, make most slaves,
Burn the most vines and men, and rob the most.
I fight against that strength, and in my turn
Slay these brave young who duteously strove.
Cruel ? ay, it is cruel. But, how else ?
To save, we kill; each blow we strike at guilt
Hurts innocence with its shock. Men might well seek
For purifying rites; even pious deeds
Need washing. But my cleansing waters flow
Solely from my intent.

> (*He turns away from the bodies to where his
> garments lie, but does not lift them.*)

                              And she must suffer !
But she has seen the unchangeable and bowed

Her head beneath the yoke. And she will walk
No more in chilling twilight, for to-day
Rises our sun. The difficult night is past;
We keep the bridge no more, but cross it; march
Forth to a land where all our wars shall be
With greedy obstinate plants that will not yield
Fruit for their nurture. All our race shall come
From north, west, east, a kindred multitude,
And make large fellowship, and raise inspired
The shout divine, the unison of resolve.
So I, so she, will see our race redeemed.
And their keen love of family and tribe
Shall no more thrive on cunning, hide and lurk
In petty arts of abject hunted life,
But grow heroic in the sanctioning light,
And feed with ardent blood a nation's heart.
That is my work: and it is well begun.
On to achievement !
   (*He takes up the mail-shirt, and looks at it, then
   throws it down again.*)
               No, I'll none of you !
To-day there'll be no fighting. A few hours,
And I shall doff these garments of the Moor:
Till then I will walk lightly and breathe high.

SEPHARDO (*appearing at the archway leading into the outer
gallery*).
You bade me wake you . . .

ZARCA.   Welcome, Doctor; see,
With that small task I did but beckon you
To graver work. You know these corpses ?

SEPHARDO.   Yes.
I would they were not corpses. Storms will lay

The fairest trees and leave the withered stumps.
This Alvar and the Duke were of one age,
And very loving friends. I minded not
The sight of Don Diego's corpse, for death
Gave him some gentleness, and had he lived
I had still hated him. But this young Alvar
Was doubly noble, as a gem that holds
Rare virtues in its lustre; and his death
Will pierce Don Silva with a poisoned dart.
This fair and curly youth was Arias,
A son of the Pachecos; this dark face . .

ZARCA. Enough ! you know their names. I had divined
That they were near the Duke, most like had served
My daughter, were her friends; so rescued them
From being flung upon the heap of slain.
Beseech you, Doctor, if you owe me aught
As having served your people, take the pains
To see these bodies buried decently.
And let their names be writ above their graves,
As those of brave young Spaniards who died well.
I needs must bear this womanhood in my heart –
Bearing my daughter there. For once she prayed –
'Twas at our parting – "When you see fair hair
Be pitiful." And I am forced to look
On fair heads living and be pitiless.
Your service, Doctor, will be done to her.

SEPHARDO. A service doubly dear. For these young dead,
And one less happy Spaniard who still lives,
Are offerings which I wrenched from out my heart,
Constrained by cries of Israel: while my hands
Rendered the victims at command, my eyes
Closed themselves vainly, as if vision lay
Through those poor loopholes only. I will go

And see the graves dug by some cypresses.

ZARCA. Meanwhile the bodies shall rest here. Farewell.
                    (*Exit* SEPHARDO.)
Nay, 'tis no mockery. She keeps me so
From hardening with the hardness of my acts.
This Spaniard shrouded in her love – I would
He lay here too that I might pity him.

*Morning. – The Plaça Santiago in Bedmár. A crowd of
townsmen forming an outer circle: within, Zíncali and
Moorish soldiers drawn up round the central space. On
the higher ground in front of the church a stake with
faggots heaped, and at a little distance a gibbet. Moorish
music.* ZARCA *enters, wearing his gold necklace with the
Gypsy badge of the flaming torch over the dress of a
Moorish Captain, accompanied by a small band of armed
Zíncali, who fall aside and range themselves with the
other soldiers while he takes his stand in front of the
stake and gibbet. The music ceases, and there is
expectant silence.*

ZARCA. Men of Bedmár, well-wishers, and allies,
Whether of Moorish or of Hebrew blood,
Who, being galled by the hard Spaniard's yoke,
Have welcomed our quick conquest as release,
I, Zarca, chief of Spanish Gypsies, hold
By delegation of the Moorish King
Supreme command within this town and fort.
Nor will I, with false show of modesty,
Profess myself unworthy of this post,
For so I should but tax the giver's choice.
And, as ye know, while I was prisoner here,
Forging the bullets meant for Moorish hearts,

But likely now to reach another mark,
I learned the secrets of the town's defence,
Caught the loud whispers of your discontent,
And so could serve the purpose of the Moor
As the edge's keenness serves the weapon's weight.
My Zíncali, lynx-eyed and lithe of limb,
Tracked out the high Sierra's hidden path,
Guided the hard ascent, and were the first
To scale the walls and brave the showering stones.
In brief, I reached this rank through service done
By thought of mine and valour of my tribe,
Yet hold it but in trust, with readiness
To lay it down; for we − the Zíncali −
Will never pitch our tents again on land
The Spaniard grudges us: we seek a home
Where we may spread and ripen like the corn
By blessing of the sun and spacious earth.
Ye wish us well, I think, and are our friends ?

CROWD.   Long life to Zarca and his Zíncali !

ZARCA.   Now, for the cause of our assembling here.
   'Twas my command that rescued from your hands
   That Spanish Prior and Inquisitor
   Whom in fierce retribution you had bound
   And meant to burn, tied to a planted cross.
   I rescued him with promise that his death
   Should be more signal in its justice − made
   Public in fullest sense, and orderly.
   Here, then, you see the stake − slow death by fire;
   And there a gibbet − swift death by the cord.
   Now hear me, Moors and Hebrews of Bedmár,
   Our kindred by the warmth of Eastern blood !
   Punishing cruel wrong by cruelty
   We copy Christian crime. Vengeance is just:

Justly we rid the earth of human fiends
Who carry hell for pattern in their souls.
But in high vengeance there is noble scorn:
It tortures not the torturer, nor gives
Iniquitous payment for iniquity.
The great avenging angel does not crawl
To kill the serpent with a mimic fang;
He stands erect, with sword of keenest edge
That slays like lightning. So too we will slay
The cruel man; slay him because he works
Woe to mankind. And I have given command
To pile these faggots, not to burn quick flesh,
But for a sign of that dire wrong to men
Which arms our wrath with justice. While, to show
This Christian worshipper that we obey ·
A better law than his, he shall be led
Straight to the gibbet and to swiftest death.
For I, the chieftain of the Gypsies, will,
My people shed no blood but what is shed
In heat of battle or in judgment strict
With calm deliberation on the right.
Such is my will, and if it please you – well.

CROWD. It pleases us. Long life to Zarca !

ZARCA.   Hark !
   The bell is striking, and they bring even now
   The prisoner from the fort. What, Nadar ?

NADAR (*has appeared, cutting the crowd, and advancing
   toward* ZARCA *till he is near enough to speak in an
   under-tone*).

                                        Chief,
   I have obeyed your word, have followed it
   As water does the furrow in the rock.

ZARCA. Your band is here ?

NADAR.   Yes, and the Spaniard too.

ZARCA. 'Twas so I ordered.

NADAR.   Ay, but this sleek hound,
Who slipped his collar off to join the wolves,
Has still a heart for none but kennelled brutes.
He rages at the taking of the town,
Says all his friends are butchered; and one corpse
He stumbled on – well, I would sooner be
A murdered Gypsy's dog, and howl for him,
Than be this Spaniard. Rage has made him whiter.
One townsman taunted him with his escape,
And thanked him for so favouring us. . . .

ZARCA.   Enough.
You gave him my command that he should wait
Within the castle, till I saw him ?

NADAR.   Yes.
But he defied me, broke away, ran loose
I know not whither; he may soon be here.
I came to warn you, lest he work us harm.

ZARCA. Fear not, I know the road I travel by:
Its turns are no surprises. He who rules
Must humour full as much as he commands;
Must let men vow impossibilities;
Gant folly's prayers that hinder folly's wish
And serve the ends of wisdom. Ah, he comes !

[Sweeping like some pale herald from the dead,
Whose shadow-nurtured eges, dazed by full light,

425

See nought without, but give reverted sense
To the soul's imagery, Silva came,
The wondering people parting wide to get
Continuous sight of him as he passed on –
This high hidalgo, who through blooming years
Had shone on men with planetary calm,
Believed-in with all sacred images
And saints that must be taken as they were,
Though rendering meagre service for men's praise:
Bareheaded now, carrying an unsheathed sword,
And on his breast, where late he bore the cross,
Wearing the Gypsy badge; his form aslant,
Driven, it seemed, by some invisible chase,
Right to the front of Zarca. There he paused.]

Don Silva. Chief, you are treacherous, cruel, devilish ! –
Relentless as a curse that once let loose
From lips of wrath, lives bodiless to destroy,
And darkly traps a man in nets of guilt
Which could not weave themselves in open day
Before his eyes. Oh, it was bitter wrong
To hold this knowledge locked within your mind,
To stand with waking eyes in broadest light,
And see me, dreaming, shed my kindred's blood.
'Tis horrible that men with hearts and hands
Should smile in silence like the firmament
And see a fellow-mortal draw a lot
On which themselves have written agony !
Such injury has no redress, no healing
Save what may lie in stemming further ill.
Poor balm for maiming ! Yet I come to claim it.

Zarca. First prove your wrongs, and I will hear your claim.
Mind, you are not commander of Bedmár,
Nor duke, nor knight, nor anything for me,

Save a sworn Gypsy, subject with my tribe,
Over whose deeds my will is absolute.
You chose that lot, and would have railed at me
Had I refused it you: I warned you first
What oaths you had to take . . .

DON SILVA.   You never warned me
That you had linked yourself with Moorish men
To take this town and fortress of Bedmár –
Slay my near kinsman, him who held my place,
Our house's heir and guardian – slay my friend,
My chosen brother – desecrate the church
Where once my mother held me in her arms,
Making the holy chrism holier
With tears of joy that fell upon my brow !
You never warned . . .

ZARCA.   I warned you of your oath.
You shrank not, were resolved, were sure your place
Would never miss you, and you had your will.
I am no priest, and keep no consciences:
I keep my own place and my own command.

DON SILVA. I said my place would never miss me – yes !
A thousand Spaniards died on that same day
And were not missed; their garments clothed the backs
That else were bare. . . .

ZARCA.   But you were just the one
Above the thousand, had you known the die
That fate was throwing then.

DON SILVA.   You knew it – you !
With fiendish knowledge, smiling at the end.
You knew what snares had made my flying steps

427

Murderous; you let me lock my soul with oaths
Which your acts made a hellish sacrament.
I say, you knew this as a fiend would know it,
And let me damn myself.

ZARCA.   The deed was done
Before you took your oath, or reached our camp,
Done when you slipped in secret from the post
'Twas yours to keep, and not to meditate
If others might not fill it. For your oath,
What man is he who brandishes a sword
In darkness, kills his friends, and rages then
Against the night that kept him ignorant ?
Should I, for one unstable Spaniard, quit
My steadfast ends as father and as chief;
Renounce my daughter and my people's hope,
Lest a deserter should be made ashamed ?

DON SILVA.
Your daughter – O great God ! I vent but madness.
The past will never change. I come to stem
Harm that may yet be hindered. Chief – this stake –
Tell me who is to die ! Are you not bound
Yourself to him you took in fellowship ?
The town is yours; let me but save the blood
That still is warm in men who were my . . .

ZARCA.   Peace !
They bring the prisoner.

                    [Zarca waved his arm
With head averse, in peremptory sign
That 'twixt them now there should be space and silence.
Most eyes had turned to where the prisoner
Advanced among his guards; and Silva too

428

Turned eagerly, all other striving quelled
By striving with the dread lest he should see
His thought outside him. And he saw it there.
The prisoner was Father Isidor:
The man whom once he fiercely had accused
As author of his misdeeds – whose designs
Had forced him into fatal secrecy.
The imperious and inexorable Will
Was yoked, and he who had been pitiless
To Silva's love, was led to pitiless death.
O hateful victory of blind wishes – prayers
Which hell had overheard and swift fulfilled !
The triumph was a torture, turning all
The strength of passion into strength of pain.
Remorse was born within him, that dire birth
Which robs all else of nurture – cancerous,
Forcing each pulse to feed its anguish, turning
All sweetest residues of healthy life
To fibrous clutches of slow misery.
Silva had but rebelled – he was not free;
And all the subtle cords that bound his soul
Were tightened by the strain of one rash leap
Made in defiance. He accused no more,
But dumbly shrank before accusing throngs
Of thoughts, the impetuous recurrent rush
Of all his past-created, unchanged self.
The Father came bareheaded, frocked, a rope
Around his neck, – but clad with majesty,
The strength of resolute undivided souls
Who, owning law, obey it. In his hand
He bore a crucifix, and praying, gazed
Solely on that white image. But his guards
Parted in front, and paused as they approached
The centre where the stake was. Isidor
Lifted his eyes to look around him – calm,

Prepared to speak last words of willingness
To meet his death – last words of faith unchanged,
That, working for Christ's kingdom, he had wrought
Righteously. But his glance met Silva's eyes
And drew him. Even images of stone
Look living with reproach on him who maims,
Profanes, defiles them. Silva penitent
Moved forward, would have knelt before the man
Who still was one with all the sacred things
That came back on him in their sacredness,
Kindred, and oaths, and awe, and mystery.
But at the sight, the Father thrust the cross
With deprecating act before him, and his face
Pale-quivering, flashed out horror like white light
Flashed from the angel's sword that dooming drave
The sinner to the wilderness. He spoke.]

FATHER ISIDOR.

Back from me, traitorous and accursed man !
Defile not me, who grasp the holiest,
With touch or breath ! Thou foulest murderer !
Fouler than Cain who struck his brother down
In jealous rage, thou for thy base delight
Hast oped the gate for wolves to come and tear
Uncounted brethren, weak and strong alike,
The helpless priest, the warrior all unarmed
Against a faithless leader: on thy head
Will rest the sacrilege, on thy soul the blood.
These blind barbarians, misbelievers, Moors,
Are but as Pilate and his soldiery;
Thou, Judas, weighted with that heaviest crime
Which deepens hell ! I warned you of this end.
A traitorous leader, false to God and man,
A knight apostate, you shall soon behold
Above your people's blood the light of flames

Kindled by you to burn me – burn the flesh
Twin with your father's. O most wretched man !
Whose memory shall be of broken oaths –
Broken for lust – I turn away mine eyes
For ever from you. See, the stake is ready
And I am ready too.

DON SILVA.   It shall not be !
    (Raising his sword, he rushes in front of the guard
    who are advancing, and impedes them.)
If you are human, Chief, hear my demand !
Stretch not my soul upon the endless rack
Of this man's torture !

ZARCA.   Stand aside, my lord !
  Put up your sword. You vowed obedience
  To me, your chief. It was your latest vow.

DON SILVA. No ! hew me from the spot, or fasten me
  Amid the faggots too, if he must burn.

ZARCA. What should befall that persecuting monk
  Was fixed before you came: no cruelty,
  No nicely measured torture, weight for weight
  Of injury, no luscious-toothed revenge
  That justifies the injurer by its joy:
  I seek but rescue and security
  For harmless men, and such security
  Means death to vipers and inquisitors.
  These faggots shall but innocently blaze
  In sign of gladness, when this man is dead,
  That one more torturer has left the earth.
  'Tis not for infidels to burn live men
  And ape the rules of Christian piety.
  This hard oppressor shall not die by fire:

He mounts the gibbet, dies a speedy death,
That, like a transfixed dragon, he may cease
To vex mankind. Quick, guards, and clear the path !

[As well-trained hounds that hold their fleetness tense
In watchful, loving fixity of dark eyes,
And move with movement of their master's will,
The Gypsies with a wavelike swiftness met
Around the Father, and in wheeling course
Passed beyond Silva to the gibbet's foot,
Behind their chieftain. Sudden left alone
With weapon bare, the multitude aloof,
Silva was mazed in doubtful consciousness,
As one who slumbering in the day awakes
From striving into freedom, and yet feels
His sense half captive to intangible things;
Then with a flush of new decision sheathed
His futile naked weapon, and strode quick
To Zarca, speaking with a voice new-toned,
The struggling soul's hoarse, suffocated cry
Beneath the grappling anguish of despair.]

Don Silva. You, Zíncalo, devil, blackest infidel !
You cannot hate that man as you hate me !
Finish your torture − take me − lift me up
And let the crowd spit at me − every Moor
Shoot reeds at me, and kill me with slow death
Beneath the mid-day fervour of the sun −
Or crucify me with a thieving hound −
Slake your hate so, and I will thank it: spare me
Only this man !

Zarca.   Madman, I hate you not.
But if I did, my hate were poorly served
By my device, if I should strive to mix

432

A bitterer misery for you than to taste
With leisure of a soul in unharmed limbs
The flavour of your folly. For my course,
It has a goal, and takes no truant path
Because of you. I am your chief: to me
You're nought more than a Zíncalo in revolt.

DON SILVA. No, I'm no Zíncalo ! I here disown
The name I took in madness. Here I tear
This badge away. I am a Catholic knight,
A Spaniard who will die a Spaniard's death !

[Hark ! while he casts the badge upon the ground
And tramples on it, Silva hears a shout:
Was it a shout that threatened him ? He looked
From out the dizzying flames of his own rage
In hope of adversaries − and he saw above
The form of Father Isidor upswung
Convulsed with martyr throes; and knew the shout
For wonted exultation of the crowd
When malefactors die − or saints, or heroes.
And now to him that white-frocked murdered form
Which hanging judged him as its murderer,
Turned to a symbol of his guilt, and stirred
Tremors till then unwaked. With sudden snatch
At something hidden in his breast, he strode
Right upon Zarca: at the instant, down
Fell the great Chief, and Silva, staggering back,
Heard not the Gypsies' shriek, felt not the fangs
Of their fierce grasp − heard, felt but Zarca's words
Which seemed his soul outleaping in a cry
And urging men to run like rival waves
Whose rivalry is but obedience.]

433

ZARCA (*as he falls*).

My daughter ! call her ! Call my daughter !

NADAR (*supporting* ZARCA *and crying to the Gypsies who have clutched* SILVA).

Stay !

Tear not the Spaniard, tie him to the stake:
Hear what the Chief shall bid us – there is time !

[Swiftly they tied him, pleasing vengeance so
With promise that would leave them free to watch
Their stricken good, their Chief stretched helplessly
Pillowed upon the strength of loving limbs.
He heaved low groans, but would not spend his breath
In useless words: he waited till *she* came,
Keeping his life within the citadel
Of one great hope. And now around him closed
(But in wide circle, checked by loving fear)
His people all, holding their wails suppressed
Lest Death believed-in should be over-bold:
All life hung on their Chief – he would not die;
His image gone, there were no wholeness left
To make a world of for the Zíncali's thought.
Eager they stood, but hushed; the outer crowd
Spoke only in low murmurs, and some climbed
And clung with legs and arms on perilous coigns,
Striving to see where that colossal life
Lay panting – lay a Titan struggling still
To hold and give the precious hidden fire
Before the stronger grappled him. Above
The young bright morning cast athwart white walls
Her shadows blue, and with their clear-cut line,
Mildly relentless as the dial-hand's,
Measured the shrinking future of an hour
Which held a shrinking hope. And all the while

434

The silent beat of time in each man's soul
Made aching pulses.

                But the cry, "She comes !"
Parted the crowd like waters: and she came.
Swiftly as once before, inspired with joy,
She flashed across the space and made new light,
Glowing upon the glow of evening,
So swiftly now she came, inspired with woe,
Strong with the strength of all her father's pain,
Thrilling her as with fire of rage divine
And battling energy. She knew − saw all:
The stake with Silva bound − her father pierced −
To this she had been born: a second time
Her father called her to the task of life.

She knelt beside him. Then he raised himself,
And on her face there flashed from his the light
As of a star that waned, but flames anew
In mighty dissolution: 'twas the flame
Of a surviving trust, in agony.
He spoke the parting prayer that was command,
Must sway her will, and reign invisibly.]

ZARCA. My daughter, you have promised − you will live
   To save our people. In my garments here
   I carry written pledges from the Moor:
   He will keep faith in Spain and Africa.
   Your weakness may be stronger than my strength,
   Winning more love. . . . I cannot tell the end. . . .
   I held my people's good within my breast.
   Behold, now I deliver it to you.
   See, it still breathes unstrangled − if it dies,
   Let not your failing will be murderer. . . .
   Rise, tell our people now I wait in pain . . .

I cannot die until I hear them say
They will obey you.

                              [Meek, she pressed her lips
With slow solemnity upon his brow,
Sealing her pledges. Firmly then she rose,
And met her people's eyes with kindred gaze,
Dark-flashing, fired by effort strenuous
Trampling on pain.]

FEDALMA.   Ye Zíncali all, who hear !
Your Chief is dying: I his daughter live
To do his dying will. He asks you now
To promise me obedience as your Queen,
That we may seek the land he won for us,
And live the better life for which he toiled.
Speak now, and fill my father's dying ear
With promise that you will obey him dead,
Obeying me his child.

                              [Straightway arose
A shout of promise, sharpening into cries
That seemed to plead despairingly with death.]

THE ZINCALI. We will obey ! Our Chief shall never die !
We will obey him − will obey our Queen !

[The shout unanimous, the concurrent rush
Of many voices, quiring shook the air
With multitudinous wave: now rose, now fell,
Then rose again, the echoes following slow,
As if the scattered brethren of the tribe
Had caught afar and joined the ready vow.
Then some could hold no longer, but must rush
To kiss his dying feet, and some to kiss

The hem of their Queen's garment. But she raised
Her hand to hush them. "Hark ! your Chief may speak
Another wish." Quickly she kneeled again,
While they upon the ground kept motionless,
With head outstretched. They heard his words; for now,
Grasping at Nadar's arm, he spoke more loud,
As one who, having fought and conquered, hurls
His strength away with hurling off his shield.]

Zarca. Let loose the Spaniard ! give him back his sword;
He cannot move to any vengeance more –
His soul is locked 'twixt two opposing crimes.
I charge you let him go unharmed and free
Now through your midst. . . .

                              [With that he sank again –
His breast heaved strongly tow'rd sharp sudden falls,
And all his life seemed needed for each breath:
Yet once he spoke.]

                              My daughter, lay your arm
Beneath my head . . . so . . . bend and breathe on me.
I cannot see you more . . . the Night is come.
Be strong . . . remember . . . I can only . . . die.

[His voice went into silence, but his breast
Heaved long and moaned: its broad strength kept a life
That heard nought, saw nought, save what once had
    been,
And what might be in days and realms afar –
Which now in pale procession faded on
Toward the thick darkness. And she bent above
In sacramental watch to see great Death,
Companion of her future, who would wear
For ever in her eyes her father's form.

437

And yet she knew that hurrying feet had gone
To do the Chief's behest, and in her soul
He who was once its lord was being jarred
With loosening of cords, that would not loose
The tightening torture of his anguish. This –
Oh, she knew it ! – knew it as martyrs knew
The prongs that tore their flesh, while yet their tongues
Refused the ease of lies. In moments high
Space widens in the soul. And so she knelt,
Clinging with piety and awed resolve
Beside this altar of her father's life,
Seeing long travel under solemn suns
Stretching beyond it; never turned her eyes,
Yet felt that Silva passed; beheld his face
Pale, vivid, all alone, imploring her
Across black waters fathomless.

                                        And he passed.
The Gypsies made wide pathway, shrank aloof
As those who fear to touch the thing they hate,
Lest hate triumphant, mastering all the limbs,
Should tear, bite, crush, in spite of hindering will.
Slowly he walked, reluctant to be safe
And bear dishonoured life which none assailed;
Walked hesitatingly, ail his frame instinct
With high-born spirit, never used to dread
Or crouch for smiles, yet stung, yet quivering
With helpless strength, and in his soul convulsed
By visions where pale horror held a lamp
Over wide-reaching crime. Silence hung round:
It seemed the Plaça hushed itself to hear
His footsteps and the Chief's deep dying breath.
Eyes quickened in the stillness, and the light
Seemed one clear gaze upon his misery.
And get he could not pass her without pause:
One instant he must pause and look at her;

But with that glance at her averted head,
New-urged by pain he turned away and went,
Carrying for ever with him what he fled –
Her murdered love – her love, a dear wronged ghost,
Facing him, beauteous, 'mid the throngs of hell.

O fallen and forsaken ! were no hearts
Amid that crowd, mindful of what had been ? –
Hearts such as wait on beggared royalty,
Or silent watch by sinners who despair ?

Silva had vanished. That dismissed revenge
Made larger room for sorrow in fierce hearts;
And sorrow filled them. For the Chief was dead.
The mighty breast subsided slow to calm,
Slow from the face the ethereal spirit waned,
As wanes the parting glory from the heights,
And leaves them in their pallid majesty.
Fedalma kissed the marble lips, and said,
"He breathes no more." And then a long loud wail,
Poured out upon the morning, made her light
Ghastly as smiles on some fair maniac's face
Smiling unconscious o'er her bridegroom's corse.
The wailing men in eager press closed round,
And made a shadowing pall beneath the sun.
They lifted reverent the prostrate strength,
Sceptred anew by death. Fedalma walked
Tearless, erect, following the dead – her cries
Deep smothering in her breast, as one who guides
Her children through the wilds, and sees and knows
Of danger more than they, and feels more pangs,
Yet shirks not, groans not, bearing in her heart
Their ignorant misery and their trust in her.

BOOK V

The eastward rocks of Almería's bay
Answer long farewells of the travelling sun
With softest glow as from an inward pulse
Changing and flushing: all the Moorish ships
Seem conscious too, and shoot out sudden shadows;
Their black hulls snatch a glory, and their sails
Show variegated radiance, gently stirred
Like broad wings poised. Two galleys moored apart
Show decks as busy as a home of ants
Storing new forage; from their sides the boats,
Slowly pushed off, anon with flashing oar
Make transit to the quay's smooth-quarried edge,
Where thronging Gypsies are in haste to lade
Each as it comes with grandames, babes, and wives,
Or with dust-tinted goods, the company
Of wandering years. Nought seems to lie unmoved,
For 'mid the throng the lights and shadows play,
And make all surface eager, while the boats
Sway restless as a horse that heard the shouts
And surging hum incessant. Naked limbs
With beauteous ease bend, lift, and throw, or raise
High signalling hands. The black-haired mother steps
Athwart the boat's edge, and with opened arms,
A wandering Isis outcast from the gods,
Leans towards her lifted little one. The boat
Full-laden cuts the waves, and dirge-like cries
Rise and then fall within it as it moves
From high to lower and from bright to dark.
Hither and thither, grave white-turbaned Moors
Move helpfully, and some bring welcome gifts,
Bright stuffs and cutlery, and bags of seed
To make new waving crops in Africa.

Others aloof with folded arms slow-eyed
Survey man's labour, saying, "God is great;"
Or seek with question deep the Gypsies' root,
And whether their false faith, being small, will prove
Less damning than the copious false creeds
Of Jews and Christians: Moslem subtlety
Found balanced reasons, warranting suspense
As to whose hell was deepest – 'twas enough
That there was room for all. Thus the sedate.
The younger heads were busy with the tale
Of that great Chief whose exploits helped the Moor.
And, talking still, they shouldered past their friends
Following some lure which held their distant gaze
To eastward of the quay, where yet remained
A low black tent close guarded all around
By well-armed Gypsies. Fronting it above,
Raised by stone steps that sought a jutting strand,
Fedalma stood and marked with anxious watch
Each laden boat the remnant lessening
Of cargo on the shore, or traced the course
Of Nadar to and fro in hard command
Of noisy tumult; imaging oft anew
How much of labour still deferred the hour
When they must lift the boat and bear away
Her father's coffin, and her feet must quit
This shore for ever. Motionless she stood,
Black-crowned with wreaths of many-shadowed hair;
Black-robed, but bearing wide upon her breast
Her father's golden necklace and his badge.
Her limbs were motionless, but in her eyes
And in her breathing lip's soft tremulous curve
Was intense motion as of prisoned fire
Escaping subtly in outleaping thought.

She watches anxiously, and yet she dreams:
The busy moments now expand, now shrink
To narrowing swarms within the refluent space
Of changeful consciousness. For in her thought
Already she has left the fading shore,
Sails with her people, seeks an unknown land,
And bears the burning length of weary days
That parching fall upon her father's hope,
Which she must plant and see it wither only –
Wither and die. She saw the end begun.
The Gypsy hearts were not unfaithful: she
Was centre to the savage loyalty
Which vowed obedience to Zarca dead.
But soon their natures missed the constant stress
Of his command, that, while it fired, restrained
By urgency supreme, and left no play
To fickle impulse scattering desire.
They loved their Queen, trusted in Zarca's child,
Would bear her o'er the desert on their arms
And think the weight a gladsome victory;
But that great force which knit them into one,
The invisible passion of her father's soul,
That wrought them visibly into its will,
And would have bound their lives with permanence,
Was gone. Already Hassan and two bands,
Drawn by fresh baits of gain, had newly sold
Their service to the Moors, despite her call,
Known as the echo of her father's will,
To all the tribe, that they should pass with her
Straightway to Telemsán. They were not moved
By worse rebellion than the wilful wish
To fashion their own service; they still meant
To come when it should suit them. But she said,
This is the cloud no bigger than a hand,
Sure threatening. In a little while, the tribe

That was to be the ensign of the race,
And draw it into conscious union,
Itself would break in small and scattered bands
That, living on scant prey, would still disperse
And propagate forgetfulness. Brief years,
And that great purpose fed with vital fire
That might have glowed for half a century,
Subduing, quickening, shaping, like a sun –
Would be a faint tradition, flickering low
In dying memories, fringing with dim light
The nearer dark.

             Far, far the future stretched
Beyond that busy present on the quay,
Far her straight path beyond it. Yet she watched
To mark the growing hour, and yet in dream
Alternate she beheld another track,
And felt herself unseen pursuing it
Close to a wanderer, who with haggard gaze
Looked out on loneliness. The backward years –
Oh, she would not forget them – would not drink
Of waters that brought rest, while he far off
Remembered. "Father, I renounced the joy;
You must forgive the sorrow."

                   So she stood,
Her struggling life compressed into that hour,
Yearning, resolving, conquering; though she seemed
Still as a tutelary image sent
To guard her people and to be the strength
Of some rock-citadel.

              Below her sat
Slim mischievous Hinda, happy, red-bedecked
With rows of berries, grinning, nodding oft,
And shaking high her small dark arm and hand
Responsive to the black-maned Ismaël,
Who held aloft his spoil, and clad in skins

Seemed the Boy-prophet of the wilderness
Escaped from tasks prophetic. But anon
Hinda would backward turn upon her knees,
And like a pretty loving hound would bend
To fondle her Queen's feet, then lift her head
Hoping to feel the gently pressing palm
Which touched the deeper sense. Fedalma knew –
From out the black robe stretched her speaking hand
And shared the girl's content.

                  So the dire hours
Burthened with destiny – the death of hopes
Darkening long generations, or the birth
Of thoughts undying – such hours sweep along
In their aërial ocean measureless
Myriads of little joys, that ripen sweet
And soothe the sorrowful spirit of the world,
Groaning and travailing with the painful birth
Of slow redemption.

                  But emerging now
From eastward fringing lines of idling men
Quick Juan lightly sought the upward steps
Behind Fedalma, and two paces off,
With head uncovered, said in gentle tones,
"Lady Fedalma !" – (Juan's password now
Used by no other), and Fedalma turned,
Knowing who sought her. He advanced a step,
And meeting straight her large calm questioning gaze.
Warned her of some grave purport by a face
That told of trouble. Lower still he spoke.

JUAN. Look from me, lady, towards a moving form
    That quits the crowd and seeks the lonelier strand –
    A tall and grey-clad pilgrim. . . .

His low tones fell on her, as if she passed
Into religious dimness among tombs,
And trod on names in everlasting rest.
Lingeringly she looked, and then with voice
Deep and yet soft, like notes from some long chord
Responsive to thrilled air, said –]

FEDALMA.   It is he !

[Juan kept silence for a little space,
With reverent caution, lest his lighter grief
Might seem a wanton touch upon her pain.
But time was urging him with visible flight,
Changing the shadows: he must utter all.]

JUAN. That man was young when last I pressed his hand –
In that dread moment when he left Bedmár.
He has aged since: the week has made him grey.
And yet I knew him – knew the white-streaked hair
Before I saw his face, as I should know
The tear-dimmed writing of a friend. See now –
Does he not linger – pause ? – perhaps expect . . .

[Juan pled timidly: Fedalma's eyes
Flashed; and through all her frame there ran the shock
Of some sharp-wounding joy, like his who hastes
And dreads to come too late, and comes in time
To press a loved hand dying. She was mute
And made no gesture: all her being paused
In resolution, as some leonine wave
That makes a moment's silence ere it leaps.]

JUAN. He came from Carthagena, in a boat
Too slight for safety; yon small two-oared boat

Below the rock; the fisher-boy within
Awaits his signal. But the pilgrim waits. . . .

FEDALMA. Yes, I will go ! – Father, I owe him this,
For loving me made all his misery.
And we will look once more – will say farewell
As in a solemn rite to strengthen us
For our eternal parting. Juan, stay
Here in my place, to warn me, were there need.
And, Hinda, follow me !

                              [All men who watched
Lost her regretfully, then drew content
From thought that she must quickly come again,
And filled the time with striving to be near.
She, down the steps, along the sandy brink
To where he stood, walked firm; with quickened step
The moment when each felt the other saw.
He moved at sight of her: their glances met;
It seemed they could no more remain aloof
Than nearing waters hurrying into one.
Yet their steps slackened and they paused apart,
Pressed backward by the force of memories
Which reigned supreme as death above desire.
Two paces off they stood and silently
Looked at each other. Was it well to speak ?
Could speech be clearer, stronger, tell them more
Than that long gaze of their renouncing love ?
They passed from silence hardly knowing how;
It seemed they heard each other's thought before.]

DON SILVA. I go to be absolved, to have my life
Washed into fitness for an offering
To injured Spain. But I have nought to give
For that last injury to her I loved

Better than I loved Spain. I am accurst
Above all sinners, being made the curse
Of her I sinned for. Pardon ? Penitence ?
When they have done their utmost, still beyond
Out of their reach stands Injury unchanged
And changeless. I should see it still in heaven –
Out of my reach, for ever in my sight:
Wearing your grief 'twould hide the smiling seraphs.
I bring no puling prayer, Fedalma – ask
No balm of pardon that may soothe my soul
For others' bleeding wounds: I am not come
To say, "Forgive me:" you must not forgive,
For you must see me ever as I am –
Your father's . . .

FEDALMA.   Speak it not ! Calamity
Comes like a deluge and o'erfloods our crimes,
Till sin is hidden in woe. You – I – we two,
Grasping we knew not what, that seemed delight,
Opened the sluices of that deep.

DON SILVA.   We two ? –
Fedalma, you were blameless, helpless.

FEDALMA.   No !
It shall not be that you did aught alone.
For when we loved I willed to reign in you,
And I was jealous even of the day
If it could gladden you apart from me.
And so, it must be that I shared each deed
Our love was root of.

DON SILVA.   Dear ! you share the woe –
Nay, the worst dart of vengeance fell on you.

FEDALMA.

    Vengeance ! She does but sweep us with her skirts –
She takes large space, and lies a baleful light
Revolving with long years – sees children's children,
Blights them in their prime. . . . Oh, if two lovers leaned
To breathe one air and spread a pestilence,
They would but lie two livid victims dead
Amid the city of the dying. We
With our poor petty lives have strangled one
That ages watch for vainly.

DON SILVA.   Deep despair

    Fills all your tones as with slow agony.
Speak words that narrow anguish to some shape:
Tell me what dread is close before you ?

FEDALMA.   None.

    No dread, but clear assurance of the end.
My father held within his mighty frame
A people's life: great futures died with him
Never to rise, until the time shall ripe
Some other hero with the will to save
The outcast Zíncali.

DON SILVA.   And yet their shout

    I heard it – sounded as the plenteous rush
Of full-fed sources, shaking their wild souls
With power that promised sway.

FEDALMA.   Ah yes, that shout

    Came from full hearts: they meant obedience.
But they are orphaned: their poor childish feet
Are vagabond in spite of love, and stray
Forgetful after little lures. For me –

I am but as the funeral urn that bears
The ashes of a leader.

DON SILVA.   O great God !
What am I but a miserable brand
Lit by mysterious wrath ? I lie cast down
A blackened branch upon the desolate ground
Where once I kindled ruin. I shall drink
No cup of purest water but will taste
Bitter with thy lone hopelessness, Fedalma.

FEDALMA. Nay, Silva, think of me as one who sees
A light serene and strong on one sole path
Which she will tread till death . . .
He trusted me, and I will keep his trust:
My life shall be its temple. I will plant
His sacred hope within the sanctuary
And die its priestess − though I die alone,
A hoary woman on the altar-step,
Cold 'mid cold ashes. That is my chief good.
The deepest hunger of a faithful heart
Is faithfulness. Wish me nought else. And you −
You too will live. . . .

DON SILVA.   I go to Rome, to seek
The right to use my knightly sword again;
The right to fill my place and live or die
So that all Spaniards shall not curse my name.
I sate one hour upon the barren rock
And longed to kill myself; but then I said,
I will not leave my name in infamy,
I will not be perpetual rottenness
Upon the Spaniard's air. If I must sink
At last to hell, I will not take my stand
Among the coward crew who could not bear

The harm themselves had done, which others bore.
My young life yet may fill some fatal breach,
And I will take no pardon, not my own,
Not God's – no pardon idly on my knees:
But it shall come to me upon my feet
And in the thick of action, and each deed
That carried shame and wrong shall be the sting
That drives me higher up the steep of honour
In deeds of duteous service to that Spain
Who nourished me on her expectant breast
The heir of highest gifts. I will not fling
My earthly being down for carrion
To fill the air with loathing: I will be
The living prey of some fierce noble death
That leaps upon me while I move. Aloud
I said, "I will redeem my name," and then –
I know not if aloud: I felt the words
Drinking up all my senses – "She still lives.
I would not quit the dear familiar earth
Where both of us behold the self-same sun
Where there can be no strangeness 'twixt our thoughts
So deep as their communion." Resolute
I rose and walked. – Fedalma, think of me
As one who will regain the only life
Where he is other than apostate – one
Who seeks but to renew and keep the vows
Of Spanish knight and noble. But the breach
Outside those vows – the fatal second breach –
Lies a dark gulf where I have nought to cast,
Not even expiation – poor pretence,
Which changes nought but what survives the past,
And raises not the dead. That deep dark gulf
Divides us.

FEDALMA.   Yes, for ever. We must walk
Apart unto the end. Our marriage rite
Is our resolve that we will each be true
To high allegiance, higher than our love.
Our dear young love – its breath was happiness !
But it had grown upon a larger life
Which tore its roots asunder. We rebelled –
The larger life subdued us. Yet we are wed;
For we shall carry each the pressure deep
Of the other's soul. I soon shall leave the shore.
The winds to-night will bear me far away
My lord, farewell !

                He did not say "Farewell."
But neither knew that he was silent. She,
For one long moment, moved not. They knew nought
Save that they parted; for their mutual gaze
As with their soul's full speech forbade their hands
To seek each other – those oft-clasping hands
Which had a memory of their own, and went
Widowed of one dear touch for evermore.
At last she turned and with swift movement passed,
Beckoning to Hinda, who was bending low
And lingered still to wash her shells, but soon
Leaping and scampering followed, while her Queen
Mounted the steps again and took her place,
Which Juan rendered silently.

                    And now
The press upon the quay was thinned; the ground
Was cleared of cumbering heaps, the eager shouts
Had sunk, and left a murmur more restrained
By common purpose. All the men ashore
Were gathering into ordered companies,
And with less clamour filled the waiting boats,
As if the speaking light commanded them

451

To quiet speed: for now the farewell glow
Was on the topmost heights, and where far ships
Were southward tending, tranquil, slow, and white
Upon the luminous meadow toward the verge.
The quay was in still shadow, and the boats
Went sombrely upon the sombre waves.
Fedalma watched again; but now her gaze
Takes in the eastward bay, where that small bark
Which held the fisher-boy floats weightier
With one more life, that rests upon the oar
Watching with her. He would not go away
Till she was gone; he would not turn his face
Away from her at parting: but the sea
Should widen slowly 'twixt their seeking eyes.

The time was coming. Nadar had approached.
Was the Queen ready ? Would she follow now
Her father's body ? For the largest boat
Was waiting at the quay, the last strong band
Of Zíncali had ranged themselves in lines
To guard her passage and to follow her.
"Yes, I am ready;" and with action prompt
They cast aside the Gypsy's wandering tomb,
And fenced the space from curious Moors who pressed
To see Chief Zarca's coffin as it lay.
They raised it slowly, holding it aloft
On shoulders proud to bear the heavy load.
Bound on the coffin lay the chieftain's arms,
His Gypsy garments and his coat of mail.
Fedalma saw the burthen lifted high,
And then descending followed. All was still.
The Moors aloof could hear the struggling steps
Beneath the lowered burthen at the boat –
The struggling calls subdued, till safe released
It lay within, the space around it filled

By black-haired Gypsies. Then Fedalma stepped
From off the shore and saw it flee away –
The land that bred her helping the resolve
Which exiled her for ever.

                        It was night
Before the ships weighed anchor and gave sail:
Fresh Night emergent in her clearness, lit
By the large crescent moon, with Hesperus,
And those great stars that lead the eager host.
Fedalma stood and watched the little bark
Lying jet-black upon moon-whitened waves.
Silva was standing too. He too divined
A steadfast form that held him with its thought,
And eyes that sought him vanishing: he saw
The waters widen slowly, till at last
Straining he gazed, and knew not if he gazed
On aught but blackness overhung by stars.

P. 237. *Cactus.*

The Indian fig (*Opuntia*), like the other *Cactaceae*, is believed to have been introduced into Europe from South America; but every one who has been in the south of Spain will understand why the anachronism has been chosen.

P. 334. *Marranos.*

The name given by the Spanish Jews to the multitudes of their race converted to Christianity at the end of the fourteenth century and beginning of the fifteenth. The lofty derivation from *Maran-atha*, the Lord cometh, seems hardly called for, seeing that *marrano* is Spanish for *pig*. The "old Christians" learned to use the word as a term of contempt for the "new Christians," or converted Jews and their descendants; but not too monotonously, for they often interchanged it with the fine old crusted opprobrium of the name *Jew*. Still, many Marranos held the highest secular and ecclesiastical prizes in Spain, and were respected accordingly.

P. 351. *Celestial Baron.*

The Spaniards conceived their patron Santiago (St James), the great captain of their armies, as a knight and baron: to them, the incongruity would have lain in conceiving him simply as a Galilean fisherman. And their legend was adopted with respect by devout mediaeval minds generally. Dante, in an elevated passage of the *Paradiso* – the memorable opening of *Canto* xxv. – chooses to introduce the Apostle James as *il barone*.

> "Indi si mosse un lume verso noi
> Di quella schiera, ond 'uscì la primizia

Che lasciò Cristo de' vicari suoi.
E la mia Donna piena di letizia
Mi disse: Mira, mira, ecco 'l barone
Per cui laggiù si visita Galizia."

P. 353. *The Seven Parts.*
Las Siete Partidas (The Seven Parts) is the title given to
the code of laws compiled under Alfonso the Tenth, who
reigned in the latter half of the thirteenth century –
1252-1284. The passage in the text is translated from
Partida II., Ley II. The whole preamble is worth citing
in its old Spanish: –

"*Como deben ser escogidos los caballeros.*"

"Antiguamiente para facer caballeros escogien de los
venadores de monte, que son homes que sufren grande
laceria, et carpinteros, et ferreros, et pedreros, porque
usan mucho a ferir et son fuerte de manos; et otrosi de
los carniceros, por razon que usan matar las cosas vivas
et esparcer la sangre dellas: et aun cataban otra cosa en
escogiendolos que fuesen bien faccionadas de membros
para ser recios, et fuertes et ligeros. Et esta manera de
escoger usaron los antiguos muy grant tiempo; mas
porque despues vieron muchas vegadas que estos atales
non habiendo vergüenza olvidaban todas estas cosas
sobredichas, et en logar de vincer sus enemigos vencíense
ellos, tovieron por bien los sabidores destas cosas que
catasen homes para esto que hobiesen naturalmiente en
sí vergüenza. Et sobresto dixo un sabio que habie
nombre Vegecio que fabló de la órden de caballería, que
la vergüenza vieda al caballero que non fuya de la batalla,
et por ende ella le face ser vencedor; ca mucho tovieron
que era mejor el homo flaco et sofridor, que el fuerte et
ligero para foir. Et por esto sobre todas las otras cosas

cataron que fuesen homes porque se guardasen de facer cosa por que podiesen caer en vergüenza: et porque estos fueron escogidos de buenos logares et algo, que quiere tanto decir en lenguage de España como bien, por eso los llamaron fijosdalgo, que muestra atanto como fijos de bien. Et en algunos otros logares los llamaron gentiles, et tomaron este nombre de gentileza que muestra atanto como nobleza de bondat, porque los gentiles fueron nobles homes et buenos, et vevieron mas ordenadamente que las otras gentes. Et esta gentileza aviene en tres maneras; la una por linage, la segunda por saber, et la tercera por bondat de armas et de costumbres et de maneras. Et comoquier que estos que la ganan por su sabidoría ó por su bondat, son con derecho llamados nobles et gentiles, mayormiente lo son aquellos que la han por linage antiguamiente, et facen buena vida porque les viene de lueñe como por heredat: et por ende son mas eacargados de facer bien et guardarse de yerro et de malestanza; ca non tan solamiente quando lo facen resciben daño et vergüenza ellos mismos, ma nun aquellos onde ellos vienen."

THE END

EPIGRAPHS

Chapter 1:

> He left me when the down upon his lip
> Lay like the shadow of a hovering kiss.
> "Beautiful mother, do not grieve," he said;
> "I will be great, and build our fortunes high,
> And you shall wear the longest train at court,
> And look so queenly, all the lords shall say,
> 'She is a royal changeling: there's some crown
> Lacks the right head, since hers wears nought but
>   braids.' "
> O, he is coming now – but I am grey:
> And he –

Chapter 2:

> A jolly parson of the good old stock,
> By birth a gentleman, yet homely too,
> Suiting his phrase to Hodge and Margery
> Whom he once christened, and has married since.
> A little lax in doctrine and in life,
> Not thinking God was captious in such things
> As what a man might drink on holidays,
> But holding true religion was to do
> As you'd be done by – which could never mean
> That he should preach three sermons in a week.

Chapter 3:

> 'Twas town, yet country too; you felt the warmth
> Of clustering houses in the wintry time;
> Supped with a friend, and went by lantern home.
> Yet from your chamber window you could hear
> The tiny bleat of new-yearned lambs, or see
> The children bend beside the hedgerow banks
> To pluck the primroses.

Chapter 5:

1st Citizen. Sir, there's a hurry in the veins of youth
That makes a vice of virtue by excess.

2d Citizen. What if the coolness of our tardier veins
Be loss of virtue ?

1st Citizen. All things cool with time –
The sun itself, they say, till heat shall find
A general level, nowhere in excess.

2d Citizen. 'Tis a poor climax, to my weaker thought,
That future middlingness.

Chapter 7:

M. It was but yesterday you spoke him well –
You've changed your mind so soon ?

N. Not I – 'tis he
That, changing to my thought, has changed my mind.
No man puts rotten apples in his pouch
Because their upper side looked fair to him.
Constancy in mistakes is constant folly.

Chapter 11:

> Truth is the precious harvest of the earth.
> But once, when harvest waved upon a land,
> The noisome cankerworm and caterpillar,
> Locusts, and all the swarming foul-born broods,
> Fastened upon it with swift, greedy jaws,
> And turned the harvest into pestilence,
> Until men said, What profits it to sow ?

Chapter 14:

> This man's metallic; at a sudden blow
> His soul rings hard. I cannot lay my palm,
> Trembling with life, upon that jointed brass.
> I shudder at the cold unanswering touch;
> But if it press me in response, I'm bruised.

Chapter 15:

> And doubt shall be as lead upon the feet
> Of thy most anxious will.

Chapter 17:

> It is a good and soothfast saw;
> Half-roasted never will be raw;
> No dough is dried once more to meal,
> No crock new-shapen by the wheel;
> You can't turn curds to milk again,
> Nor Now, by wishing, back to Then;
> And having tasted stolen honey,
> You can't buy innocence for money.

Chapter 19:

> Consistency ? – I never changed my mind,
> Which is, and always was, to live at ease.

Chapter 22:

> Her gentle looks shot arrows, piercing him
> As gods are pierced, with poison of sweet pity.

Chapter 25:

> Your fellow-man ? – Divide the epithet:
> Say rather, you're the fellow, he the man.

Chapter 34:

> The fields are hoary with December's frost.
> I too am hoary with the chills of age.
> But through the fields and through the untrodden woods
> Is rest and stillness – only in my heart
> The pall of winter shrouds a throbbing life.

Chapter 35:

> *M.*   Check to your queen !
> *N.*   Nay, your own king is bare,
> And moving so, you give yourself checkmate.

Chapter 36:

> See now the virtue living in a word !
> Hobson will think of swearing it was noon
> When he saw Dobson at the May-day fair,
> To prove poor Dobson did not rob the mail.
> 'Tis neighbourly to save a neighbour's neck:
> What harm in lying when you mean no harm ?
> But say 'tis perjury, then Hobson quakes –
> He'll none of perjury.
>   Thus words embalm
> The conscience of mankind; and Roman laws
> Bring still a conscience to poor Hobson's aid.

Chapter 38:

> The down we rest on in our aëry dreams
> Has not been plucked from birds that live and smart:
> 'Tis but warm snow, that melts not.

Chapter 41:

> He rates me as the merchant does the wares
> He will not purchase – "quality not high ! –
> 'Twill lose its colour opened to the sun,
> Has no aroma, and, in fine, is naught –
> I barter not for such commodities –
> There is no ratio betwixt sand and gems."
> 'Tis wicked judgment ! for the soul can grow,
> As embryos, that live and move but blindly,
> Burst from the dark, emerge regenerate,
> And lead a life of vision and of choice.

Chapter 44:

> I'm sick at heart. The eye of day,
> The insistent summer noon, seems pitiless,
> Shining in all the barren crevices
> Of weary life, leaving no shade, no dark,
> Where I may dream that hidden water lie.

Chapter 45:

> We may not make this world a paradise
> By walking it together with clasped hands
> And eyes that meeting feed a double strength.
> We must be only joined by pains divine,
> Of spirits blent in mutual memories.

Chapter 46:

> Why, there are maidens of heroic touch,
> And yet they seem like things of gossamer
> You'd pinch the life out of, as out of moths.
> O, it is not fond tones and mouthingness,
> 'Tis not the arms akimbo and large strides,
> That make a woman's force. The tiniest birds,
> With softest downy breasts, have passions in them,
> And are brave with love.

Chapter 47:

> The devil tempts us not − 'tis we tempt him,
> Beckoning his skill with opportunity.

Chapter 49:

> Nay, falter not — 'tis an assured good
> To seek the noblest — 'tis your only good
> Now you have seen it; for that higher vision
> Poisons all meaner choice for evermore.

Chapter 51:

> The maiden said, I wis the londe
>   Is very fair to see,
> But my true-love that is in bonde
>   Is fairer still to me.

Epilogue:

> Our finest hope is finest memory;
> And those who love in age think youth is happy,
> Because it has a life to fill with love.

Chapter 4:

>| *1st Gent.* | Our deeds are fetters that we forge ourselves. |
>| *2d Gent.* | Ay, truly: but I think it is the world |
>| | That brings the iron. |

Chapter 6:

> My lady's tongue is like the meadow blades,
> That cut you stroking them with idle hand.
> Nice cutting is her function: she divides
> With spiritual edge the millet-seed,
> And makes intangible savings.

Chapter 8:

> Oh, rescue her ! I am her brother now,
> And you her father. Every gentle maid
> Should have a guardian in each gentleman.

Chapter 9:

>| *1st Gent.* | An ancient land in ancient oracles |
>| | Is called "law-thirsty:" all the struggle there |
>| | Was after order and a perfect rule. |
>| | Pray, where lie such lands now ? . . |
>| *2d Gent.* | Why, where they lay of old − in human souls. |

Chapter 13:

1st Gent.   How class your man ? – as better than the most,
              Or, seeming better, worse beneath that cloak ?
              As saint or knave, pilgrim or hypocrite ?
2d Gent.   Nay, tell me how you class your wealth of books,
              The drifted relics of all time. As well
              Sort them at once by size and livery:
              Vellum, tall copies, and the common calf
              Will hardly cover more diversity
              Than all your labels cunningly devised
              To class your unread authors.

Chapter 14:

Follows here the strict receipt
For that sauce to dainty meat,
Named Idleness, which many eat
By preference, and call it sweet:
    First watch for morsels, like a hound,
    Mix well with buffets, stir them round
    With good thick oil of flatteries,
    And froth with mean self-lauding lies.
    Serve warm: the vessels you must choose
    To keep it in are dead men's shoes.

Chapter 15:

Black eyes you have left, you say,
   Blue eyes fail to draw you;
Yet you seem more rapt to-day,
   Than of old we saw you.

Oh I track the fairest fair
   Through new haunts of pleasure;
Footprints here and echoes there
   Guide me to my treasure:

Lo ! She turns – immortal youth
   Wrought to mortal stature,
Fresh as starlight's aged truth –
   Many-namèd Nature !

Chapter 17:

The clerkly person smiled and said,
Promise was a pretty maid,
But being poor she died unwed.

Chapter 18:

Oh, sir, the loftiest hopes on earth
Draw lots with meaner hopes: heroic breasts,
Breathing bad air, run risk of pestilence;
Or, lacking lime-juice when they cross the Line,
May languish with the scurvy.

Chapter 20:

> A child forsaken, waking suddenly,
> Whose gaze afeard on all things round doth rove,
> And seeth only that it cannot see
>   The meeting eyes of love.

Chapter 23:

> "Your horses of the Sun," he said,
>   "And first-rate whip Apollo !
> Whate'er they be, I'll eat my head,
>   But I will beat them hollow."

Chapter 27:

> Let the high Muse chant loves Olympian:
> We are but mortals, and must sing of man.

Chapter 28:

> *1st Gent.* All times are good to seek your wedded home
>   Bringing a mutual delight.
> *2d Gent.*   Why, true.
>   The calendar hath not an evil day
>   For souls made one by love, and even death
>   Were sweetness, if it came like rolling waves
>   While they two clasped each other, and foresaw
>   No life apart.

Chapter 31:

How will you know the pitch of that great bell
Too large for you to stir ? Let but a flute
Play 'neath the fine-mixed metal: listen close
Till the right note flows forth, a silvery rill:
Then shall the huge bell tremble – then the mass
With myriad waves concurrent shall respond
In low soft unison.

Chapter 34:

1st Gent.   Such men as this are feathers, chips, and straws,
            Carry no weight, no force.
2d Gent.   But levity
            Is casual too, and makes the sum of weight.
            For power finds its place in lack of power;
            Advance is cession, and the driven ship
            May run aground because the helmsman's thought
            Lacked force to balance opposites.

Chapter 40:

Wise in his daily work was he:
    To fruits of diligence,
And not to faiths or polity,
    He plied his utmost sense.
These perfect in their little parts,
    Whose work is all their prize –
Without them how could laws, or arts,
    Or towered cities rise ?

470

Chapter 43:

> This figure hath high price: 'twas wrought with love
> Ages ago in finest ivory;
> Nought modish in it, pure and noble lines
> Of generous womanhood that fits all time.
> That too is costly ware; majolica
> Of deft design, to please a lordly eye:
> The smile, you see is perfect – wonderful
> As mere Faience ! a table ornament
> To suit the richest mounting.

Chapter 44:

> I would not creep along the coast, but steer
> Out in mid-sea, by guidance of the stars.

Chapter 47:

> Was never true love loved in vain,
> For truest love is highest gain.
> No art can make it: it must spring
> Where elements are fostering.
>   So in heaven's spot and hour
>   Springs the little native flower,
>   Downward root and upward eye,
>   Shapen by the earth and sky.

Chapter 48:

> Surely the golden hours are turning grey
> And dance no more, and vainly strive to run:
> I see their white locks streaming in the wind –
> Each face is haggard as it looks at me,
> Slow turning in the constant clasping round
> Storm-driven.

Chapter 49:

> A task too strong for wizard spells
>   This squire had brought about;
> 'Tis easy dropping stones in wells,
>   But who shall get them out ?

Chapter 51:

> Party is Nature too, and you shall see
> By force of Logic how they both agree:
> The Many in the One, the One in Many;
> All is not Some, nor Some the same as Any:
> Genus holds species, both are great or small;
> One genus highest, one not high at all;
> Each species has its differentia too,
> This is not That, and He was never You,
> Through this and that are AYES, and you and he
> Are like as one to one, or three to three.

Chapter 55:

Hath she her faults ? I would you had them too.
They are the fruity must of soundest wine;
Or say, they are regenerating fire
Such as hath turned the dense black element
Into a crystal pathway for the sun.

Chapter 57:

They numbered scarce eight summers when a name
    Rose on their souls and stirred such motions there
As thrill the buds and shape their hidden frame
    At penetration of the quickening air:
His name who told of loyal Evan Dhu,
    Of quaint Bradwardine, and Vich Ian Vor,
Making the little world their childhood knew
    Large with a land of mountain, lake, and scaur,
And larger yet with wonder, love, belief
    Toward Walter Scott, who living far away
Sent them this wealth of joy and noble grief.
    The book and they must part, but day by day,
        In lines that thwart like portly spiders ran,
        They wrote the tale, from Tully Veolan.

Chapter 59:

They said of old the Soul had human shape,
But smaller, subtler than the fleshly self,
So wandered forth for airing when it pleased.
And see ! beside her cherub-face there floats
A pale-lipped form aerial whispering
Its promptings in that little shell her ear.

473

Chapter 64:

1st Gent.   Where lies the power, there let the blame lie too.
2d Gent.   Nay, power is relative; you cannot fright
            The coming pest with border fortresses,
            Or catch your carp with subtle argument.
            All force is twain in one: cause is not cause
            Unless effect be there; and action's self
            Must needs contain a passive. So command
            Exists but with obedience.

Chapter 67:

            Now is there civil war within the soul:
            Resolve is thrust from off the sacred throne
            By clamorous Needs, and Pride the grand-vizier
            Makes humble compact, plays the supple part
            Of envoy and deft-tongued apologist
            For hungry rebels.

Chapter 70:

            Our deeds still travel with us from afar,
            And what we have been makes us what we are.

Chapter 72:

            Full souls are double mirrors, making still
            An endless vista of fair things before,
            Repeating things behind.

Chapter 73:

> Pity the laden one; this wandering woe
> May visit you and me.

Chapter 78:

> Would it were yesterday and I i' the grave,
> With her sweet faith above for monument.

Epigraph:

> Let thy chief terror be of thine own soul:
> There, 'mid the throng of hurrying desires
> That trample o'er the dead to seize their spoil,
> Lurks vengeance, footless, irresistible
> As exhalations laden with slow death,
> And o'er the fairest troop of captured joys
> Breathes pallid pestilence.

Chapter 2:

> This man contrives a secret 'twixt us two,
> That he may quell me with his meeting eyes
> Like one who quells a lioness at bay.

Chapter 8:

> What name doth Joy most borrow
> When life is fair ?
>   "Tomorrow."
> What name doth best fit Sorrow
> In young despair ?
>   "Tomorrow."

Chapter 9:

> I'll tell thee, Berthold, what men's hopes are like:
> A silly child that, quivering with joy,
> Would cast its little mimic fishing-line
> Baited with loadstone for a bowl of toys
> In the salt ocean.

Chapter 10:

1st Gent.
> What woman should be ? Sir, consult the taste
> Of marriageable men. This planet's store
> In iron, cotton, wool, or chemicals –
> All matter rendered to our plastic skill,
> Is wrought in shapes responsive to demand:
> The market's pulse makes index high or low,
> By rule sublime. Our daughters must be wives,
> And to be wives must be what men will choose:
> Men's taste is women's test. You mark the phrase ?
> 'Tis good, I think ? – the sense well winged and poised
> With t's and s's.

2d Gent.   Nay, but turn it round:
> Give us the test of taste. A fine *menu* –
> Is it to-day what Roman epicures
> Insisted that a gentleman must eat
> To earn the dignity of dining well ?

Chapter 13:

> Philistia, be thou glad of me !

Chapter 14:

> I will not clothe myself in wreck – wear gems
> Sawed from cramped finger-bones of women drowned;
> Feel chilly vaporous hands of ireful ghosts
> Clutching my necklace; trick my maiden breast
> With orphans' heritage. Let your dead love
> Marry its dead.

Chapter 18:

> Life is a various mother: now she dons
> Her plumes and brilliants, climbs the marble stairs
> With head aloft, nor ever turns her eyes
> On lackeys who attend her; now she dwells
> Grim-clad up darksome alleys, breathes hot gin,
> And screams in pauper riot.
>   But to these
> She came a frugal matron, neat and deft,
> With cheerful morning thoughts and quick device
> To find the much in little.

Chapter 22:

> We please our fancy with ideal webs
> Of innovation, but our life meanwhile
> Is in the loom, where busy passion plies
> The shuttle to and fro, and gives our deeds
> The accustomed pattern.

Chapter 26:

He brings white asses laden with the freight
Of Tyrian vessels, purple, gold, and balm,
To bribe my will: I'll bid them chase him forth,
Nor let him breathe the taint of his surmise
On my secure resolve.
                                    Ay, 'tis secure:
And therefore let him come to spread his freight.
For firmness hath its appetite and craves
The stronger lure, more strongly to resist;
Would know the touch of gold to fling it off;
Scent wine to feel its lip the soberer;
Behold soft byssus, ivory and plumes
To say, "They're fair, but I will none of them,"
And flout Enticement in the very face.

Chapter 27:

Desire has trimmed the sails, and Circumstance
Brings but the breeze to fill them.

Chapter 30:

No penitence and no confessional:
No priest ordains it, yet they're forced to sit
Amid deep ashes of their vanished years.

Chapter 37:

Aspern.   Pardon, my lord – I speak for Sigismund.
Fronsberg. For him ? Oh, ay – for him I always hold
            A pardon safe in bank, sure he will draw
            Sooner or later on me. What his need ?
            Mad project broken ? fine mechanic wings
            That would not fly ? durance, assault on watch,
            Bill for Epernay, not a crust to eat ?
Aspern.   Oh, none of these, my lord; he has escaped
            From Circe's herd, and seeks to win the love
            Of your fair ward Cecilia: but would win
            First your consent. You frown.
Fronsberg.   Distinguish words
            I said I held a pardon, not consent.

Chapter 44:

       Fairy folk a-listening
       Hear the seed sprout in the spring,
       And for music to their dance
       Hear the hedgerows wake from trance,
       Sap that trembles into buds
       Sending little rhythmic floods
       Of fairy sound in fairy ears.
       Thus all beauty that appears
       Has birth as sound to finer sense
       And lighter-clad intelligence.

Chapter 45:

Behold my lady's carriage stop the way,
With powdered lacquey and with champing bay:
She sweeps the matting, treads the crimson stair,
Her arduous function solely "to be there."
Like Sirius rising o'er the silent sea,
She hides her heart in lustre loftily.

Chapter 49:

Ever in his soul
That larger justice which makes gratitude
Triumphed above resentment. 'Tis the mark
Of regal natures, with the wider life,
And fuller capability of joy –
Not wits exultant in the strongest lens
To show you goodness vanished into pulp
Never worth "thank-you" – they're the devil's friars,
Vowed to be poor as he in love and trust,
Yet must go begging of a world that keeps
Some human property.

Chapter 57:

Deeds are the pulse of Time, his beating life,
And righteous or unrighteous, being done,
Must throb in after-throbs till Time itself
Be laid in stillness, and the universe
Quiver and breathe upon no mirror more.

Chapter 67:

> The godhead in us wrings our nobler deeds
> From our reluctant selves.

APPENDIX

The Legend of Jubal and Other Poems

In March 1874, George Eliot wrote to Blackwood that she was preparing a collection of poems which 'Mr Lewes wishes me to get published in May.' *The Legend of Jubal*, which came out in early May, contained ten poems. When the Cabinet Edition was in preparation, her publisher advised her to add further verse, as he felt the volume needed filling out. Another four poems were included: 'A College Breakfast–Party', which had first come out in *Macmillan's Magazine* in July 1878, 'Self and Life', 'Sweet Evenings Come and Go, Love' and 'The Death of Moses'. The ordering of the poems in the two volumes was as follows:

1874	1878
The Legend of Jubal	The Legend of Jubal
Agatha	Agatha
Armgart	Armgart
How Lisa Loved the King	How Lisa Loved the King
A Minor Prophet	A Minor Prophet
Brother and Sister	Brother and Sister
Stradivarius	Stradivarius
Two Lovers	A College–Breakfast Party
Arion	Two Lovers
'O May I Join the Choir Invisible'	Self and Life
	'Sweet Evenings Come and Go, Love'
	The Death of Moses
	Arion
	'O May I Join the Choir Invisible'

When *The Legend of Jubal and Other Poems* was reissued in this revised form, it bore the title *The Legend of Jubal and Other Poems, Old and New*.

INDEX OF FIRST LINES

First lines of songs from *The Spanish Gypsy* are in italics.

SKOOB LITERATURE

Francis Lathom: The Midnight Bell
First published in 1798 and one of the novels listed in Jane Austen's *Northanger Abbey*, *The Midnight Bell* is a story of loneliness, persecution and family secrets.   1 871438 30 6 (pbk)

Peter Teuthold: The Necromancer
First published in 1794, *The Necromancer* unfolds a series of mysterious events set in the Black Forest.   A group of friends investigates and uncovers a criminal secret society.
1 871438 20 9 (pbk)

Forthcoming Titles

David Gascoyne: The Collected Journals 1936-1942
David Gascoyne has been a major force in British poetry for over fifty years. These journals cover his involvement with the Communist Party, his time in Paris and his period as an actor with ENSA. This edition includes an introduction by Kathleen Raine.
1 871438 45 4 (hbk)   1 871438 50 0 (pbk)

George Crabbe: The Borough
George Crabbe (1754-1832) was born in Aldeburgh, Suffolk and served as a doctor's apprentice.   Befriended by Edmund Burke and Dr Johnson, he lived to be admired by both Scott and Byron. This edition of *The Borough* is accompanied by an essay on Benjamin Britten's *Peter Grimes*, the opera which took its plot from Crabbe's poem, by Michael Kennedy, Britten's biographer.

Peter Will: Horrid Mysteries
Admired by Shelley, satirised by Thomas Love Peacock, read by Jane Austen's father and Catherine Morland in *Northanger Abbey*, Peter Will's novel is based upon the fictional memoirs of the German author Karl Grosse, who awarded himself the title of Marquis and was an odd mixture of genius and confidence trickster. *Horrid Mysteries* is the account of a secret society and one man's loss of everything in his attempt to investigate it; is it benevolent and far-seeing or wicked and power-seeking?

SKOOB ORIENTAL

A Mandarin's impressions of Australia 1899-1912, by Hwuy-Ung, mandarin of the fourth button
In his travels in turn-of-the-century Australia, Hwuy-Ung found much that was strange to him. In letters home, he records his experiences.

GEORGE ELIOT

Collected Poems